HORSE
ANSWERS

GW00722410

First published in Great Britain in 1995 by Boxtree Limited

Text © Emap Pursuit Publishing
Photographs © Emap Pursuit Publishing

1 2 3 4 5 6 7 8 9 10

All rights reserved. Except for use in a review, no part of this book may be reproduced, stored in a retrieval system or transmitted in any form or by any means, electronic, mechanical, photocopying, recording or otherwise, without prior permission of Boxtree Limited.

Designed by Design 23

Printed and bound in the UK by
Bath Press Colour Books, Glasgow for

Boxtree Limited
Broadwall House
21 Broadwall
London SE1 9PL

A CIP catalogue entry for this book is available from the British Library.

ISBN 1 85283 918 X

HORSE ANSWERS

Horse Care, Riding and Veterinary Advice

Published in
association with

YOUR HORSE

B❧XTREE

Contents

The Experts

J. Matthew J. Tong, BVSc, Cert EP, Cert VR, MRCVS
has a special interest in horses and is one of Your Horse magazine's
veterinary advisers.

Karen Bush, BHSII (T)
has many years' experience of teaching riding and of handling
and schooling horses.

Teresa Hollands, BSc (Hons), MSc
is an equine nutritionist.

Don Cassell
is a journalist specialising in legal matters.

Foreword

There have been many, many books published about horses, and horse owners and riders could be forgiven for thinking that everything that could have been said has been said. Not so. There has never been a book quite like this one.

What makes this book different is that it answers questions continually being asked by owners and riders just like you! And for that reason it will quickly become an essential aid in the day-to-day care and riding of your horse, an invaluable problem solver which will soon make you wonder what you did without it.

Not only will this book solve your particular horsey headaches, by enabling you to share in the experiences of other horse owners and riders it will help prepare you for future problems.

Horse Answers is an extension of the extremely popular section of the same name appearing in Your Horse magazine, Britain's biggest selling equestrian monthly. Sales of Your Horse have grown enormously in recent years, not least because of the introduction of Horse Answers. The Horse Answers format, now well established and known and trusted by Your Horse readers, is in fact the most popular feature among the magazine's expansive audience, meeting its needs more accurately than any other component.

Like the section from which its takes its name, this book will solve many of the most common problems you are likely to experience – and some less common ones too. For ease of reference it has been split into four clearly identifiable sections – horse care, riding, veterinary and legal and financial matters. Colour coded bars on the pages will also help you find your way around and the index beginning on page 173 will further assist easy reference.

All questions have actually been asked by readers of Your Horse and answers and advice are provided by specialists, each recognised in their field. More information on the specialists can be found opposite. All answers have been approved by Your Horse Editor, Lesley Bayley.

We hope Horse Answers will save you time and money and enhance your enjoyment of your horse. It is destined to become an indispensable handbook.

Melvyn Bagnall,
Publisher of Your Horse magazine.

*Your Horse magazine, containing more Horse Answers,
is on sale on the 21st of each month.

Horse Care

Careful grooming

I have just bought an eight-year-old chestnut gelding who has a beautiful long, thick tail. Could you give me any advice on keeping it looking nice and thick, as all my horses seem to end up with wispy tails.

The answer to keeping your gelding's tail thick and luxuriant lies in very careful grooming! Don't use a brush when caring for it each day but gently tease out any tangles and bedding with your fingers. If the tail becomes very muddy, wait until it is dry, when you can tease out the tangles as before, then carefully brush it out, strand by strand, using a soft body brush. This does take time so be patient. Don't use a comb, dandy brush or plastic curry comb as this will break off the hairs, leading to a wispy appearance. When you wash the tail, brush it out carefully when dry as described above. Using an equine hair gloss product will give it a lovely silky sheen and help prevent it becoming massively tangled, making it easier for you to care for.

Won't get caught

I recently bought a 13-year-old gelding knowing that when he was younger he had been hit around his head and ill-treated. However, his last owner had no trouble with him. I've been finding it very hard to catch him even when he has a headcollar on. He will turn his back on me and put his ears back.

Particularly since your gelding has been mistreated in the past, it may be that he simply isn't completely sure of your yet, even though you may not have given him any cause to distrust you. It can take time with some horses to acquire their confidence. Try to give him some incentive for being caught - offer an edible treat of some kind, encouraging him to keep his head to you rather than his quarters, and even to approach you. Once you have caught him, try to bring him to a feed – even if it is only a handful of cubes in his feed bowl – and avoid riding him for at least half an hour afterwards so he has a reason for looking forward to being caught, and doesn't always associate it with being worked.

Rubber trick

Could you tell me how to fit bit rubbers or dummies on a bit? I have tried many times but have been unable to stretch them enough to get them over the bit. Also, is it OK to put them on a bridle with a flash, drop or any other noseband?

Putting on bit rubbers is easy - when you know how! Take a length of baler twine, thread it through the hole in the centre of one rubber and tie the ends securely together so the twine forms a loop. Take a second piece of twine and do the same thing again. Next, put your foot on the bottom of one loop of twine while pulling upwards on the other loop - this will stretch the rubber so it forms a long slot which you can then push the bit ring through with your spare hand. Yes, you can use them with flash, cavesson, drop or grakle nosebands!

Rug rumpus

My gelding will not wear any of his rugs and particularly dislikes his N.Z. He bucks and will not let me put it on him. Could you give me some advice?

It sounds as though your gelding is worried by the whole process of being rugged up - presumably he is not bothered about being saddled up. It may be that he has been frightened or caused extreme discomfort by a rug in the past. Tie him up in the stable or ask someone to hold him for you, and quietly approach him with a neatly folded lightweight rug. Let him sniff at it, and speak reassuringly to him; as he settles, gently stroke it along his shoulder and back. When he is quite relaxed about this, slide the rug, still folded, across his withers and unfold it so that it hangs down either side. Keep reassuring him and keep hold of the rug, so if he panics it does not slide back or to the side, which could frighten him more when he feels the movement. Once you have got to this stage, carefully remove the rug, refold it and repeat the whole process until he is unbothered by it. The next step is to quietly unfold the rug backwards over his back and quarters. Make sure any attached straps are secured (surcingles and belly straps can be tied in a knot) so they do not dangle down and bump against his legs or under his belly and frighten him. Make your movements quiet and slow, stopping when necessary to reassure and relax him again. Quietly secure chest and surcingle straps, checking they are neither too loose nor too tight.

Initially start off by using a rug manufactured from a light, non-rustly fabric which conforms well to his shape, as this will be easier to manage and less frightening for him, particularly when he moves. Even when he becomes more confident, do take care both when rugging and un-rugging him. Remove rugs by unfastening and securing dangling straps before folding them forward and slipping them off – a moment's carelessness when you are a little abrupt could easily put you back. You may not solve this problem overnight but hopefully, with persistence and patience, matters will improve.

Pulling power

I have a problem with pulling manes. Given a long, thick mane of even length, I understand you pull from the underneath to get the required thickness for plaiting. How do you go about shortening the top layer if it is still too long? I also do not understand how pulling hair out from the root shortens the mane as well as thinning it. And what do you do with the new hair that grows underneath? When I pull my pony's mane I only seem to thin and not shorten it.

If you pull the hairs lying on the top of the mane they will form an upright fringe along the crest, so doing this should be avoided - it can look most odd when plaited! Brush out the mane thoroughly and pull the longest hairs (this will shorten as well as thin it), a few at a time, from the underside. Aim to achieve the right thickness along the length of the neck, so don't concentrate just on those areas where the mane is sparser and more easily pulled nearer to withers. Once you have got the mane to the right thickness, if you find it is still too long you can use an old clipper blade to shorten it by taking a lock of hair at a time, pulling it taut and slicing downwards with it. This will give a neat, more natural effect than using scissors.

When pulling the mane, don't be tempted to do too much in one go as this will lead to soreness and your horse may well rub, totally destroying the effect you have laboured to achieve! Do a little each day instead, preferably after exercise when your horse is still warm, as the hairs will be easier to pull out.

Difficult to lead

question **Q**

My 22-month-old filly is difficult to lead – she throws her head in the air, sometimes rears, and then takes off at full speed. I always use a headcollar as I am nervous of hurting her mouth with a bridle. I feel she should be walking out on roads now for her education but I am worried that I will not be able to control her.

answer **A**

It is vital that your youngster does not learn that she is stronger than a human, so if necessary enlist the help of someone who is strong enough to deal with her so she does not realise that she can lift you off the ground or cart you about whenever she pleases.

Another tack you can take is to go back to basics, leading her round in the stable, where she cannot charge off anywhere – rather like a mini lungeing lesson.

You may find it easier to control her when out in a field by using a 'controller' halter (although some horses do not like the sensation of it tightening on the head) or by using a normal headcollar and passing the headrope from the back D, anti-clockwise around the nose and through the back D again, but making sure that it does not interfere with her breathing.

If absolutely necessary, introduce her to a bit, and use a coupling or thread the leadrope through the nearside cheek ring and clip it to the offside ring to lead her.

Although you are reluctant to bit her at the moment, there is no reason why you should not do this if you are having trouble – it is important for you to be in control.

Until you have sorted out the leading problem you should not attempt to take her on the roads, and when you do decide to do so, stick to quiet lanes and have a quiet, sensible horse as escort to give her confidence.

Improving paddocks

question **Q**

The paddocks we have were previously a building site. Our soil is mainly ash and is bone dry in summer, so the grass is slow to grow and is yellowy. Is there anything which can be applied to improve the grass and/or soil? Would nitrogen fertiliser be of any use?

Also, do you know of any laws regarding microlights near bridleways? They fly very low and my pony has already bolted.

answer **A**

As regards your grazing, you should contact the ADAS department of your local Ministry of Agriculture, Fisheries and Foods (MAFF) – you will find the number in your local Yellow Pages directory under 'Government Offices'.

It is important when trying to improve grazing that individual characteristics and previous history plus any underlying problems are taken into account; it is not always simply a case of applying fertilizers willy-nilly, so the advice of a local ADAS officer who can make a visit will be invaluable.

Regarding the microlight problem, contact your local council about this. Alternatively (or if you do not get much help), you could try getting in touch with the Access and Rights of Way department at the British Horse Society, British Equestrian Centre, Stoneleigh, Kenilworth, Warwickshire, CV8 2LR.

TOP TIPS

Hay Care

When soaking hay use clean water for each batch of hay – this is because the water becomes contaminated. Empty and clean your soaking bin each time.

Use a large weight to keep your hay totally submerged - otherwise it is not being effectively soaked. If your soaking bin is small, turn the hay so that it is all soaked.

Shelter bedding

question

Could you advise on the floor covering in and around my field shelter? The floor is stony soil but it does get muddy around the entrance and inside. Previously I have used straw successfully, but my pony has developed COPD (Chronic Obstructive Pulmonary Disease) so an alternative must be found.

Would sawdust, shavings or wood chips serve the purpose? Which would be best and how much would be needed?

answer

You could use shavings to form a semi-deep litter bed inside your field shelter, although without the dimensions of the shelter it is impossible to say how many bales you would need. Although you will find that deep litter is not normally recommended for horses with respiratory problems, since this is a shelter rather than a stable, ventilation shouldn't be a problem!

Drainage is important if the bedding is to be successful, however, so if you can afford it you might think of laying a base inside. Looseweave asphalt laid over fine gravel, on top of clinker and rubble, might be an option – the urine will drain away into the earth – or use old bricks laid on gravel with about half an inch between them.

Field shelters need some form of bedding inside

Safe spuds?

question

Is it safe to feed potato peelings? Is white wine vinegar really good for horses?

answer

Potatoes (including peelings) should not be fed to horses as they can be poisonous; cider vinegar is often used by people to help with arthritic complaints. Obviously you should not attempt home veterinary remedies if your pony has a problem, but should consult a vet.

Molasses – and more

question Q

I would be grateful if you could advise me on the effect that molasses has on horses. I have a 16.2hh 17-year-old ID/TB mare who is highly strung. She became unrideable about four months ago so I took her to the local equine veterinary hospital for tests. They have given her the all clear: no pain, no hormone problem etc.

They thought that she was a very nice forward going horse, asked about her food, exercise etc. and watched her being ridden. We have now been given ACP tablets for her, to be given before she is ridden out. This does seem to help as she no longer rears or swings her body about when we turn for home. Could you advise on the following points:

1. What effect will the ACP tablets have?

2. Does molasses 'heat up' a horse that has a forward going, highly strung nature?

3. Would a change of diet help, e.g. a straightforward cool mixture?

4. We are moving to our own fields with one other mare (to which mine is very attached) and two geldings. Will this cause a problem with mares and geldings sharing?

5. The new fields which we have purchased are on a bridlepath away from the main road. Will the local police or fire brigade advise on safety?

6. The field was sprayed, by the previous owner, to get rid of a bad ragwort problem. We have pulled most of it and intend to harrow and reseed this spring. Will it be all right for horses to graze on this summer?

7. Is 3½ acres enough for four horses if the muck is taken off the field regularly and the land is then harrowed?

answer A

ACP is used as a sedative and tranquilliser; if you are worried about the effects of long term use, consult your vet. If you prefer, it may be possible to use a homoeopathic alternative – if you wish to explore this possibility, contact the Alternative Veterinary Medicine Centre, Stanford-in-the-Vale for a list of homoeopathic veterinary practitioners who may be able to help you with your mare.

I would not have thought that a small quantity of molasses would have been responsible solely for your mare's behaviour, but it is an energy-giving food, and it may just be possible that she is allergic to it in the same way as hyperactivity in children can be caused by certain food substances. You could always try omitting it from her diet to see if there is any change, feeding a non-molassed chaff instead.

Keeping mares and geldings together should not cause any problems, although some people do have definite views on keeping the sexes segregated. The only time you might have problems is if you have a mare who tends to flirt and be a real nuisance when in season, but personally I have never had any trouble in keeping both sexes turned out together.

You could contact your local police station or Horsewatch group about making your premises secure, and your local fire service should be able to offer advice on fire precautions.

You might also find it helpful to obtain a copy of Book 6 in the BHS *Manual of Stable Management* series, entitled *The Stable Yard* (£7.95 published by Threshold Books) which will tell you more about construction etc.

The grazing you have should be adequate, with good, careful management, for your horses; if you have any specific queries, contact the ADAS adviser at your local Ministry of Agriculture, Fisheries and Food – you will find the number in your area Yellow Pages directory under the 'Government Offices' heading.

TOP TIP

Steaming Hay
Steaming hay in a plastic dustbin is just as efficient but less hassle than soaking it. Simply pour boiling water over the haynet, pop the dustbin lid on securely and leave for an hour or so.

Algae build-up

question

Are there any steps I can take to prevent algae growing around the sides of my water trough? At present I have to empty and scrub the trough weekly; since it is an automatic water trough, I thought the trough and water should stay cleaner for longer.

What are the negative consequences of horses drinking water from a trough dirty with algae? Are there any positive consequences?

answer

Regular scrubbing-out of water troughs is advisable to prevent the build-up of algae and sediment, which might otherwise cause a tummy upset; some horses may refuse to drink from them at all if algae is really allowed to build up.

Although using a mild solution of disinfectant may help to prevent such a rapid build-up, some horses may be deeply suspicious of the smell and turn their noses up; since there is no way of monitoring the water intake, regular scrubbing with a stiff brush and clean water may ultimately be the best solution.

Drainage systems

question

I am considering constructing either an indoor or an outdoor school for exercising my horses. The problem is, how should the ground be prepared beforehand?

For a sand school, can you put the sand directly on the topsoil after draining it, or is it essential to remove the topsoil? Should there be a layer of stones about one foot below the surface to assist drainage?

answer

You can make an exercise ring fairly simply by laying soiled bedding (droppings removed first) directly on top of grass or soil. This will give a surface which will enable you to work in all but the very worst of weather in walk and trot at least. Straw can, however, become a little slippery when it is wet, and care should be taken.

For a more permanent surface or an indoor school, you will need to construct a proper, level base to ensure correct drainage. The construction of such a base depends to a certain extent upon the type of surface you ultimately intend to lay.

Bear in mind, however, that whatever surface you choose, it will only be as good as the base you lay, so you shouldn't attempt to take short cuts here. The construction of the base will also be determined by the soil structure and location you have in mind.

Back problems?

question

I have a 13-year-old horse on loan who had not worked for two years. She was fine when I started riding her but I have now noticed that two of her vertebrae are prominent. I ran my fingers down either side of her spine and she sank about a foot but showed no signs of pain.

She doesn't sink when I mount, she isn't lame or stiff in any way when walked out. The vet is baffled. What do you think I should do?

answer

The problems you describe in your letter are common in horses who have a saddle-related problem. We are concerned that when she sinks as you run your fingers down her spine, you have not recognised this as a sign of discomfort or pain. This reaction is not normal unless you put considerable pressure close to the spine. We do see this in horses who have bruising and muscular problems due to ill-fitting saddles.

If you want more information about this, or wish to discuss your horse's saddle in more depth, please contact a reputable master saddler.

Saddle reactions

My four-year-old New Forest x Arab mare moves away when she sees me approaching with her saddle, although she does stand to be saddled and when I tighten the girth. However, if I run my hand along her back she shivers. My instructor has put it down to her lack of muscle, because she is fine when ridden.

The saddle I have came with her and is a 16¹/₂-inch G.P. (General Purpose). I use a numnah but can only push it up into the gullet at the cantle end, not the pommel.

I feel that the reactions from your mare when you go to tack her up could well be indicating some problems with the fit of the saddle. Obviously it is difficult to give you a proper assessment when I haven't seen the horse and saddle, but in my experience horses do not object to the actions of their riders or handlers unless they have good reason.

You mention that your saddle is a 16¹/₂-inch G.P. Unfortunately, this information is not enough, as the major influence on the comfort of your horse is the width of the saddle. If the saddle is fairly new it will have stamped on the stirrup bar an N, M or W to indicate whether it is Narrow, Medium or Wide. In my experience, based on her breeding a Narrow or Medium width will not be wide enough for your mare. Also, we feel that you need to consider the long term implications of such a young and inexperienced horse being 'trained' (albeit unintentionally) to associate discomfort with being ridden.

As far as the numnah is concerned, obviously if the gullet of the saddle is not wide enough it will be hard to keep any numnah up sufficiently.

First-hand experience

I have been a regular weekend rider on and off for the past ten years or so and I now feel that as I am financially secure with a good career, I would like to have my own horse.

Having simply had lessons and hacked out on a regular basis, my knowledge of stable management is very limited; however, I am willing to learn and feel that I have sufficient time at weekends and during summer evenings to keep a horse part livery at a local stable.

Please advise me how I should go about purchasing a horse for myself and the best way of arranging the proper care.

You are honest enough to admit that your knowledge of stable management is fairly rudimentary, so it might be an idea to start remedying this before taking the plunge into horse ownership!

Ask at local riding schools as to whether they run (or are planning to run) any courses on this – you could also ask whether it would be possible to help out at weekends and evenings so that you can pick up some first-hand practical knowledge. Theory is one thing, but some practical experience will help even more!

This will also give you a chance to find out whether horse owning is really for you – it can be fairly time consuming, and it's best to find out in advance whether you really enjoy turning out on a cold, dark, wet night to tuck up your horse for the evening before it's too late to change your mind!

Your idea of initially keeping your horse on part livery is an excellent one, incidentally, as you will be able to learn the ropes with help if necessary.

Learning to load

question

When we bought my pony some friends collected him for us in their lorry. We have since tried to load him in our trailer but without success. It's a huge battle to get him in and he immediately leaps out. What can we do?

answer

Lots of horses and ponies are mildly (and some very badly) claustrophobic and this often accounts for difficulties in loading. A lorry is larger, and generally more inviting than a trailer; it is also more stable when travelling, and there are a number of animals who are reasonably happy in a lorry, but which flatly refuse to go into a trailer.

You will need to teach your pony to load into your trailer, since it will obviously be inconvenient to rely on your friend all the time! Be patient and take your time; try to load him every single day, encouraging him to walk gradually further up the ramp, offering him a feed in a bucket.

Make sure the trailer is located on level ground and doesn't rock around; put plenty of bedding down inside (and on the ramp) and bandage or put travelling boots on your pony to protect his legs. If there is a partition, remove it so there is more space inside for him. You don't say whether you have a front unload ramp, which would be ideal; if you do, put it down so he can see right through and doesn't feel trapped.

Once you can get him to step into the trailer for his feed, lead him right through and repeat all over again. Once he is happy about this, try halting him in the trailer, letting him eat his feed and then unloading him; gradually build up the time you spend with him halted in the trailer and then try asking someone to put up the rear ramp – make sure they stand to the side of it whilst doing this.

If he is happy with this, put up the front ramp too, but remember to take everything in gradual stages. It might be helpful, if there is no-one at your yard who can assist you, to contact the centre you bought him from, and to ask someone to come over for a couple of hours to help you with this problem. You could also enquire as to whether this problem with trailers is one he has always had, and whether there is a reason for it, such as a bad experience previously.

Once he is happy to load and unload, ask your Dad to take him for a short drive, taking it very slowly and returning to the yard the first couple of times, where you can unload and then load him again. Make sure you have a breast bar up though!

Getting your pony's confidence will take lots of patience and perseverance, but try to get into the habit of taking him in each day if possible and giving him his feed inside the trailer rather than in his stable, so he looks forward to going in, rather than dreading it.

Native needs

question

Will my part-Welsh mare need a N.Z. rug? She lives out permanently on a very open field as she cannot be exercised at the moment.

answer

Natives are usually fairly hardy, but crossing them can reduce their toughness and ability to live out during the winter. Especially since the field is open, she will appreciate the protection of a New Zealand rug, but you should also try to provide some kind of shelter from wind and rain.

Just because she cannot be ridden at the moment does not necessarily mean that she can fend happily for herself in all weathers! Try to get hold of a copy of *The Horse in Winter* by Susan McBane, which will give you all the information you need about caring for your pony properly during the winter months.

18

Difficult to bridle

Before I bought him my horse had been neglected. He is very sensitive about his ears as he suffered from untreated rain rash. Although his ears are healing, putting a bridle on is virtually impossible. As soon as you go near his ears he goes crazy. I've tried various approaches, e.g. taking the bridle to bits, but to no avail.

He is okay with a headcollar and will let me stroke his ears. It seems as though the bridle problem is because he anticipates pain. Should I persevere or give him a break and hope he gets over this fear?

It sounds as though you have worked hard at putting your horse's condition right again; continue with your policy of gently handling his head and ears at every opportunity. For the moment at any rate, when bridling up, just use an absolutely basic bridle; remove the browband altogether, take off the bit and slide the remaining headpiece and cheekpieces over his head like a headcollar.

Attach the bit to the offside cheekpiece, pop it in his mouth and attach it to the nearside cheekpiece, and do up the throatlash. You will find that cheekpieces with buckles will be easier to manage than hook stud billets.

Have the bit adjusted so that it is a little on the low side whilst putting it on (although not so much that it bangs against his front teeth), so that you do not inadvertently pull the headpiece into the base of his ears; once you have got it buckled on, adjust it to a more correct height.

If you find that the bridle tends to slip back from the poll, make up a simple browband from a strip of cloth or broad nylon tape (like the sort headcollars are made from) and add a piece of Velcro to the ends, so that you can slip it into place and fold the ends over to secure it.

Once he is more confident about having his ears handled and folded forwards, you could try putting on the bridle again in a more conventional way, although initially you may have to undo a cheekpiece whilst putting the headpiece on.

Just take things quietly though, as it will take some time for him to come to realise that it isn't going to hurt!

Horses at home 1

I am now able to keep my horses at home and would appreciate advice re. stabling, suitable hedging and pasture care.

There are a couple of books you would find helpful: try *Pasture Management for Horses and Ponies* by Gillian McCarthy and Book 6 in the BHS *Manual of Stable Management* series – *The Stable Yard,* which will give you more information on caring for your paddocks and on setting up your stabling.

The BHS also publishes a number of useful free leaflets on *Ragwort; Control those Weeds; Poisonous Plants and Trees* and *Planning Concessions* – send a large sae for them to the BHS British Equestrian Centre, Stoneleigh, Kenilworth, Warks, CV8 2LR.

> ## *TOP TIP*
>
> ### Drying Horses
> If you have just bathed your horse, use a sweat scraper to remove excess water. Then, using an old thin rug with a cotton lining, place this over the horse and pat him all over so that the rug lining soaks up the remaining water. This process takes only a couple of minutes but the result is a horse which can then quickly be dried off completely by the usual method of walking him around.

Horses at home 2

We have moved house and now have a third of an acre. There are also some outbuildings and I am planning on keeping my Shetland and my 14.1hh Connemara cross at home.

What is the smallest size of stable I would need for the Shetland? Is it worth putting the third of an acre to grass? I have to keep the ponies off too much grass and a friend suggested putting another surface down and just feeding hay. Any help would be appreciated.

A third of an acre isn't really sufficient to keep your two ponies on; even if it were seeded for grazing, it would get so churned up in the winter that it would be pointless. However, it would certainly be a useful area in which to turn them out during the day (and far better than keeping them stabled all the time), and since they are such good doers it would also enable you to control their waistlines fairly efficiently.

Against this you will need to set the cost of supplementary feeding with hay. If you have the time, there is of course no reason why you couldn't lead them out in hand each day to ensure they get some fresh grass as well.

As regards stabling, minimum dimensions of 10ft x 10ft for the Shetland and 12ft x 10ft for the other pony should be sufficient, providing room to lie down as well as allowing

for adequate ventilation; as a general rule, the height should be twice that of the horse at the withers.

Check with your local planning authority that you are allowed to convert your building into stabling, and don't forget that you will need to make arrangements for the disposal of your manure; even two small ponies on a diet can produce an amazing amount in a remarkably short space of time!

There are several books and leaflets available which will help you with all this: *One Horse/ One Acre?; Planning Concessions - Stabling within the Curtilage; Winter Shelters, Needs, Hints on Construction* are all available free from the British Horse Society, British Equestrian Centre, Stoneleigh, Kenilworth, Warwickshire CV8 2LR (send a large sae).

Try also *The Stable Yard* (BHS *Manual of Stable Management* series Book 6 £7.95) and *The Design and Construction of Stables* by Peter C Smith (J A Allen £7.95).

TOP TIP

Fence Check
Check daily that fencing is secure. Horses tend to try and go wandering in winter, usually because they are cold, hungry or, in some cases, just plain bored.

Weight-carrying capacity

My mare is a 14.2hh threequarter Arab, quarter Dartmoor and is a medium stocky build. Am I too heavy for her at 11$\frac{1}{2}$ stones? I am currently dieting.

Both Arabs and natives are usually pretty strong provided the conformation is good, but it does sound as though you may possibly be pushing it a little bit by riding her at your current weight.

A lot obviously depends on your mare's build and conformation as to how much weight she can happily cope with, and you might

find it best to ask a good instructor to take a look at you together to assess this at first hand (it is difficult really to comment without seeing her), and to give you some idea of a maximum weight.

Your plan to diet is good, as apart from not overstressing your mare, you will also find that a trimmer figure will actually help you to improve your riding (as well as giving you a psychological boost), so stick at it! Do have a chat with your GP about this though, so you can work out a sensible plan which won't incur any health problems for you.

Coping with 'bargers'

question

I have just bought a 16.2hh Irish Draught who is impeccable in every way except for barging his way out of his box. Do you have any ideas on how to curb his enthusiasm?

answer

At16.2hh your horse is a big strong chap, and you will not be able to control him through relying on your own strength! When leading him out of his box, rather than sticking to a headcollar, use a bridle, or a sliphead with a Chifney on it, which will give you more control.

Make sure that you use a long lead rope, and take the precaution of wearing gloves and a hard hat for your own protection. Do take care that the habit has not arisen through his feeling crowded – if the doorway is very narrow for example – and try to ensure that the doors are opened fully and are not allowed to blow back on his hips as he walks through, as this will encourage him to rush forwards in panic.

To prevent him from barging out of the stable whilst you are going in or out (and trying to leave him inside!) fit a breast bar on the inside of the doorway. Fixed like a slip rail, this will enable you to open the door and duck underneath it without him being able to push past you. Close and bolt the door before removing the slip rail on those occasions when you want to take him out.

Spend some time teaching him to move backwards when asked to, so that you can begin to encourage him to move back away from the door when you enter as well; you can do this by standing to one side of him, taking a fold of skin at the front of his chest and twisting it gently, pushing backwards at the same time, asking him to 'Back'.

Claustrophobic?

question

My five-year-old gelding used to live in a barn-type stable. Now he's in an ordinary stable and he's banging the door and pawing the ground. He can see the other horses but this does not seem to make any difference.

answer

Door kicking and pawing at the ground is usually an expression of psychological frustration – I assume that he is turned out to graze for some part of the day and not kept continually stabled or in the barn? If not, then it would be wise to do so, and this habit is very understandable!

You could try leaving him in the stable with something to keep him occupied when he has to be in – a haynet, a swede suspended on a rope to nibble at and a toy such as a football or a plastic squash container half filled with water and hung up for him to play with.

There is also a possibility that he is a little claustrophobic and, whilst he doesn't mind the larger barn area, is unable to cope with the more confined stable, in which case you will simply have to continue using the barn instead.

Mark of the Prophet

question

I noticed a horse advertised for sale in a magazine which had a 'Prophet's Thumb Mark'. What is this?

answer

A 'Prophet's Thumb Mark' is a dimple mark usually seen on the neck, but sometimes on the shoulders and occasionally the hindquarters; they are most often found on Arabs and TBs. It is believed by some to be a mark of quality and a sign of good luck.

Bitting difficulties

question

My gelding gets his tongue over the bit. He is ridden in a vulcanite snaffle and a flash nose-band. He is not comfy in a metal bit as he tilts his head and chews one side of the bit. I am considering changing to a hackamore. What do you suggest?

answer

Before changing bits, ask your vet to check your gelding's mouth and teeth, as a problem here will cause difficulties. Check also that the bit is adjusted sufficiently high up – if it is very low it will encourage this problem.

Using a grakle noseband, rather than a different bit, may be the solution, as the higher pressure point will help stop him from being able to open his mouth sufficiently to manoeuvre his tongue over the bit.

If necessary, try using this in conjunction with a rubber tongue port. Another option you could try is an Australian cheeker, which helps to keep the bit up in the mouth, and is useful for horses which try to put their tongues over the bit.

If it is found that he has a mouth problem which means that, temporarily at least, he is better off without a bit, you could try opting for a Scawbrig, which is the mildest of this family, fitted with the noseband three or four fingers' width above the nostrils so it cannot hamper breathing.

Tenses when saddled

question

My mare has always been cold backed, but recently when I've saddled her up she tenses up and when I mount she snorts and jogs off. My instructor says everything's okay but my horse is not the sort to be naughty without a reason. Do you think there's something wrong or am I over-reacting?

answer

It would certainly be worth asking your vet to check over your mare's back since there may possibly be a physical problem at the root of this.

You should also ask your saddler to check the fit of her saddle – bear in mind that the stuffing can settle with time, horses can change shape with work and it may not be as good a fit now as when you first bought it.

The fact that she has not reacted in this way in the past, but only recently, would seem to indicate the presence of some kind of physical problem.

Young rearer

question

I have a home-bred two-year-old gelding who is causing problems at the moment. He has always reared, ever since being a foal, but the problem is getting worse. He is quite excitable and at the smallest excuse he rears up and tries to come down on me, attempting to wrap his legs around my neck. I have tried throwing water at him, using a schooling whip on him, even pulling him over – but all to no avail. What can I do?

answer

Whatever the reason for your gelding's behaviour, it sounds as though you need some expert and strong assistance, as trying to deal with this on your own will sooner or later lead to you becoming injured.

It might be possible to begin remedying the problem by attaching a lunge rein to either side of his headcollar and having someone on each side keeping him anchored at a distance from the other person, but obviously you will need to enlist some experienced, professional, strong help, and the sooner you can do this, the better. Do wear hard hats and gloves for protection.

Which studs?

I regularly compete in small cross country and showjumping events but my pony loses confidence when the going is very slippery and muddy. It has been suggested that I use studs – but which ones should I use and when?

Studs can help give better purchase, thus giving the horse or pony more confidence, as well as helping it stay on its feet. Studs come in all shapes and sizes, and you should select the right sort for the ground conditions; you can buy them from most saddlers, or your farrier can supply them if asked.

Squarer studs are normally used for soft going, whilst rounded jumping studs – which are more pointed – are used when the ground is harder; these sharper studs give more 'cut' on firmer ground.

If you are in doubt as to which sort you should use, you should be able to get advice at a good saddlers or from your farrier.

Freezemarking and grazing youngsters

I have a four-month-old filly. At what age can I get her freezemarked? When she is weaned she will live with two donkeys and some cows. Will this be okay or should I rent a field with some horses?

When a farrier was asked to trim the feet of my eight-month-old donkey he refused, saying that they should not need doing until the donkey was a year old. Is this right?

Farmkey do not recommend freezemarking until horses and ponies are a minimum of twelve months old; if done before this the mark apparently doesn't take as well and can become distorted.

As regards grazing your youngster with cows and donkeys: ideally, other horses would be a better option if you have the choice, especially if the cows are turned out on dairy pasture – fine for cows having to produce a high milk yield, but less than perfect for horses, whose nutritional needs are different. If you do graze your filly with cows, they should be dehorned. When sharing grazing with donkeys, you should make sure that you worm against lungworm.

If your donkey's feet are long and becoming chipped, then yes, they should be trimmed and rasped to keep them healthy and in a good shape.

Before your horse is freeze-marked, the area where the markers are applied is clipped

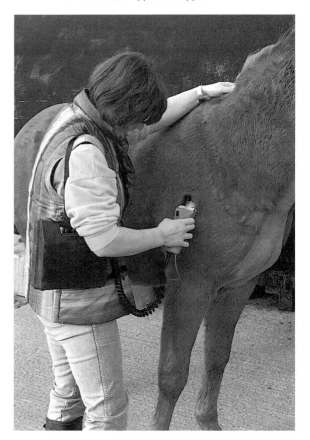

Rubber bedding

My horse is bedded on shavings as she cannot have straw. However, she has recently started to eat the shavings and has had a serious attack of colic and a blocked bowel as a result. I am now considering rubber bedding – where can I get hold of some?

It sounds as though rubber flooring might be a wise solution, although you might also investigate possible causes of this behaviour, such as lack of fibre, boredom etc.

If you are a regular reader of *Your Horse* magazine you will have seen various reports and items on rubber floor coverings which will help you in making your choice. You will find contact addresses for these with the relevant articles; you will also find a list of suppliers and manufacturers in the British Equestrian Directory under the heading 'Floor Coverings' – the reference section of your local or county library may have a copy of this publication.

Greedy guts!

My horse is greedy and messy when he eats! He bolts his food and paws the ground furiously at the same time, with the end result that much of his feed ends up in his bed or the field, whilst he tends to suffer slightly from digestive upsets.

How I can solve this problem?

Try adding chaff to your horse's feed – not only will this provide extra fibre, it should also help to slow him down! Put a couple of large, clean, smooth stones in his feed bucket – these will prevent him bolting his feed as he'll have to pick it out carefully.

It may be worth fixing a manger on the stable wall, or fence, to stop him from knocking his bucket over.

Grass guide

How do you know if your horses are on 'good grazing' or not? How can you find out if the grass is too rich for your horse? Is it harmful to graze horses on a field containing winter wheat?

Good grazing is full of timothy, ryegrass, herbs, clover, fescue and meadow grass. It should be regularly topped, well drained, well fenced, not over-grazed and have the droppings picked up regularly.

Poor grazing is full of mud, soil, weeds, nettles, thistles, droppings and ragwort, and is over-grazed.

Horses keep weight on, or get fatter, on good grazing and lose weight on poor grazing.

Grass that is high in soluble carbohydrates (starch) is not suitable for fat ponies which do no or little work; however, it may be ideal for competition horses and stud animals who have limited access to the grazing.

If your horses or ponies are putting on weight rapidly (check using a weight-tape), will not be caught because they are enjoying the grass too much, are not interested in other types of food or their droppings are loose, then there is probably too much feed value in the grass relative to their needs.

Winter wheat used regularly to be grazed by sheep in the winter, as they padded the plants down and encouraged more robust growth. Sheep do not pull the wheat out by its roots, nor trample it like horses do.

Farmers would not appreciate horses grazing a valuable crop. If, however, you have a grass field with some straggling winter wheat coming through then there is no problem!

LOADING A HORSE SINGLE HANDED

Do you have trouble loading your horse? Take comfort from one reader who has overcome such problems single-handed.

My horse refused to be loaded into a trailer. It seemed, moreover, from any source of advice I consulted, that I could expect to achieve a measure of success only with the aid of an assistant, a combination of ropes and pulleys, and the timely application of a stable broom!

Unconvinced of their lasting efficiency, I determined to devise a method which would enable me to load and travel my horse single-handed.

So successful has my method proved that my mare, Larky, now walks calmly and unaccompanied up the trailer ramp with no encouragement from me and watches, disinterestedly, while I raise the ramp behind her. She now travels as steady as a rock and emerges calmly and unaided.

First things first
The first step I took was to remove all internal partitions from the double, rear unload trailer and put it in the field with Larky. I left the groom's door open and the ramp down.

Larky made it abundantly clear that the trailer's presence posed a threat to life and limb, but when hunger eventually overcame her she plucked up enough courage to approach her feed bucket, which was placed inside.

I then led Larky around the trailer several times, encouraging her to sniff and touch it with her nose.

Every time she explored the trailer a little further, Larky was rewarded with a Polo mint. From the beginning the connection between the trailer, food, reward and praise was established.

Successive meals were eaten, firstly, with the bucket on the foot of the ramp but all Larky's feet firmly on terra firma, then progressively further towards the interior of the trailer, until Larky was obliged to stand fully inside it if she wanted her meal.

I theorised that ultimate success in the venture depended largely not only on Larky's co-operation, but also upon her making a positive contribution to the procedure – she had to do much of the work herself.

These early lessons were invaluable in teaching her that she could safely enter and remain alone in the trailer without my reassuring presence.

Slow progress
After a week or so she would confidently enter the trailer to reach the food bucket at the far end. Occasionally she would back out after taking a mouthful of feed if something outside distracted her. I did not try to discourage or prevent her from coming out, deducing that if she knew she could exit if she wanted to, she would never be afraid to re-enter and never feel trapped.

The next step was to tie the feed bucket to a ring at breast height and for a few days Larky ate her feeds by taking a few mouthfuls, reversing out and walking in again as she pleased. She was still completely loose, but by this stage I thought that she could no longer be frightened of the trailer itself. The next step was to persuade Larky to walk in confidently when I wanted her to and to stay in!

Leading in
I removed the trailer from the field and parked it out of sight and earshot of Larky's companions. From her stable Larky watched her feed bucket disappear into the trailer. I then led her, with an extra-long rope, purposefully towards the ramp. As predicted, Larky stopped halfway up the ramp.

I was not unsympathetic. After all, why should a horse strongly motivated by instincts of self-preservation, voluntarily enter a small, dark, confined cubicle, mysteriously suspended above the ground.

Although Larky could see her feed waiting inside the trailer, she could not bring herself to be led in to reach it. Occasionally she would creep forward, snatch a mouthful and then engage reverse gear again. It was clear that she was still frightened.

Turning point
I tried the 'get tough' treatment, to no avail. My patience was now beginning to wear dangerously thin, but I refused to castigate a horse still obviously in a state of trepidation. I was more than ready to compromise and had to settle for holding the feed bucket whilst Larky took a step further inside the trailer than she had done previously. That session was the turning point.

Gradually, over the next week with two or three sessions a day, I managed to get her right into the trailer and to stand there for increasingly longer periods without her backing out. If she did back out, I would walk her straight back in. Progress was painstakingly slow, but perseverance was the key.

Raising the ramp

The next hurdle to overcome was for me to edge down the ramp and leave Larky inside so that the ramp could be raised. After several days I found that I could remain at the foot of the ramp whilst she quietly ate her feed within. I wanted this routine well established before entertaining any thoughts of raising the ramp.

The first time I tried lifting the ramp, Larky went into reverse. I dropped the ramp immediately and let her exit.

With practice, the exits became less frequent until after a week she stood still whilst I raised the ramp inch by inch until it was fully raised. After securing it, I quickly went in through the groom's door and heaped Polos and praise upon Larky. I had no idea what she would do next. She could easily panic, since this was the first time she was unable to come out when she wanted to. Thankfully she did not panic – not then nor since.

I then let the ramp down – standing to one side for safety. Larky came out extremely hastily, but we had done it! As usual, she went back out into the field the instant she did what was asked of her.

Trial journey

After a week or so of simply putting Larky into the trailer and leaving her in there for increasingly longer periods with the ramp up, I felt that the time was right to take her on her first journey.

Well booted and bandaged, she allowed herself to be led in easily, if a little suspiciously. I did not tie her up, nor did I fasten the breeching strap, but I left the partition in place. I drove her round for 10 minutes at no more than 15mph

before taking her home. Through the little window at the front of the trailer I could see Larky looking anxiously behind her, but otherwise she travelled steadily.

On returning home, I entered through the groom's door to move the central partition to one side to allow Larky more room to emerge. I dropped the ramp as quickly as I could and she shot out, snorting. I always left the head collar rope over her neck before letting her out and caught it as she emerged. She never tried to run off once out of the trailer, knowing there were Polos on hand! However, I always made sure that the yard gate was safely shut before unloading.

After a few more, longer, journeys I deemed it safe to unload her somewhere quiet and take her for a short hack before reloading and coming home. No problems. We clearly had this thing licked!

First show

We went to our first show, just to hack round quietly and let Larky get used to the sights and sounds. After an hour or so I thought that she would be glad to get back to the refuge of the trailer. Little did I know! It took one and a half hours to get her in it. Unbelievably, since that day I have had no problems. I now only have to let the ramp down and she marches straight in.

TOP TIP

Always try to be quiet, calm, patient and reassuring, but above all, be determined. Never try to cure a loading problem when you are short of time – or feeling fractious due to other pressures.

Confidence and trust need to be established so your horse will load happily every time

Trailer light

question

Should trailers have a lit interior light when travelling in the dark?

answer

The interior light, if there is one, must be working, but it need not be on when you are travelling a horse after dark. If there is no interior light in your trailer, you must carry some form of lighting with you to check on the horse when travelling in the dark, such as a torch.

'Snaking' trailer

question

What should I do if my trailer begins to 'snake' when I'm towing it?

answer

'Snaking' is caused by a variety of things, e.g. strong wind, passing lorries, incorrect tyre pressures or a problem in the suspension system.
   There are several things you should do when snaking occurs – and also things you shouldn't:

Do
• Take your foot off the accelerator and let the car slow down on its own until the snaking stops.
• Let the steering wheel move slightly in your hands whilst at the same time maintaining a straight, or slightly curved, course ahead.
• If going down a hill when snaking occurs, apply the brakes lightly and gently to control speed.

Don't
• Try to accelerate out of snaking – this will make it worse!
• Use your brakes – jack-knifing or over-turning may well result from this action.

TRAILER TIPS

Trailers
Before looking at trailers, ask horsey friends and acquaintances if they can recommend certain makes or dealers to buy from/ask for advice.

Out-of-town trailer towing speed limits are 50mph on single carriageways, 60mph on motorways and dual carriageways – all unless lower limits are signed. If you are towing you cannot go in the third or fourth lanes of a motorway.

Ensure that you always attach the break-away safety cable!
Always carry a spare wheel and a suitable jack.

If you are travelling just one animal in a two-horse trailer, travel it on the right-hand side for better stability and a smoother ride.

Breeding natives

question

I would like to breed from my Connemara-cross mare. Could you tell me where I could find a stallion and also recommend a book which will help me during the pregnancy?

answer

There are some breeders listed in the BETA British Equestrian Directory who you could contact. You could also try contacting the breed society direct at English Connemara Pony Society, 2 The Leys, Salford, Chipping Norton, Oxon OX7 5FD Tel: 0608 643309.
   As regards a book, I would strongly recommend *First Foal* by Jane van Lennep and published by J A Allen.

Cooling down

When my mare sweats she seems to take ages to cool down. Although I walk her quietly for as long as possible at the end of a ride, there are occasions when she is hot and sweaty. This happens in winter as well. How could I best cool her off? Should I rug her and if so, which rugs? In winter could she then be turned out in a New Zealand rug?

If your mare returns home hot and sweaty, walk her round with a light sheet over the top of an anti-sweat sheet to cool her down; once she is warm as opposed to hot she can be stabled wearing this clothing, or thatched with straw beneath the rug.

Once she is dry she can be turned out again in her New Zealand rug, or made comfortable in her stable. Do not turn her out whilst still wet, however, as water is a good conductor of heat – sweat will also cause the coat to lie very flat and close to the skin, further reducing its insulating qualities.

Whilst she is drying off you may find it necessary to change the rugs and/or thatching if it becomes very wet. If you have the time you can also help dry her to an extent using old towels – but don't strip off all the rugs whilst doing this; instead, fold them forwards or backwards over the shoulders and quarters whilst working on different areas.

Terrified of people

I bought two unhandled Shetlands. One has been fine but I cannot even catch the other. He has just started to eat from your hand but he will not let you touch his body.

I did try shutting him up for 24 hours without food or water but he turns his backside and kicks! I wondered whether the experience of being gelded has terrified him for life? Any suggestions welcome!

It does sound as though your Shetland has had a bad time of it at some time to be so frightened of humans. If possible, shut him in your stable again (use food and one of the other ponies as a lure if necessary).

Have a chat with your vet and see if he can give you some sedatives which can be administered orally in a small feed – you will need a sufficient dosage to knock him out as much as possible.

If he is dozy enough this should give you the opportunity to get a headcollar on him which can be left on, although obviously you should be careful when doing this, as if he is still awake enough to object his movements will be unco-ordinated and less predictable.

Next, you will have to embark on an inten-

sive programme of handling: leave him without food and water, and make frequent visits, offering him food and water each time. Insist that he apprroaches you to take it, talking soothingly to him.

If he turns to kick, withdraw the food and water and leave, visiting again an hour later and trying again. When he takes the food and drink speak soothingly to him, and slowly and gently try to stroke his neck; if he tries to turn and kick, reprimand him with your voice and, depending on your assessment of the situation, either withdraw again with the food, or encourage him to approach you and try again.

This will take a lot of time and patience, but hopefully, with persistence you will gradually be able to stroke and 'finger nibble' a more extensive area of the neck and take hold of the headcollar without him becoming anxious, and ultimately work your way towards the shoulders.

Until he is relaxed and confident about being handled all over it would be best to leave hoof trimming and leading lessons for the moment.

HORSE CARE

Loaning a horse

question

I have been riding for six months and thoroughly enjoy it. I would love to ride more and am considering having a horse on loan – could you advise what this actually entails and how to go about it?

I have also read that rescued horses are offered for loan or sale. How do I find out more about this?

answer

Although having a horse of your own would enable you to practise your riding more, it is advisable to reach a certain level of competence before embarking on this – otherwise even the most equable of equines will soon learn to take advantage of you!

Ideally you should be able to work in walk, trot (both rising and sitting) and canter confidently and with control on both reins, and have mastered simple school movements including turns, circles and serpentines.

It is also wise to have done a little hacking, as it can be very different from riding in an enclosed area: there are many more hazards to be aware of.

Have a chat with your instructor, telling him/her of your plans eventually to purchase or loan a horse or pony, and ask him/her to tell you when it is felt that you are ready for such a commitment.

Your instructor would also be a good person to ask for advice in finding a suitable horse or pony, and it would be a good idea to take him/her with you when looking at prospective purchases to ensure you make the right choice.

He/she will also be able to advise you on the costs of keeping a horse or pony in your area. You will also find there are a number of books which cover in detail all the queries you have raised; have a look in the reference section of your local library.

As regards taking a 'rescue' horse or pony on loan from a charity, there is often a waiting list, and potential loanees are stringently vetted for suitability; experienced owners and riders are usually preferred as offering the best homes to animals which may have behavioural problems as a result of past treatment.

Kicks out

question

My TB gelding had not been handled much when I bought him so I was wary of him. He hates having his stomach or the inside of his back legs brushed and he kicks out at me. He doesn't mind having leg straps on rugs done up so I think he is just being evil. I would be grateful for some advice.

answer

Kicking is most frequently in self defence – if something causes pain, or startles a horse – rather than from aggression. Check that there is nothing physical which could be causing him discomfort – although be careful when doing this that you don't get kicked for your pains!

Have someone hold a forefoot up and take hold of his tail, leaning down on it slightly to inhibit a kick, and look carefully to see if there are any abrasions, skin lesions, cuts etc.; if he

is a bit furry, probe very gently with your fingers to see if you can feel anything.

Wear a hard hat, and try to keep your head out of the direct line of fire. If there are no physical problems, it might be worth asking yourself whether you are the source of the discomfort; remember that the skin in these areas is very thin and sensitive, and if you use a stiff brush it will hurt.

Teasing out mud and sweat which has accumulated can also tweak painfully at the hairs; take your time and if necessary use a soft cloth or even just fingers to groom, rather than a brush – fingers are more sensitive and can be more gentle than the softest of brushes.

Start off with just minimal grooming until he is more tolerant and you can be more thorough.

Pulling tails

Please could you tell me the correct way to pull a tail? How far down the dock should I pull? Do I only pull hairs from the sides, so the centre part is left normal length?

Pulling a tail well takes practice and experience – the best way to learn is really to ask someone to demonstrate to you. You should only pull tail hairs from the sides, leaving the hairs on the top long.

Use a short-toothed comb, wind a few hairs around it (just a few at a time – less painful for the horse, easier to pull out, and less likely to leave a large bald patch) and pull them out with a quick, sharp tug.

Pulling after exercise when the horse is still warm usually makes the task easier; some horses will take exception, however, so be careful.

Remove hairs evenly from either side of the dock; step back every now and then to assess this and ensure you don't get carried away and overpull from one area, leaving it looking bald.

How far down the dock you pull depends on what suits your horse best, but don't get too carried away – about halfway down should be sufficient.

Spread your tail pulling over several days rather than tackling it in one go, otherwise your horse may feel sore, making him strenuously resist having it done next time, and leading to him rubbing, leaving him with a stubbly-looking loo-brush effect.

Once you have pulled the tail,

dampen the hairs slightly and put a tail bandage on for a couple of hours to help it look neat and nicely shaped.

As the hairs begin to grow out, use fingers and comb to keep it tidy; the short hairs you cannot get hold of can be removed using a small pair of pliers if necessary.

If your horse really objects, leave his tail unpulled and learn how to plait it instead – it will ultimately be kinder to him!

29

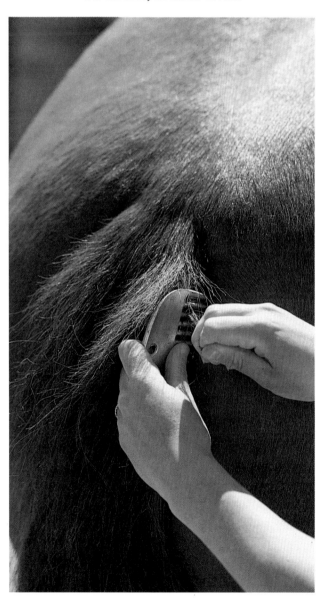

Pull tails carefully or you could upset your horse

Breeding options

question

I have a 14hh Welsh Section D mare I would like to breed from. My aim is to produce something about 15.2hh with good bone for eventing. I would appreciate any advice.

answer

Breeding your own foal can be a satisfying but expensive way of producing what you want – and there is no guarantee that the offspring will do the job you want. No matter how careful you are it may prove to have no real aptitude or talent for jumping.

If you specifically want a youngster to bring on to do some cross country work it might be best to buy a four- or five-year-old which you know will have ability in that sphere to some degree: it will also be cheaper in the long run.

However, if you specifically want to breed from your mare because you want one of her progeny, you will find *First Foal* by Jane van Lennep (J A Allen) or *Foal to Full Grown* by Janet Lorch (David & Charles) of great assistance in selecting a stallion and caring for your mare and the resultant youngster.

Saddles for flat-backed horses

question

I have a Welsh Cob x TB who is very flat backed. His saddle seems to fit him and is certainly comfortable for me, but it will not stay put!

When the saddle is placed on my horse's back the cantle won't sit down. When I ride, the saddle tends to move from side to side. If I jump, it slips forward on to his neck and if he puts his head down it tips up.

I had thought of putting a pad under the pommel to make the cantle sit down. What do you think? I would like to do long distance riding and some hunter trials but the saddle problem is putting me off.

answer

It is evident that your saddle does not fit your horse. We are looking for a secure fit to the horse's back, where the saddle does not roll, lift up in trot or move around unduly. By placing a pad under the pommel you will alter the balance of the saddle completely, thus causing pressure elsewhere.

I can honestly say that with a correctly fitting saddle you shouldn't experience any difficulty. With your horse's stature, I think it would be advisable to have a saddle with an extra girth strap, called a 'point strap'. This will help to stop the saddle running up the horse's neck.

From the pics and info you supplied, you would be looking for a wide-fit saddle, possibly an Ideal H & C (Highland & Cob) G.P. saddle which would allow you to do all your jumping and long distance riding – but it may be necessary to reflock the panel to fit and you would need an extra-deep rear gusset.

Buying a lorry

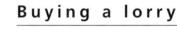

question

I would like to buy a small horsebox but am confused by the terms, e.g. plating. Could you advise?

answer

There is a lot to cover regarding points to look for when buying a horsebox, and with regard to legal requirements. Try to get hold of copies of *Transporting Your Horse or Pony* by Chris Larter and Tony Jackson (David & Charles) and *Transporting Horses by Road* (BHS/Threshold publication) which will explain all the complexities to you! Your local library may have, or be able to obtain, copies of these books if you do not wish to purchase them.

Teaching a youngster to lead

My filly foal is almost six months old and I have been trying to teach her to lead since she was a month old. She either pulls forward or walks into me, sometimes both together! I have tried teaching her with her mother but that didn't help so I always take her on her own now. Any ideas?

Since you have now presumably weaned your youngster, you might find it easiest to teach her to lead in the stable – provided she is relaxed and happy about being in there.

Take the leadrope in your left hand, holding it about six inches from the headcollar, and facing sideways on to her. Hold the end of the leadrope in your right hand where it will not trip either of you up; be careful not to coil it tightly round your hand, and do wear gloves and a hard hat as a precaution.

Encourage her to walk forwards a few steps around the stable, and then to halt; if she tries to walk into you, you can gently but firmly push her away from you with your right hand on her shoulder. Halt after a few steps and praise her, then repeat a couple of times, which should do for one lesson.

If lessons can be learnt at an early age you will make life easier for both you and the youngster later on

In the confines of a stable she should be less inclined to want to pull forwards away from you, but be ready in case she does. Use tugs on the rope to halt her (not a continuous pull), calm her (halt if necessary) and then repeat the few steps of walk and halt again. Once you can lead her in walk and halt around the stable without trouble, try the lessons outdoors.

Tethering problem

A pony I know is tethered in a field where there is no shelter. Should I speak to the owner about this?

Tethering is not the ideal system of grazing as there is no access to shade or shelter, the animal needs to be moved regularly, can escape unless properly secured, and even if a bucket of water is left within reach, it inevitably gets knocked over at some point.

The BHS publish a free booklet entitled *Code of Practice for Tethering Horses and Ponies* which you might like to write for. The address is: British Horse Society (Welfare Dept.,), British Equestrian Centre, Stoneleigh, Kenilworth, Warwickshire, CV8 2LR – don't forget to include a large sae.

This will give you more information: if you feel, having read it, that the pony is suffering, then contact your nearest equine welfare organisation – lots of the horse charities you see advertised in magazines have their own welfare officers who can then investigate the matter further. It would not necessarily be best for you to approach the owner personally.

Naughty or frightened?

My 13.2hh pony will walk into my roomy rear load trailer, stand still for a minute or so and then bolt out. He is so quick we cannot get the tail gate up in time. Is he just being naughty?

Your pony may be claustrophobic and unable to cope with close confinement for very long: this is more common than people realise. He may simply be anxious – you will need to ask an experienced instructor or transporter to visit and help you as it is impossible to comment on the pony's behaviour without seeing him 'in action'. Whether the pony is frightened or just naughty will influence the kind of tactics used – but your adviser on the ground will be able to assist you.

To hog or not?

I may hog my daughter's Shetland/Dartmoor-cross pony as he has a thick mane. Would this be likely to affect points awarded in a Handy Pony style and appearance or turnout class? If the mane was hogged should the pony's tail be plaited or pulled?

Native types very often have thick, coarse manes, as you describe! Before you take the somewhat drastic step of hogging it, do bear in mind all the benefits that a mane offers, even if it does look like an unruly thatch!

Although it will not affect the judging in Handy Pony classes, it does help the rider when mounting – and provides a handy emergency hold on other occasions!

The forelock helps keep flies out of the eyes in summer, and the whole mane helps with weatherproofing the neck area in winter. Admittedly, a very thick mane can prove a problem if it gets in the way of the reins (or if the rider cannot see past it!) but this can be overcome by either putting in a long running plait along the crest, or by patiently doing some judicious thinning and shortening of the mane over a period of time.

If you do hog the mane, it takes some time to grow through again, and if you allow it to do so will still be just as thick as before, and may be difficult to train over to one side.

A plaited tail looks smart with a hogged or plaited mane, and you will have the advantage of being able to leave the tail unpulled, helping to keep the pony warm in winter, and flies away from the dock in summer.

Suitable grazing?

question

I may be moving to a property which has six acres of winter wheat. As the hydroponic grass growers use barley I wondered whether it would be detrimental to graze horses on winter wheat until such time as grass is available?

answer

An equine nutritionist has indicated that graz-

ing your horse on winter wheat is not advisable because wheat is nutritionally richer than grass and the higher protein content may cause problems. Where hydroponics are concerned, the intake is controlled, but this would be impossible to monitor in a field.

Hydroponic grasses are enjoyed by horses

Stable coverings

question

I have converted an old cow shed into stables and would appreciate help on the paint and timber treatments which would be suitable.

answer

There should be no problem in painting the interior of your new stabling with something like Snowcem, but whatever product you

eventually decide to use on the walls do check with the manufacturer that it is not toxic to horses. Fortunately, lead-based paints are not so common nowadays, but these, for instance, should be avoided. Creosote could be used for the timber.

Arena surfaces

We are planning to build a manège but are uncertain as to what type of surface to use. The area we are planning to use drains well but we will not be able to dampen down any surface.

There are three main types of surface, the cheapest being wood chip or bark, which will gradually break down with use, requiring topping up after about 18 months and annually thereafter (depending on the amount of use).

PVC-type materials offer a non-degradable surface, but need some kind of binding agent, such as sand, to reduce scattering of the particles and offer a firmer and more stable surface.

Sand-based surfaces are the most expensive but are reputed to have the longest life expectancy; they are good for jumping, but on their own can give a rather 'dead' feel if concentrating on dressage work.

Both shavings and sand will require regular watering in dry weather, and with all surfaces droppings will need to be removed and the arena then raked to maintain levelness.

It sounds as though the most suitable surface for you to use would be a PVC-type material laid on, or mixed with, fine sand, which will retain moisture better.

As an all-weather surface represents a considerable investment – even if you know of contractors who may be able to do the job for you cheaply – it is wise to do your homework first.

Do make sure bases are correctly constructed; if you try to skimp on this (and as it is the most expensive part, it can be tempting), the surface will not perform well for you and problems will ultimately arise.

Contact the manufacturers of the different surfaces, enquiring about specific requirements for bases for each material, and try to visit yards with different all-weather surfaces, as personal recommendation is less biased than that of manufacturers who will obviously prefer to promote their own products.

Hates the rain

My five-year-old gelding has always shown a dislike for rain but this is gradually getting worse. He refuses to come out of his stable and when I do get him out, he puts his head between his knees and starts to half rear. He refuses to walk through puddles and dislikes the wind as well. Is there anything I can do?

Few horses enjoy being worked in wet weather, especially if it is windy as well, or if they are very fine coated; however, you cannot allow it to become an excuse for bad behaviour.

Most horses do settle once they have warmed up and done a little work. It might be worth lungeing your horse for 15 minutes or so before actually riding him in such weather conditions, to help get him more settled and resigned to it all, but without risk to yourself.

Do try to avoid keeping him hanging around for too long. Check what you are wearing too – rustling long waterproofs etc. may cause him to be a little anxious.

Kimblewicks explained

My 13.2hh pony is impossibly strong on occasions and I ordered a kimblewick for him. What I had in mind was the one with a Cambridge mouth and plain D rings. I actually received a Uttoxeter kimblewick which has two slots on the bit rings, the lower setting being, I believe, more severe.

Could you explain the difference between

these two bits and what purpose the Cambridge mouth serves? I am also a little concerned as to whether two reins should be used on the Uttoxeter style.

answer With a Cambridge-mouth kimblewick the position of the rider's hands affects the amount of curb action; with raised hands there is less, with the hands lowered it is increased.

The shape of the mouthpiece, with a port, allows more room for the tongue, but this in turn puts more pressure on the bars of the mouth than a mullen mouthpiece.

A kimblewick with slots on the bit rings allows the severity of the bit to be varied by selecting either the higher or lower slot; it is also possible to use two pairs of reins so that you can opt for a milder or severe action depending on the circumstances.

Mixed grazing

question Is allowing my horses to graze with cows dangerous?

answer Mixed grazing can be beneficial – or alternatively following horses on with sheep or cattle as it helps to reduce the worm burden, and as they are less selective feeders than horses they will graze back the coarse tufts of grass, helping to create a better sward.

Where mixed grazing is carried out, the

horses may become infected with a type of stomach worm shared by cattle, sheep and horses, but your vet will be able to advise you about a suitable wormer to deal with this.

It is important, however, that the cattle are dehorned, and that the pasture is not of dairy grazing quality which is not ideal for horses. You should also check that the fencing is stockproof.

TOP TIPS

Winter

Soak only enough sugar beet for feeding the following day. If you soak too much it tends to go off before you can use it all up. Label beet nut bins clearly so no-one makes the possibly fatal mistake of feeding them instead of pony nuts. Sugar beet can be prevented from freezing by soaking it in a picnic-type coolbox.

Lag all water pipes and stand taps well. Box-in a stand tap and pack straw around the lagging, along with a stone hot water bottle when temperatures fall below freezing. Fill water containers/tanks as a standby so that you don't get caught out by a 'big freeze'.

Spreading salt grit does help prevent yards from becoming skating rinks, but be warned that salt can damage concrete.

Keep a plumber's and electrician's telephone number handy, as you can count on fuses to blow and pipes to leak at the most inconvenient times! It's a good idea to know where the electric fuse box is and how to change the fuse if necessary.

If your horse suffers from mud fever, try using Mud Fever Leggings (£19.50 a pair) from Lansdown. Contact Jane Whittle on 0272 324609 for details on how the leggings work. Or write to Lansdown Rugs, Beechwood Cottage, Lansdown, Bath, Avon, BA1 9DB.

36

Dangerous 'play'

When I approach my three-year-old filly she charges up to me, rears and bucks in my face. I thought at first that she was just playing, but she keeps doing it and it frightens me.

What starts off as a game can all too often turn into something more serious, which is why it is important not to encourage youngsters to 'play' with humans.

This habit will need some firm handling to nip in the bud, but as you have now become apprehensive and frightened by her, I suggest that you obtain some 'on the spot' assistance from an experienced person. This sort of behaviour is not to be tolerated, and you must get some help with her as soon as possible.

Horses need to play with their own kind, not with humans

Cleaning synthetic equipment

How should I clean synthetic knee boots?

Synthetic equipment can often be cleaned by rinsing in water, or washing using a non-biological washing product; some can even be put in the washing machine, although hot temperatures should be avoided as they can melt the fabrics or their linings – it depends on the material used.

You should follow the manufacturer's instructions as to washing and general care; if you have lost them, contact the saddler you bought the items from, who should be able to help you.

Aggressive gelding

My gelding is great with humans but very aggressive towards other horses. He has been turned out with other horses – at first successfully, but then the horses were moved around which has resulted in kicking matches and injuries.

The other livery owners do not want him in the field with their horses so he now has a paddock on his own – but he is unhappy without company.

It takes time for the social hierarchy to be sorted out when new horses are introduced to established groups, or if two groups are put together. Sometimes this can result in more than just nips and threats, particularly where space is limited in relation to the size of the group.

If an aggressor continues to persist, the only solution is to isolate him from the rest of the group before a really serious injury does occur; and it is understandable if the other owners are reluctant to expose their animals to risk and expensive veterinary treatment.

It is a little unfair on your horse perhaps, but you do have to consider the well-being of the other horses, and the feelings of the owners.

Would it perhaps be possible for one or both of the group he was with before, and which he was evidently quite amenable to, to be turned out with him so as not to deprive him totally of equine company?

In the meantime you could try riding out with horses from the new group, and perhaps trying to reduce his 'boss' status in their eyes, by adopting such tactics as approaching , talking to and making a fuss over them first before going to yours.

This might help as a more long term solution, provided it can be arranged in safe surroundings (such as whilst they are in their stables) and in such a manner that all the horses can observe what is happening, including yours.

Baby food

I felt sorry for a young native pony at a sale and bought it. The vet says it is only three months old. What is the best diet for it and how much per day?

The best diet for a three-month-old foal is obviously its mother's milk. If it has just been taken from mum, then it can stay on a milk replacer, such as Equilac, for another couple of months. It can also have a handful of Pasture Mix, or similar feed, plus Surelimb every day.

Do take advice from your vet, as it is impossible to be specific about a suitable diet without knowing a lot more about your foal.

TOP TIP

Safe Move
Moving your horse to a new yard? Follow these tips to promote his health and safety:
● **Dispose of any old bedding you find in his new stable – it may be mouldy or contaminated.**
● **Disinfect the stable.**
● **Disinfect any drinking or eating bowls.**
● **Check the stable for any projections or** sharp edges which could cause injury.
● Are the windows safe? Are there grilles to prevent the horse getting at the glass/plastic?
● How secure is the door? Are the bolts and hinges strong? Is there a bottom bolt as well?
● Check out the grazing arrangements – you ought to have surveyed the fields and their suitability before deciding on the yard.
● Find out which horses in the field kick etc.!

question

answer

Too thin

I have a real problem with my 16hh, seven-year-old TB gelding. Whatever I feed him he simply does not put enough weight on. He looks very poor and has poverty lines on his quarters, although he seems bright and lively enough.

The vet has checked him over for a physical ailment and worms and given him the all clear. My gelding is out during the day and in at night. What diet and what quantities would be suitable for him?

Weight gain (or weight loss) needs to be done slowly. It will take up to six months for a weight increase to be seen, if you are being sensible about it!

Make sure that your hay is of good feed value (cut early in the season and fresh smelling). It may be worth getting your hay analysed to ensure you are getting what you pay for!

Let him have ad-lib hay (as long as it does not prevent him from eating his energy feeds). Good grazing will also be beneficial.

TOP TIPS

Feed Management for thin horses
- Feed your horse slow-releasing energy feeds.
- Make sure he has company.
- Keep to a constant routine.
- Feed him in peaceful surroundings.
- Ensure he is not being bullied.
- Check he is warm (rug him up when necessary).
- Make sure his water supply is clean, accessible and always there. A horse will stop eating if he does not have access to water.

Recommended diet – assuming he is in light work:
Summer:
- Good grazing.
- 4lbs Fiber P or Alfa-A.
- 3lbs low energy feed, e.g. Pasture Mix, Horse & Pony Nuts, All-Rounder, Cool Mix.
- 1lb extruded barley.
Split the above feeds into three feeds a day.
- Hay at night.

Winter:
- Ad-lib hay in stable and field.
- 4lbs Fiber-P or Alfa-A.
- 4lbs low energy diet (as in summer).
- 2lbs extruded barley.
- 1lb (dry weight before soaking) sugar beet shreds.
- 5 tablespoons of soya oil.
- Possibly some Haylage at night.
Split the daily ration as suggested into four feeds.
NB: If your gelding has been in this condition for a long time and your vet has checked him once over, then it may be worth getting a second opinion.

Fence chewer

question

answer

My gelding has started to eat the post and rail fencing in his field. I have tried putting Cribox on his 'favourite' areas but it is difficult to cover all the fencing.

Fence chewing is an irritating habit as well as an expensive one, considering the cost of good post and rail fencing. Protect fencing by applying a coat of creosote or a product such as 'Bitter Apple'. If you use creosote, allow it

to dry before turning the horses out in the field: otherwise it can cause blistering. You could also try giving your horse a broad spectrum mineral/vitamin supplement in case a deficiency is at the root of the habit.

Convalescent diet

I've just bought a 'rescue case' from a sale. The mare is a 16.2hh, fine TB-type and is vastly underweight. She's approximately 11-years-old and is very nervous. I've heard that in such cases a normal diet is unwise, as is feeding her up too quickly, as all sorts of digestive problems can arise.

Can you advise me what I should feed the mare on, and in what quantities?

All changes in diet should be made slowly. I suggest you treat your mare in the same way as you would yourself if you'd had a bad digestive upset.
• Feed little and often, mainly fibrous feeds – give her small haynets.
• Let her graze for an hour at a time. Let her have company, but make sure she is not bullied.
• Give her a total of 4lbs of hard feed a day for the first fortnight, split into four feeds. Use Pasture Mix and Alfa-A (keeping fibre levels up)

or Convalescent Diet, plus Alfa-A.
• It may be useful to add Yea-Sacc to her diet as this helps stabilise the hind-gut.
• Let her have a few carrots and apples in her feed.

Build up feed and grazing very gradually and expect to see a gradual weight increase, so she regains good condition over a six to eight-month period.

Obviously you will get the vet to check her over, to make sure it is just a malnourishment problem that has caused weight loss. The vet can advise you on worming, teeth, etc.

I would caution anyone buying a case like this from a sale. The horse may be underweight because it has cancerous tumours, or total worm infestation which may cause it to have colic and die.

Although you may feel sorry for and buy a neglected horse, it is not a wise thing to do if you are inexperienced and unprepared for the care it needs

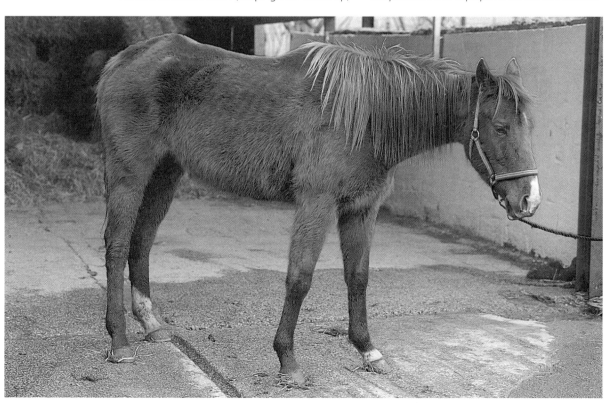

question

answer

New horse 'blues'

I cannot catch my new horse – even when I take food to him – yet he still comes to his old owner! I have had him for almost a month – what can I do?

Your relationship with your new horse is still in its early days; the fact that the previous owner can catch him without difficulty illustrates this. He evidently knows, trusts and respects her but he obviously doesn't feel that he knows you quite as well!

People often forget that getting used to a new owner can be quite as hard for the horse as vice versa; routines, feeds, field companions and work are often different, as well as the actual location and person caring for and exercising them, and this can often lead to teething troubles and a few misunderstandings initially.

When you think about it, it is a fairly major upheaval for a horse – you might compare it to being sent away to boarding school, where you don't know anyone, have a confusing timetable, and perhaps don't know some of the schoolwork; some adapt quicker than others!

Be patient, and try to have a chat with the previous owner about this problem. See if you can follow a fairly similar daily routine to the one she had, and do try to avoid only catching him up when you are riding – even though this may mean sacrificing some riding time and social activities in the meantime.

Horses are very quick to learn this. It will only be in the short term – and if you have to spend hours catching him, your riding time will be very short anyway. Spend time getting to know him as a person, grooming him and perhaps leading him out for a bite of grass.

You could also ask the previous owner if she could come with you to catch him for a couple of days, with you gradually taking over the initiative and encouraging him to transfer his trust and dependence to you. Be prepared to reimburse her for her time if necessary; and even if it isn't mentioned, a small gift such as a box of chocolates would probably be appreciated!

Consider the work you do with your horse as this could also have a bearing on his attitude to you; avoid doing really demanding activities, concentrating instead on activities he finds fun.

Banishing ragwort

question

answer

Is it illegal to have ragwort on your land? If so, how do we get rid of it?

Ragwort is extremely poisonous; one of the dangers is that the effects are cumulative – that is to say that a small intake over a long period is as dangerous and fatal as a large intake on one occasion.

As there is no specific treatment, the best policy is prevention, by removing the plant altogether. Pulling by hand is not only back breaking work, but not terribly effective, as sections of the root may be left in the ground and will re-grow even more vigorously; wilted plants are also more palatable, and should be removed from the grazing area and burnt.

The most practical solution for most people is to spray using the herbicides MCPA or 2,4-D every autumn or every second spring.

Ragwort is classified as an injurious weed and specified in the Weeds Act 1959; the MAFF have powers to serve clearance notices on agricultural land. Where domestic gardens, roadside verges and waste land are concerned the local authorities should have bylaws which can be enacted if required; difficulties can occur on other types of land with regard to enforcement.

For further information you may like to read the leaflet *Ragwort* available free from the British Horse Society, British Equestrian Centre, Stoneleigh, Kenilworth, Warwickshire CV8 2LR – please enclose a large sae with your request.

Clipping considerations

I have a Section D cob and am receiving different advice as to his winter living arrangements. I plan to hunt him occasionally, have lessons in an indoor school twice a week and hack out the rest of the time. He seems to be happier living out than being stabled. What would be the best arrangement for him?

As you intend to hunt occasionally as well as continue with your hacking activities and twice-weekly lessons it would be advisable to have him clipped, which would necessitate rugging him up both when stabled and when out in the field.

The clip need not be too drastic; a trace chip would probably be fine since you wish to keep him out during the day, only bringing him in to the stable for the evening. This would enable him to work without becoming unduly distressed, hot and sweaty, or losing condition – as well as making it easier to cool him down with less danger of chilling after exertion.

Unhappy with Tack

I am concerned about my mare's saddle as she appears unhappy when tacked up and has gradually become less easy to work on the bit. I broke her in two years ago and she did well in dressage competitions but she does not listen to me so well now. Her current saddle has a gullet which tapers towards the cantle. If I do not use a numnah my mare bucks in canter. I was considering buying a synthetic saddle. What do you suggest?

It sounds highly probable that your problems are related to saddle fit; your youngster will be a very different shape now to that when she was unbroken, and now she has acquired more musculature along her top line, a saddle which was previously a good fit may now be starting to pinch.

The gullet of the saddle should not taper towards the cantle, but rather be of the same width along its length, otherwise pinching will also occur – the horse's backbone does not narrow in this area after all!

My personal opinion is that if a saddle is a good fit, the material it is made of is largely irrelevant, although the synthetic types can make the horse's back sweat rather more than a leather one, which should be borne in mind if you are planning long distance work.

With any saddle, no matter how good the fit, there is inevitably going to be a certain amount of movement from it on the horse's back, and when using synthetic saddles this can lead to some friction being caused by the material, which can rub the hair up the wrong way, so if you opt for this type of saddle, do use a numnah to eliminate the effect.

Even with a leather saddle a numnah can be a good idea – some horses dislike the touch of a saddle without one (particularly if clipped out completely along the back in winter) and it does help to reduce labour in keeping the saddle lining clean: it is far easier to change a dirty numnah than to clean the lining every time you ride.

However, the numnah should be no more than a thin cloth type, so that the fit of the saddle is not changed; it must be pulled well up into the whole of the gullet, and care taken that rubbing is not caused by any tapes attached to secure it to the saddle, particularly since these are usually stitched on with nylon thread which can be very abrasive on sensitive skin.

If you are using a thick numnah this might be the reason why your mare does not buck when you use it – it may be helping to reduce the pinching effect caused by the narrowing of the gullet. However, this is not ideal – far better to sort out a new saddle.

If you would really prefer to stick with a leather saddle, why not ask your saddler about the chances of a trade-in against your current saddle? This would help you to offset the cost of a new or secondhand saddle.

STEP BY STEP GUIDES

42

QUARTERING YOUR HORSE

1. Tie your horse up using a quick release knot. Ensure you don't tie the leadrope directly to a solid object – fasten baling string to the tie rig and attach the leadrope to that. Pick your horse's feet out, from heel to toe, into a container or skip. Check the state of his shoes and feet. Take this opportunity also, to check your horse's legs for signs of injury, mud rash, etc.

2. Brush off mud and loose hairs from the body with a dandy brush or other tool, eg. a rubber pimple pad or mitt, whichever you and your horse prefer. Use softer brushes or pads, eg. a body brush, on the face and other sensitive or bony areas. Whilst brushing off, check your horse for signs of injury or if he's 'off-colour'.

3. To avoid tack rubbing, take particular care cleaning areas where it will fit, ie. the saddle and girth area, legs where boots or bandages will fit, between the forelegs if a martingale or breastplate is used, and the head.

TOP TIP

Putting Vaseline or udder cream on dry heels and lower legs before turning your horse out will help repel mud and help prevent mud fever.

4. Once the body is done, brush the mane and tail out with a body brush or your fingers. Then dampen the mane and dock with water to 'lay' them, ie. flatten and shape the hairs neatly.

5. Sponge off obvious stable or grass stains with equine shampoo. Unless you use 'Bascule' shampoo, ensure you rinse all soap off. Dry washed areas with a towel.

6. Sponge your horse's eyes, nose, udder or sheath and dock (using a different sponge for the last three 'bits'). Use tepid water. Alternatively, use Targa's Under Tail Wipes and Equine Face Wipes. Dry off sponged areas. In cold weather, apply a little Vaseline to help prevent drying and chapping.

7. A slick of hoof oil, or other preferred hoof preparation, completes the job. Alternatively, you can use vegetable oil.

Wet weather riding

It's all very well brushing off a dry horse, but what should I do if I want to ride my horse in bad weather and he comes in from the field wet and extremely muddy?

It It's all very well brushing off a dry horse, but what should I do if I want to ride my horse in bad weather and he comes in from the field wet and extremely muddy?

Ideally your horse can be brought in an hour or so before you ride to give him chance to dry off a bit. If he's been rolling, the last thing you want to do is put a saddle on a wet back that's covered in gritty mud! It's essential that the back and girth area id dry so that all traces of mud can be brushed off.

wearing a NZ rug in winter and a light waterproof turnout rug during summer if the weather is wet will help keep the back dry and clean.

Muddy legs can either be left to dry before the mud is brushed off, or, if time is short, wash the legs but ensure that you dry them well. Muddy tails and manes can be rinsed, but try to avoid getting any more of the horse wet - especially in cold weather.

Types of hedging

I rent my paddock from the local council. The fencing is post and wire but they have now asked for a fence which provides more of a screen. I have persuaded them that hedging would be better than their suggestion of seven foot panelling but I have to submit types of hedging I would be planting. Can you advise?

Hedging can provide a useful windbreak and afford shelter and shade; suitable varieties include blackthorn, hawthorn, and holly. Faster growing species can be incorporated if you want to see quicker results; you could also think of putting in a few trees which can either be allowed to grow as trees or used to form the hedges themselves. Alder and sycamore are options, (and rapid growing) or may and beech can be used.

Hedges do offer a habitat for wildlife; it is important to remember however, that a number of hedgerow plants which are poisonous may also thrive, so you will need to look out for these.

Hedging can take a long time to grow and to become substantial enough to give either shelter or to screen off the field, and will need protection whilst young from being nibbled. If you are planning to plant close to the existing fence, you will need to erect a secondary fence (possibly a temporary one) about a metre inside the hedge, whilst trees will need a guard around the trunks to stop the bark from being chewed off. Once maturing well, the hedges will benefit from being trimmed and laid.

Mix nuts with chaff

I have always thought pony nuts should be fed with bran or chaff but manufacturers say their nuts should be fed as a complete food. Can you advise?

I am in total agreement with you, that nuts/ pellets should always be fed with a chop or chaff.

Research work at universities have measured the amount of time a horse chews pellets, coarse mixes, extruded feed and hay. The feed the horse eats quickest are pellets.

He does not chew them very effectively. It takes a horse three times longer to chew hay compared to concentrates, if you feed the same weight. It is very important a horse chews, because he only produces saliva whilst he is actually chewing - a horse's mouth does not water at the sight/smell of food. Saliva is vitally important as it acts as a lubricant to stop the horse choking.

 question

Puddle phobia

My problem is my huge, strapping eight-month-old heavyweight section D filly who flatly refuses to walk through puddles of water.

Normally she has the calmest, most placid temperament imaginable, but show her a puddle and she just becomes unhinged! She would never follow her mother through before she was weaned but she has never been frightened by water: in fact she adores being bathed and having water thrown over her legs. We have dug the front of her stable out and flooded it – she walks through that into her stable without any problems!

 answer

Why all the urgency over leading your youngster through water? It is not an essential part of her training at this stage; far better to leave it until she is older, more established in her work and when you can control the situation more than you can from the ground!

If you try to force the situation now, whether successfully or not, you are only going to create phobias for the future. When she is older you can gradually introduce it not as a 'lesson'– which can lead to friction and unnecessary trouble – but when an occasion lends itself: on a rainy day going through a shallow flooded section of road with an older, wiser friend, or through a shallow river or properly constructed schooling water fence, rather than specifically aiming her through puddles she can dodge round.

There are any number of horses who are competent water jumpers, but who nevertheless try to avoid walking through puddles on the way in from the field! In the meantime, you can always bathe her since she enjoys it, but allow the water to run long enough to build up into a puddle around her which she then has to walk out of.

 question

Picking out feet

I have recently been advised not to attempt to pick out a horse's feet all from the same side. Could someone please explain the basis for this remark?

I was taught to pick out each hoof whilst standing on the nearside and it is much simpler. It does not cause a problem for the horse if he is trained to accept it.

answer

In reply to your query, I'm afraid that I disagree with the practice of picking out all the feet from one side, for the following reasons:

1. Some horses can become confused by this practice, leading to a lot of anxious shuffling about, which doesn't exactly help matters and can lead to trodden-on toes!

2. Particularly when dealing with more awkward horses, it is very difficult to remain in control and keep hold of a foot on the opposite side from the handler – the horse can easily snatch it away or kick out.

3. When picking out the feet furthest away, the handler inevitably leans inwards in order to see clearly what they are doing – putting their head in a vulnerable position.

4. The further away legs end up being drawn inwards, rather than being lifted upwards in a straight line, which can make balancing difficult for some horses – just as pulling a leg too far out to the side can.

5. If the horse attempts to snatch a foot away on the far side it can end up injuring the opposite leg.

6. When lifting a back foot, the handler inevitably passes their arm across the back of the closest leg to reach the further away one, placing it in a vulnerable position if the horse kicks out.

7. If the horse is reluctant to lift a foot it can be very difficult to encourage it to do so.

Riding through water can be fun for both horse and rider! Do check first, though, that the footing is safe and without holes and that the water is not too deep

Supplementary feed

question

Could you advise on how much to feed my 14hh part-Arab pony? In summer she has a tendency to become fat. I ride her five days a week, sometimes for two to three hours. How much hard food should I give her before taking her to shows to jump?

In winter she has pony mix, nuts, molassed chaff and sugar beet as well as hay, but I am not sure how much to give her.

answer

Do not be tempted to feed your horse if: a) she has enough energy to do the job/work

you want from her, and b) she is well covered/prone to being overweight.

Horses, like people, have varying metabolisms and your horse obviously isn't expensive to keep.

If she starts to lose weight, then do think about supplementary feeding, similar to what you would feed in the winter. I suggest you read Robert Eustace's book on *Explaining Laminitis* and its prevention. It emphasises why we should not be tempted to overfeed.

Putting on weight

question

I have a 13.2hh part-TB gelding which I showjump. I have had him for five months and have tried all kinds of fattening foods but they contain too much energy. The low energy foods do not help him to put on enough weight.

answer

Horses need energy: if you feed more energy than they are using then they will either put on weight or become more excitable – the reaction will depend upon the natural temperament of the horse and the type of energy you are feeding.

If you are looking to put on weight, then

you need mostly slow-releasing energy. These are things such as hay, and fibre-feeds. I would recommend you try Alfa-A, Fiber-P or Meadow Sweet together with sugar beet. You sound as though you have tried lots of feeds in five months. You must make changes of food slowly, over a period of two weeks.

Do have your pony's teeth checked by an equine dentist, and then at least once a year. I presume you worm him regularly?

It is best to put weight on a horse slowly. I really need to know your horse's heart girth measurement or weight and exactly what work he is doing to advise you properly.

Linseed values

question

Please can you give me any information on feeding Linseed Lozenges and their suitability for show horses, including youngstock?

answer

I do not know of the specific product Linseed Lozenges that you refer to; however, if you send me a label I can comment critically.

I can tell you what nutrients linseed per se provides for a horse:

Protein	219g/kg or 21%
Oil	316g/kg or 31%
Fibre	76g/kg or 7.6%
Lysine	7.7g/kg or 0.7%
Phosphorus	5.2g/kg or 0.5%

Although high in protein, it is not very good quality protein. Most people use linseed as a source of oil or as a 'treat' in a mash.

You must boil linseed to remove an enzyme which causes a poisonous reaction. If it is processed linseed you are buying then do check the oil levels, as often the oil is removed.

Very few books give recommendations on quantities of linseed to feed but I suggest 4oz a day is sufficient. You may be better off adding 4 tablespoons of soya oil a day to the rations.

Weight watching

question

I have a 15.2hh Arab who is 12 years old. I have difficulty putting and keeping weight on him. He is wormed every eight weeks and has his teeth rasped regularly.

At present his morning feed is a bucket of Hi-Fi with ½lb oats and ½lb bran. He's turned out to grass until 4pm when he has 1lb of horse and pony nuts, 1lb cool mix, 1lb soaked sugar beet, 1lb barley, 1lb bran with a double handful of chaff and 1lb of chopped vegetables.

At 8pm he has 1lb each of nuts, mixed flakes, soaked sugar beet and bran with 2lbs barley, chopped veg, salt and limestone flour. He has a constant supply of seed hay and is bedded on straw. He never eats all his hay and is getting thinner, not fatter. His droppings sometimes smell strange compared to those of another horse on the same feed.

During the week he is only ridden for an hour on one day and then for two hours each day at the weekend.

answer

The first thing we have to remember as horse feeders is that we are really feeding the bacteria in the lower gut and if these aren't healthy then neither is the horse.

There are 10 times the number of bacteria in the horse's gut than there are cells in the whole of the horse's body, i.e. millions and millions.

A horse therefore needs a very constant

> ### TOP TIP
>
> **Feed Check**
> Weigh your horse's feed so you know exactly what he is getting. Ensure all your feed is kept in vermin proof containers and mark each feed clearly so that anyone could make up your horse's ration without getting the foods mixed up.

diet, so you must decide which feeds your horse prefers and divide these into three feeds of the same ingredients.

Your horse is on a lot of cereals for the work he is doing and his bacteria will be more adapted to cereals, which is why he is not eating his forages (alfalfa and hay).

I suggest that you turn him out as much as possible and in the summer months feed him per day: 4lbs Hi-Fi, 4lbs either barley or a compound, plus 8lbs hay if you bring him in. In winter feed him per day: 15 – 20lbs hay, 4lbs Alfa-A, 5lbs concentrates.

Bran acts a laxative and this will not help his droppings. Horses' metabolisms do vary and this may be why your other horse seems fine on the same type of diet. However, I would recommend you swop both horses onto a more consistent diet. You may like to try some Yea-sacc ,a product that has been scientifically researched and acts as an aid to digestion – a bit like Rennies.

Licences for entires?

question

I recently bought a colt who is now a lovely, well mannered 11.1hh pony. I was thinking of keeping him entire – do I need a special licence? I would keep him with my gelding and he would not serve mares. He would go to local shows to compete.

answer

You do not need a licence in order to keep a stallion, but I would suggest that you examine your motives for doing so. Castration prevents unwanted pregnancies, makes the horse safer

and easier to handle, he can live a pleasant lifestyle turned out in mixed company with no worries, and he will also grow more.

The handling and safety aspect particularly is something which should concern you if a child is to ride him, as well as coping with him at shows. Don't be sentimental about leaving him entire, or use him as an interesting experiment for yourself; it won't necessarily be in his best interests!

STEP BY STEP GUIDES

Ticklish tummy

question Q

answer A

I have a young pony who tries to bite when I brush his tummy or the top of his hind legs. He has also started fidgeting about and stamping his hind legs. I am now worried that he may kick me. I tie him up short but it doesn't seem to make any difference.

Your pony is obviously very sensitive and ticklish under his tummy and between his back legs – lots of ponies are. He is trying to let you know this by attempting to nip and stamping his back feet – but it doesn't sound as though you are really listening to what he's

telling you!

Tying him up is a good idea to stop him nipping – but if you carry on making him too uncomfortable he'll only find another way of trying to stop you (like kicking!) Use the softest possible brush to do these tender areas – even if he is very muddy, take a little longer rather than trying to do it quickly with a stiffer brush.

If he is still touchy, just use your fingers or a soft cloth and gently work the dirt away instead. Wear a hard hat (just in case!), be careful, be thorough – and be considerate!

PUTTING ON A TAIL BANDAGE

1. Brush out the tail. Dampen the hairs at the dock using a water brush.

2. Fleecy side to the tail, lay the top of the tail bandage diagonally across the top of the tail.

3. Wind the bandage firmly once round the dock. (pic 1)

4. Fold down the free end, as shown. (pic 2)

5. Bandage over the free end to secure it in place. Continue to bandage diagonally down the dock.

6. Overlap the layer above as you go. Use even pressure, and ensure that the bandage is wrinkle-free.

7. Bandage to the end of the tail bone, or slightly beyond, before bandaging back up the tail.

8. Continue to bandage diagonally back up the dock with light, even pressure.

9. At the top of the dock, bandage straight round and down until all the bandage is used up. Flatten the tapes out, then wrap them round the tail once. (pic 3)

10. Tie the tapes in a bow, loose enough so you can just get a finger underneath them.

11. The fastened tapes should lie half-way down a wrap. Tuck the tape ends under the fastened tape.

12. Fold the bandage wrap above the tape down over it to neaten the appearance.

13. Gently mould the tail into its normal, slightly curved shape. If the bandage is too tight, moulding will be difficult, so re-bandage. (pic 4)

Removing the bandage
1. Undo the tapes and gently slide the bandage off.

Newcomers

question

Can you advise on the best way to introduce a horse/pony into an established group? Is it best to keep mares and geldings separate? Whatever I do I always seem to end up with a kicked horse.

My old mare recently had a pony put in the field with her and if I hadn't intervened she would have seriously injured the pony. She has never behaved like this before.

answer

It can sometimes be a bit traumatic introducing a newcomer to a group of horses, and inevitably there is some bickering as they establish a pecking order. It is always advisable to keep an eye on things for a while before leaving them to their own devices, as sometimes things go beyond what is acceptable, and a horse may need rescuing promptly.

In such a situation it may be necessary either to isolate the instigator of the attacks, to find alternative grazing with more congenial company for the horse which is not accepted, or to rotate the victim and aggressor's time out at grass so they are never out together, e.g. one out in the morning, in during the afternoon and vice versa.

This might give the 'victim' of the bullying a chance to pal up with another member of the group, so that it then has a 'minder' if you decide to try them all together again at some point in the future.

Area of grazing can sometimes be a factor in bullying: if it is relatively small, a new horse may find it more difficult to be accepted by the dominant one.

As regards grazing mares and geldings together, people have definite thoughts on the subject, some saying that each sex should be segregated.

I have never experienced any difficulties in grazing mares and geldings together, except on the odd occasion when a mare has been in season and exhibited aggressive tendencies or become a real nuisance through flirting, during which periods time out in the field has been divided between them.

TOP TIPS

Grooming a Stranger

If you are grooming a strange horse or one known to be sensitive about its hind legs, ensure you hold the animal's tail (with the hand nearest the horse) and place this hand just above the hock. You will then receive an early warning signal if the animal tries to kick.

Solo jumper

question

I have had my horse for two years and he's been wonderful. However, in the last couple of months he has started jumping out of his field. He has company in the field and there have been no problems until this jumping out started. He jumps into empty fields or into others with different horses in – once there he grazes quietly. I've tried changing his companions, grazing him well away from the others, making the fencing six feet high – but he still does it. He's kept at livery and I'm worried we will be asked to leave.

answer

Once horses have started jumping out of fields, it is difficult to stop them unless there is an obvious cause for the problem, e.g. incompatible company, inadequate grazing, loneliness. It doesn't sound as though any of these is a cause for your fellow though!

The obvious solution is to use electric fencing to either widen or increase the height of the fence, which you have also tried, but again with no success, and it sounds as though persisting with this could be dangerous if he became entangled with it.

The only other solutions I can suggest are either to hobble or tether him – in which case he should not be turned out with another horse as he could get into trouble if picked on. Hobbles or a tether also need to be introduced with great care and initially he will need to be supervised.

Alternatively, I have heard it suggested that making a flap (of leather or some other sturdy material which cannot be blown up by wind) which fits to the headcollar and hangs down over the eyes has been known to work; the horse cannot see ahead when the head is lifted, only when lowered, and is therefore discouraged from attempting to jump out.

I am unable to vouch personally for this, however, and whether you try it or not will be dictated by your horse's personality and temperament. Obviously there could possibly be problems if he was startled or frightened by something; he would also need to be given time to get used to it under close supervision.

The only other answer is to keep him stabled all the time, leading him out to graze each day on a lunge line, although this will obviously be less satisfactory as well as time consuming.

Stable scare

question

My pony had to have part of her top lip removed by the vet. This was done in her stable and since then she has refused to go into it again. I did entice her in with feed but she then reversed out at high speed. She has a field shelter which she uses, but what if I need to leave her in the stable for the vet or farrier?

answer

It does sound as though your pony associates the stable with the vet's visit; horses tend to have long memories for such experiences. Are you at a yard, or do you just have use of one stable? If you are at a yard it might be interesting to see if she will go into a different stable (when you could perhaps arrange a swap), or whether she is now anxious about all stables as opposed to just that one.

Trying to force her into a stable is most likely to confirm her worries rather than alleviate them, no matter what treats she finds in there. Patience would seem the only answer, although you could try depriving her of water and then using it as enticement to step into the stable; obviously you must be sure that any other horses in the field do not suffer as a result of this.

If it really becomes necessary in the meantime to confine her in a smaller area, perhaps you could adapt your field shelter, which she is evidently quite happy about, fitting it with slip rails across the entrance.

question **Q**

Jaws!

My 14-year-old mare is very snappy when handled. When she is in season she is very flirty with the geldings and although Regumate helps to calm her it is very expensive.

She hates being groomed and tacking up, rugging up etc. is also pretty dodgy – you need to avoid her teeth! When ridden she is very tense. She's better in a double than in her snaffle but out hacking she just sets her jaw whenever I take any contact. I'm a BHSAI and I feel my riding is not upsetting her.

Do you think all this behaviour is related? Is there anything I can do? I know that in the recent past she has not been badly handled. My vet has suggested putting her in foal. Would she be too old?

answer **A**

Regarding your question about breeding from your mare, if she is fit and healthy there is no reason to suppose that she will have problems in foaling, provided she has first been checked out by your vet – sound, healthy mares tend to have sound, healthy foals, regardless of their age.

Don't forget that many mares have foals in their teens if they have been leading active working lives, or have been used as competition horses. Although mares do not have a menopause, fertility does decline with age, however.

What you should think about when deciding whether to take your vet's advice is the future foal: don't breed from your mare just because you want to try to sort out her mareishness! There is no guarantee that the situation will change for good, and be any different except in the short term.

You must decide whether she is good enough to breed a nice foal from, whether it will have a home; also, good temperament is vital in a mum to be. A foal will be in her company for many months and will be influenced very much by her temperament and behaviour – cross, aggressive mares often lead to foals of a similar sort.

Breeding is not a cheap option either; you might find that ultimately it is more practical either to segregate her from the geldings when in season or to continue with the Regumate.

Most mares do tend to be more sensitive than geldings, and need more tactful handling; however, sex shouldn't become an excuse for allowing bad behaviour.

As an AI you probably know how important it is for horse and rider to be temperamentally suited to each other, and this also applies where mares and geldings are concerned. Some people get on better with them than others – and this is not meant in any derogatory way where your own skills are concerned. If you are really a gelding sort of person, then stick to them rather than forcing yourself to put up with something you really don't enjoy or get on with!

Even as a professional person, do not feel you have to keep a horse if you are not having fun with it; even professional people are allowed to enjoy themselves! Obviously if she is a talented competiton horse you may feel it is worth living with – the decision however, is ultimately yours.

Where the mouth problem is concerned, I assume you have had her teeth checked, but don't forget that 'mouth' problems can also be caused by physical discomfort in other regions and it might be worth getting her thoroughly checked over.

Providing all is well, try to avoid using a double to get through the resistance; remember it is a tool which should be used to help refine your riding once you have achieved submission in a snaffle – don't use a sledge-hammer to crack a walnut!

I feel that the mouth problem is more of a schooling one, although her temperament may contribute to her difficulty.

Always softening the hand when she resists is not the answer, however, and will never achieve any acceptance of the contact.

I am not suggesting that you make the contact rigid, but rather maintain a certain elastic tension, with 'feels' and 'eases' on the rein to

52

encourage salivation and relaxation of the jaw. If you always give in when she resists the situation will never improve.

This is a problem with which you need some assistance – from an experienced instructor and preferably one who specialises in dressage and is used to dealing with difficult horses.

Don't be embarrassed about having lessons with her even though you have got your AI – we never stop learning, after all!

question

Restoring harness

I have been restoring some driving harness which was initially very hard but is now quite supple. What could I use to achieve a really good shine on the harness?

answer

Driving harness is treated differently from other items of saddlery in that boot polish is used on the outside of the leather to produce a hard shine, whilst saddle soap and leather dressings are used on the underside to nourish it and keep it supple.

As boot polish will harden and dry out leather, attention must be paid to the regular dressing and oiling of the underside. An eye should also be kept on the stitching as boot polish will rot it relatively quickly – since it is old, you should check it carefully anyway for soundness.

Metal furniture can be cleaned using metal polish, but take care not to let it come into contact with the leather – neither should it be used on the mouthpieces of bits. If you have any patent harness, it should be cleaned with a proper patent cleaner, following the given instructions.

TOP TIPS

Saddles

Saddles must fit securely – otherwise the horse's back is damaged as the saddle bounces up and down.

Fasten your girth to the first and third girth straps as this will secure the saddle more efficiently.

If your saddle is too narrow at the front it will put pressure either side of the withers and cause bruising in this area. Check to establish whether the points of your saddle tree are digging into the horse's shoulders. It's important that your saddle is wide enough for your horse – what you certainly do not want is to gain the necessary height at the pommel at the expense of the saddle width.

When trying a new saddle use a leather or lampwick girth, as these are firm and will give more security than some of the more modern materials.

You may need to get the flocking on a new saddle altered to ensure that the saddle gives a secure fit.

If you have a short-backed horse a saddle with a straight-head tree, as opposed to a cut-back head, will give an extra inch for the rider without compromising on the length of the saddle.

Your saddle should be checked and balanced a couple of times per year to account for changes in the shape of your horse.

Ensure you ride at both your flatwork and jumping lengths in your new saddle when trying it out.

The saddle should fit the horse first and the rider second – if the saddle is a poor fit for the horse it may hurt him, but it's easy for you to compromise.

Mane problems

My horse's mane was hogged and now it is growing back it is very thick and difficult to plait. How should I go about thinning it?

Once a mane has been hogged, it invariably grows back thicker and coarser than previously, and as it takes some time for it to be trained back into a neat appearance, most people tend to keep it hogged!

This causes some problems in the summer if flies are a real pest, although fly fringes offer a good substitute forelock, and in the winter a detachable hood can be used to replace protection against the elements.

When growing the mane out, lay it over each day using water and, when it is long enough to do so, put in stable plaits to train it over to the side you want.

Care needs to be taken with this if your horse is inclined to rub, or graze under fences when out in the field, as the hairs will be broken off short.

When you judge it is long enough you can start thinning it (which will also help encourage it to lay over better) by pulling a few hairs at a time from the underside of the mane.

Make sure you don't do too much at once as this will cause soreness (better to do a little each day), or concentrate too much on one area – try instead to achieve a uniform thickness

Plait the mane to train it to lie over to the correct side of the neck

question

answer

54

You can't farm against water!

I have real problems with my five-acre field becoming waterlogged in places, due to underground springs. What would be the best drainage system? How much, approximately, would it cost to have someone come and sort the drains out?

Use a contractor who is familiar with the particular requirements for draining permanent pasture – local farmers may recommend a contractor.

Arable field drains are spaced quite wide apart and are fairly deep to be well below crops. Permanent pasture drains, however, need to be close together and near the surface, with a suitable 'gravelly' fill above the pipes. Special sand is usually placed above the

gravel.

Mole drains may be suitable on some pasture, whilst some graziers favour subsoiling. If the latter is used on horse pasture, ensure that the dangerous deep slits often left by the machine are closed by flat rolling.

Costs vary enormously on piped drainage schemes. The shapes and undulations in a field's surface make it difficult to give estimates unseen. At worst, costs could top £4000 per acre, but most jobs do not cost a quarter of that and can make an impossibly wet paddock a pleasure to use.

For DIY hire of machinery and contractors in your area contact Bill Baker of AFT on 0473 215624.

Comparing chassis

question

answer

What sort of chassis is most suitable for a horsebox?

PRB Horseboxes suggest that you don't buy a $3\frac{1}{2}$ ton chassis to transport more than one horse, $5\frac{1}{2}$ ton chassis, such as the Dodge 50, LT 50 or Ford Daily, are more stable for two horses. If practical, a HGV (over 7.5 tons) will give horses a better ride due to stiffer suspension and where features such as air suspension can be considered.

Do put as much of your budget as possible into having a good chassis – there's no point using a cheap second-hand, unsuitable chassis that will not last and having a beautiful body built on it!

Avoid buying a four-cylinder engine chassis if you are transporting more than one horse regularly – always look for six-cylinder instead.

PRB have their own opinion on chassis types:

Ford Cargo 0811 or 0813: The ideal horsebox chassis. Quick enough, reliable, readily available parts and not expensive. Very stable when loaded. The 0813 is slightly more pow-

erful, though not significantly so. The 0809 is a four-cylinder. E-reg onwards gives better drive due to disc brakes all round.

Leyland Roadrunner: Quicker than the Cargo, but not as stable. The cab seats leave a lot to be desired. D-reg onwards is preferable as the Cummings engine replaced the Leyland one.

Mercedes 0814: Without a doubt, the nicest drive of the three – but not so good for horses, as the soft suspension gives a rolling motion in transit unless the box is fully laden. More expensive to purchase and repair.

Wilcox Coachworks recommend that you get an experienced commercial vehicle mechanic (preferably one that has experience of horseboxes!) to check the engine over for you before you buy a second-hand vehicle.

Chassis come in two categories, HGV and non-HGV: HGVs have a gross weight of over 7.5 tons and to drive one you will need to take the HGV driving test. A non-HGV lorry has a gross weight of less than 7.5 tons and can be driven on an ordinary driving licence.

Peace of mind 'on the road'

My friend's lorry seems to be forever breaking down. I'm thinking of getting a lorry myself – how can I ensure I don't have the same problems?

Have your lorry serviced regularly – even if the mileage is small. Diesel engines require regular servicing – and it's always preferable to take your box to a reputable horsebox firm for this. Check your water and oil levels every time you use your lorry – commercial diesel engines use more oil.

A winter and summer service will ultimately save you a great deal of money and hassle.

TOP TIP

WEIGHTS AND LOADING CAPACITIES FOR HORSEBOXES

It is vital to ensure that you are within your carrying capacity. Not only is it illegal to be overweight, it is also extremely unsafe. Be careful that you don't buy a box that exceeds its carrying capacity before it's even got a horse on board – you'd be surprised how often this occurs!

Weight can quickly mount up, so when buying a box consider everything that you'll want to carry in it – not just the horse.

Example 1:
The Horsemaster Universal Two has a carrying capacity of 1230kg.
Average horse – 500kg.
Average adult rider – 70kg (11st).

Full tank of fuel – 60kg.
Tack, grooming kit, etc. – 15kg.
Therefore, with two horses, two adult riders with tack and a full tank of fuel you will only have another 15kg leeway.

Example 2:
The Horsemaster Champion Grand Prix (a three-horse box) has a carrying capacity of 2280kg.
Three horses – 1500kg.
Three riders – 210kg.
Fuel – 115kg.
Tank of water – 115kg.
Three sets of tack – 69kg.
This leaves 271kg for feed and anything else you want to take.

Conversion checks

I know of a lorry that has been converted into a horsebox. It is extremely reasonably priced and appears to be in a good, sound condition. Is there anything I should beware of? Are seat belts compulsory?

Don't buy a box van conversion if you can buy a purpose-built horsebox within your budget. It really is safer to buy from a reputable horsebox company who have their own mechanical department. This way the quality will be assured and the resale value will be high, age being largely immaterial, providing the vehicle has been well looked after.

Remember that flooring should, ideally, consist of thick rubber matting over an oak or aluminium planked base. Plywood and tongue and groove softwood will soon rot if left wet.

Ex-furniture and bread van conversions should be avoided at all costs – they are not designed at all to carry heavy and potentially dangerous animals such as horses! A purpose-built vehicle, on the other hand, has been designed and built for the job of carrying equines safely and comfortably.

Tell-tale signs of a conversion job are aluminium skirts on a glassonite body, and/or an untidy join where a Luton joins the box van.

Seat belts are not compulsory by law, but many people, especially those with children, prefer them to be fitted for safety's sake.

RUGGING UP

6. Leg straps are usually crossed over, as shown, with the attaching clips facing away from the horse. Always use a fillet string on summer sheets and stable rugs.

1. Ensure your horse is tied up, or held by a competent person. Fold your rug (stable or New Zealand) in half, as shown. If leg straps are attached, fasten them up so they cannot dangle and bang against your horse's legs. Similarly, secure surcingles inside the folded rug. Then place it gently on your horse's neck.

2. Slide the rug back into place until the wither patch lies correctly on the withers. Then fold back the rest of the rug over the quarters. Do not pull the rug forwards again or the hairs will lie the wrong way, causing discomfort. If you need to adjust the fit, fold the back half of the rug up over the front, take it off and start again.

3. Go to the horse's offside and take down the surcingle(s). Return to the nearside and fasten the surcingle(s) so that the rug is secured in place.

4. Next, fasten the breast strap(s).

5. Lastly, fasten the leg straps.

Taking rugs off

1. Ensure the horse is tied up or held. Unfasten any leg straps and fasten them to their keepers to prevent them dangling and banging against your horse.

2. Undo the breast strap.

3. Unfasten the surcingle, then go to the offside and fold the surcingle up and over the rug.

4. Return to the nearside and fold the back half of the rug up and over the top half.

5. Lift the rug gently off the horse.

TOP TIP

The easiest, most effective and cheapest way to clean rugs is to take them to a garage and use a hand-held 'jet wash' for cars. The jet literally blasts all hair and dirt off the rug. Ensure you rinse soap out thoroughly before taking your rugs home to dry.

Riding

Riding 'oldies'

question

I have owned my 14.2hh gelding for 20 years – he is now 28. He is ridden lightly twice a week which he seems to enjoy. Do you think he should be ridden at his age? What is the average age ponies live to?

answer

With regard to your gelding's ridden exercise, be guided by his enjoyment and ability to perform the work. If he seems to enjoy it and shows no evidence of discomfort or distress then by all means carry on.

The average age to which a horse lives lies somewhere between 20 and 25 years; there are of course instances of horses living to ages nearly double this, but these are the exception.

Bouncy trot

question

I just cannot sit to my new horse's trot. He trots very long and I just bounce all over the place with no rhythm whatsoever. My vet says the horse is fine but that he does have a funny action. I can only assume that he has been used in trotting races. He also tends to bob his head after a while, although he is not lame.

answer

It is difficult to comment on the trot without actually seeing it – if he lunges, it might be a good idea for you to watch him on the lunge as it will give you a better view of his action! Having some lessons with him from an experienced instructor would certainly be of help to you both; as already mentioned, it is very dificult to decide just what needs to be done without seeing you both in action.

Polework, transitions, half halts, slowing the speed and circle work may all be of benefit – but you do need someone on the ground to help you decide just what the best approach will be.

Overcoming tractor 'phobia'

question

My horse is perfect apart from his dislike of tractors. Is there any solution to this?

answer

A good idea is to try to keep up regular lessons as it not only helps prevent bad habits from creeping in, but will also ensure that your horse remains obedient and disciplined, even under more trying circumstances – such as meeting tractors. This is not an unusual anxiety for many horses, and fortunately most drivers are quite considerate. However, it would be better still if you could rely more on your horse and less on the driver!

It would be well worth doing some 'tractor training'; chat to a local farmer and see if it would be possible to arrange a morning or afternoon when he could bring a tractor to your yard, or for you to go to his farm (obviously you will have to pay him for his time, but it will be worth the effort).

Let your horse get used to the tractor whilst it is stationary and switched off, patting and reassuring him and allowing him to inspect it, and perhaps even to eat a feed out of a bucket placed on it. Next, try the same with it stationary but with the engine running, and finally riding along whilst it passes you at increasingly close distances.

By going about things in this way you will have plenty of time to reassure your horse, and will be in a safer environment than on the roads.

It would be a good idea to ask an instructor to come along as well to help you – and perhaps you know of one or two other people with horses who would like to join in, which could also offset the costs a little?

On the bit

My horse would work on the bit with his previous owner but I cannot get him to do this. I have lessons but they do not seem to help much. Also, how can I stop my legs slipping back?

Learning how to ride a horse 'on the bit' comes with time, patience, experience and practice. Achieving a correct outline is also very much to do with establishing balance, rhythm, impulsion, suppleness and acceptance of both hand and leg, not just a case of positioning the horse's head, so these factors have to be considered as well.

Since you are not having much success with your lessons at the moment, why not discuss this with your instructor? You may find that not only will you get more help but he/ she should be able to demonstrate how to achieve this by riding your horse for you, explaining what he/she is doing. It sometimes helps for you to walk alongside, feeling the contact on the reins which is necessary and their action. If you do not meet with success after trying this tactic, change to a different instructor who can give you the help you want.

As regards your problem with your legs, this may be due to any number of things, including riding with your stirrups too long, gripping up with your lower legs, tipping forwards or bending your knees too much – the precise cause for it can only really be diagnosed at first hand, seeing you ride, so again your instructor is really the person to ask about this.

59

Lively ride

My 17-year-old gelding has always been a forward going ride. However, over the last couple of months he has become very wound up when being ridden. He jogs constantly, puts in small bucks and feels like he will bomb off any minute. I have been using the same tack but the problem has arisen recently. I have checked his teeth and they are okay. Do you think it could have been due to a change over from ordinary to vacuum-packed hay?

It would seem from your letter that you need to go through a process of elimination to find the root cause or combination of causes of your problem. For instance:

a) It should not be difficult to find and purchase some good-quality hay. If you gradually change the pony back from the vacuum-packed hay to ordinary hay and his behaviour changes, then you may have the answer to your question.

b) Have you by any chance had your saddle re-flocked at any time during this last year? Has the pony been wearing the same saddle since he was young? If so, you could have a saddle problem due to him changing shape now he is getting into more mature years. Have you had the saddle checked by a saddler for signs of a broken tree? Has your pony put on a lot of extra weight which could be making his saddle feel tighter to him?

The other possibility that might need investigating is that the pony could need his back checked. You would have to talk to your vet. about this and ask him to recommend a chiropractor.

TOP TIPS

Teeth Grinder
If your horse grinds his teeth when you ride him there could be a number of reasons for this: a poorly fiting bit; excitement; resistance to your aids; annoyance. Once established, teeth grinding is difficult to stop, so at the first sign of it, try to establish the cause and act to remedy the situation.

question

Knocks his fences

I own a nine-year-old gelding who, when I bought him a year ago, was very green and had received very little schooling. He had been hunted but that's all. He has shown ability in the showjumping ring, is bold, keen and never stops. He makes a good shape over the fence and really seems to enjoy it.

However, he continually knocks fences – whether they are 2ft 3in or 3ft 3in. Sometimes it is my fault, but not always. With the help of my instructor we have tried hitting him when he knocks a fence and raising the front pole of a spread, but to no avail.

I have been told not to hunter trial him as this will make him long and flat. Any ideas?

answer

Generally, most horses do not like hitting fences, but some are naturally more careful than others, and these are the ones who make the best (and safest) showjumpers in the long run.

Unfortunately, there is no way in which you can teach a horse which really doesn't care about hitting its fences to be more careful – they can be frustrating in that one day they will jump beautifully and on another day they

just can't be bothered to make the effort.

However, no amount of bashing or whatever will improve the situation and may only succeed in putting the horse off the idea of jumping altogether. Quite often this sort of horse does have a healthy respect for the unyielding nature of solid fixed fences and will make a good hunter or cross country horse. Maybe this is the field he is better suited to, rather than showjumping?

Although he may get a little longer and flatter when going across country there is no reason why you should not jump him in two different styles: on a longer, more onward-bound stride when going across country and on a shorter, rounder, bouncy stride when tackling showjumps, so that he learns that they are two different disciplines to be treated differently.

There can of course be other reasons for carelessness such as being bored, not being able to make the height or width, insufficient impulsion, or even because he is busy fighting to get to the fence whilst you are trying to steady him, so that he is not entirely concentrating on the job in hand. However, these are all things your trainer should have picked up if they are the cause. Incidentally, it is not the wisest thing to raise the front rail of a spread higher than the back rail, and it can in fact be very dangerous if the horse does not see the width of it.

Things might improve a little with further schooling aimed at getting him more athletic and stronger – this will involve flatwork as well as gymnastic work over fences – but if he continues to be this careless and your heart is set on showjumping it might be better to consider selling him on and buying something else a little better suited to your purposes.

Horses generally respect solid fences

First horse advice

question

I am interested in buying a foal for my first horse and would like your advice on this. I have 10 years' riding experience and have my own land to keep a horse on. It has been eight years since I last rode but I suppose it's like riding a bike, you never forget.

answer

I wonder whether you have really thought through your plan properly? Assuming you go ahead and buy a foal, although you will technically begin and continue its training immediately (in terms of teaching it to lead, tie up, have its feet handled etc.) you won't be starting its ridden education until it is about 3¹/₂ years old. Then work will initially be for short, steady periods and you won't be doing much serious work with it until it is four, and nothing really strenuous until it is five.

It is a long time to wait for a horse you can have fun with, and even then there is no guarantee that it will be good at the particular activities you may by then have set your heart on.

To bring on a youngster successfully you do also need experience – not just of having ridden and hacked out 'made' horses but of youngsters too. They are NOT like bicycles, and if you haven't ridden properly for eight years then it would be extremely inadvisable for you to pursue this path. It is not a case of 'brushing up' but of being fit, competent and knowledgeable, able to cope correctly in any contingency!

I'm sorry to sound so pessimistic, but especially since this will be your first horse you really would be far better off buying something already made, and increasing your experience before purchasing a youngster. Before buying even an older horse, it would be a good idea to have a course of regular lessons (as opposed to hacks) at a reputable riding establishment!

Annoying habit

question

My six-year-old daughter's 12.2hh pony continually puts her head down when being ridden off the lead rein. How can I get her out of this habit?

answer

Ideally your daughter should ride a positive half halt when she feels the pony beginning to drop her nose, and firmly ride her on with her legs; however, this might be expecting rather a lot of a six-year-old!

Apart from keeping things fun for children at this age, she is also going to be lacking in strength – ponies can not only be very determined, but extremely strong for their size! Your best bet is to use grass reins; if these cause her to bear down against the bit, attach them from the

Strong ponies may need grass reins so that their riders can enjoy their riding

bit rings, through the ends of the browband and down to the front saddle dees.

Don't forget that they shouldn't interfere with the headcarriage, or be used when jumping!

question

Youngster's progress

I own a three-year-old Welsh Section D gelding who was backed at two-and-a-half. He is worked lightly now and has just started tackling some small jumps.

This is my first youngster and I'd appreciate some help on a programme of work and development for him. He's a spirited lad – would more work now calm him down a bit?

62

answer

It sounds as though your youngster is doing well at the moment, but do beware of overdoing things; bear in mind that he is still immature both physically and mentally and still in the process of growing.

You should be aiming to educate him rather than work him so hard that it tires him – this will only make him inclined to be fractious and mutinous, and there is no point in undoing all the work you have achieved with him so far.

Provided he is obedient, it would probably be a good idea to start to introduce some hacking; do always, at this stage, take a sensible and steady horse with you as escort.

These hacks needn't be long – up to half an hour will be more than enough, especially if you are still lungeing for fifteen minutes before riding.

Especially with brighter horses, it is some-

times difficult to give them enough to think about and keep their minds occupied without running the risk of overstretching them physically, and doing some hacking will broaden his horizons and solve this problem to a large extent. It will also help to keep him sweet!

You could do this three times a week, alternating with lungeing and short schooling sessions. Twenty minutes on the lunge should be quite enough – less if he is being sensible and you want to ride him as well; remember it is a very demanding exercise which can take its toll on the joints at his age if you aren't careful.

Ridden work may last from ten minutes to twenty minutes, depending on how he is going and feeling. Try always to finish on a good note, but if things don't always go entirely to plan, don't feel you have to ride him into the ground and achieve perfection at all costs – there is always another day!

Whilst it will probably do no harm to have an occasional pop over a small fence, don't do too much as he has not yet finished growing. Be patient and wait until he is more mature before working on this in earnest or making your fences larger, as it imposes considerable strain on the hock joints.

question

Rebuilding confidence

My biggest problem is that I lack confidence in myself. When hacking out, and despite going out with another horse and rider, I fear being carted off. As I live in a remote place taking lessons is not easy.

answer

Your lack of confidence seems to include not just the fear of falling off but concerns your ability to control the horse as well. Presumably you have some grounds for your anxiety.

What would help you a great deal would be to have lessons on your own horse to develop your control and position. Lunge lessons would also help.

Although you live in an isolated area, so lessons may be a problem, you could look further afield and perhaps take your horse to a riding centre for a week so you could have tuition.

Although this may be a little expensive it would be well worth the outlay if you find a good yard, as riders often get more from an intensive series of lessons than from occasional ones.

When you return home again you will find yourself with a much more positive attitude and increased confidence so you can enjoy your horse – which is why we all keep horses anyway.

Lethargic cob

I have a young cob who is 100% in every way except when I ride on my own or in front on a ride. He's then very lethargic and slow at the canter and he will not gallop. I understand that because he's young he's apprehensive about what's around the corner or in the bushes, but even though I use spurs and carry a crop it doesn't seem to make any difference. He's perfect at the walk and trot and if he's behind a fast horse he's okay.

His tack has been checked and is fine. What has annoyed me is that he gallops flat out around the field and yet when I call him in he walks slowly to me in zig-zags (due to the fact his field is on a hill) and I can see he's just lazy. I know he is young and some people will say give him time, but what I don't want to do is let this become a permanent habit.

Do you think it's because he's a cob and it's just his nature, or am I doing something wrong?

There are several things to consider here: first of all, it is not advisable to gallop a horse or pony unless it is fit as damage can easily occur to the wind or limbs.

Secondly, your horse is still a bit of a baby and he may feel insecure and anxious when being asked to move ahead of, or away from, his friends.

Further schooling independently of other horses will help to overcome his natural desire to remain with the herd, where he feels safe.

Increasing his fitness and making sure he is not overweight will also help a little.

As he is a cobby build, he may not be the most athletic type either and may tend to be short striding, and a bit stuffy in faster gaits; although he may hurtle after the other horses when following, this may well be out of sheer anxiety not to be left behind, rather than from natural inclination.

Spurs should be used as a refinement of your leg aids rather than as a way of applying more severe ones, unless riding a horse which through poor schooling has become 'dead' to the leg – as your chap is still young this should not be the case.

You would do better to abandon the spurs before you come to rely on them too much, and to work more on improving his response to light leg aids and increasing his ability, through good schooling, to respond to them quickly and correctly.

If you are unsure how to go about this, have some lessons from a good instructor. As regards his approach when calling him in from the field, if it is uphill he can't really be blamed for going slowly (especially if he suspects that you may want to ride him), and at least he does come when you call, rather than making you walk across to catch him!

Your cob sounds as though he has many good points – a sensible, kind type by all accounts – so don't be too quick to write him off!

Suitable saddles

I would like to do small jumping competitions at local shows as well as Best Turned Out and Mountain and Moorland classes. Could I use a G.P. saddle for everything?

A G.P. saddle should be fine for your local showing classes, and will be far safer and more practical for jumping than a straight-cut showing saddle!

TOP TIPS

Jogging Problem
Check out your riding position if your horse jogs all the time. His jogging could be caused by you gripping upwards with your lower leg. This problem is highlighted even more if the horse is a sensitive type.

question Q

Conflicting instructions

I own a 16hh, six-year-old Irish Draught x Hanoverian gelding. My problem is that I find it difficult to get my horse to work for me as he is very lazy, or I am not riding him properly.

I had a lesson with someone who told me that my saddle did not fit properly (which I already suspected). She has also told me to ride in a completely different way.

I had a very successful lesson in that my horse worked very well, used his hind legs instead of pulling himself along, and worked in a very good outline. I am just a bit confused about what way I should be riding him. The new instructor has said to use my leg by kicking on off, on off and backing it up with my whip, and my regular instructor has told me to keep my leg still and wrapped round the horse and to squeeze every time I sit in the saddle.

I am just a bit scared that I am going to give my horse 'dead sides' by kicking on and off but the new instructor has said this will not happen, that I will soon be able to use a soft leg and the horse will respond. She said that the way I have been riding him has resulted in 'dead sides' and this is why he is not going forward – I must admit that this is how I have been feeling.

My gelding is a very big horse and everyone says that I do not ride him forward enough (he has a wonderful nature and I find it hard to 'get after him'). The other thing the new instructor told me to do was to play on the bit as this would encourage my horse into an outline and it certainly worked.

She also told me to do lots of half halts to encourage him to shorten and work more together and from behind. My regular instructor has taught me to get him into an outline by taking more weight on the rein but I feel that in doing this I am pulling him into an outline. I never feel that he is very soft and she has never told me to do half halts. I am very confused, can you help?

answer A

All horses are individuals and need to be treated and worked as such. What works well for one horse will not necessarily do for another; gently closing your legs on a flighty free-moving horse will be sufficient to send it forward and a kick would most likely result in it setting off like a scalded cat!

On your chap, however, it appears that you can squeeze until you are blue in the face and nothing happens – except that you get very tired, and your position probably worse! With such horses you need to vibrate your leg and to reinforce it with your stick if necessary – gradually he should become more responsive, but it all takes time.

It is not so much that what your first instructor teaches is incorrect, as unsuitable for your horse at this moment in time and more appropriate advice for a well-schooled animal. Your new instructor seems to be assessing your horse more accurately, and her techniques are evidently working well for you both; although, as you say, both your instructors are qualified (and may even hold identical qualifications) the new one may be more experienced or knowledgeable, and this is what pays off at the end of the day.

Don't confuse yourself by going to different instructors until you are sufficiently experienced yourself to be able to do so and extract the pieces of information you find helpful, and discard those which aren't. Stick with the one you feel can help you both to produce good results – it will be less confusing for your horse too than adopting inconsistent styles of riding!

TOP TIP

Unlevel Hands

If one of your riding problems is unlevel hands try carrying a jumping whip horizontally across your hands so that it rests between your thumb and first fingers. You can spot when your hands become unlevel as the whip will show up any small movement.

question

Schooling is the key

I recently bought a 10-year-old TB. In canter, and sometimes in trot, she tucks her nose into her chest, snatches at the bit, sets her jaw and then does some huge bucks. Everyone who sees her says the bucks are not malicious and it does not happen every time.

I ride her in a jointed snaffle, flash noseband and running martingale. I have had her mouth, back and tack checked – all are fine. She tends to hold her head high and I wondered whether more schooling and/or a stronger bit was needed?

answer

It does not sound as though the answer to your problems lies in a different bit, but rather, as you state, in spending some time schooling her quietly.

It sounds as though she lacks confidence in the bit and the rider's hands – not necessarily your fault, but one which you will have to resolve. This results in her carrying her head very high, or drawing her head back away from the contact, avoiding rather than accepting it.

Using a stronger bit will not create more confidence but only succeed in frightening her more, and probably result in you having less control and more difficulty in straighten-

> ### TOP TIP
>
> #### Go for Goals
> Set yourself goals for your riding so you have something to focus on and aim towards. For example, a long term goal might be a placing in the top three at your local riding club jumping competition, a medium term aim may be a week's jumping course with a good instructor, whilst your goal for this month's riding might be to improve your horse's suppleness and balance through regular schooling exercises.

ing her out. It would also be sensible to have a vet check her back and teeth properly again, and a saddler look at her tack; although you have had her examined, it can be easy to miss some problems.

Really, you need to have some lessons with her as well as to spend some time schooling; make some enquiries about good freelancers in your area who can either come to you, if you have schooling facilities at home, or who can offer facilities you can go to.

So long as your mare has a kind nature and sensible temperament, it shouldn't take too long for you to begin to see results.

question

Severe stitch when trotting

answer

When riding at trot I get severe stitch in my right-hand side. All my instructor does is tell me to relax but that's not easy.

Getting a stitch is a common condition caused by overuse of the muscles of the abdominal wall. These muscles usually contract while running or walking quickly to help us retain an upright posture – if they are used excessively and become tired, the muscle fibres become deprived of oxygen.

If you do get a stitch, walk or halt and rest for a while – the pain will usually ease within a few minutes. It will help you to avoid getting a stitch in the first place if you are able to

follow your instructor's advice – breathing regularly and relaxing, although not in a floppy, collapsed sort of way.

As you are finding out, maintaining a good and effective position when riding isn't easy, but takes a lot of practice! By improving your general suppleness (ask your instructor for some exercises you can do) you should be able to improve your posture, rather than trying to compensate for weaknesses and ending up getting a stitch as a result.

It may be that you need to do some overall tidying up, so ask for some assistance with this – but avoid trying so hard that you end up becoming tense and breathing poorly.

question

answer

Novices together

I am not very experienced and I have a four-year-old mare. I no longer have lessons but mum thinks it would be a good idea to start again.

Other people at the stables ride my pony without any trouble but when I ride she drags me about. If we're in a lesson she just follows the other ponies.

To be honest, young ponies and inexperienced riders really don't make a good combination – you are at least aware of your inexperience (and honest enough to admit it!), however, which is a start.

Yes, you do definitely need to have lessons together – at least your mum is prepared to back you in that respect! They will also help to give you more confidence when riding, so will be well worth the investment.

Do be careful about how much work your pony does though; whilst you are establishing her work it might be best if she didn't get used by the school on group lessons – she won't be learning anything from continually following the tails of other ponies, or from being ridden by other novices.

In addition, she is still young, so will tire easily, which may make her irrritable and unco-operative when you want to ride. This may mean that you will have to contribute towards her upkeep in the meantime, but this will ultimately be for her own good as well as yours.

question

answer

Scared to ride

I love horses but I'm scared when riding them. I think this dates back to an instance when I was young and a pony bolted with me. I have now been riding for eight years but I am very worried about cantering.

Have a word with your riding instructor – who may not even be aware of your worries, particularly if you are the sort of person who has a reasonably good position. Sometimes a rider can look more competent and confident than they really feel!

If possible, try to have a couple of private lessons – you can then work more intensively on the problems which really worry you. For example, since cantering is one of your great anxieties, you could practise exercises such as going into canter and returning to trot after just a few strides; once you know you can stop when you wish, you will gradually begin to feel happier about cantering for increasingly long periods of time.

By sorting out your problems in private lessons, you should feel happier when riding in a group lesson again – but it is up to you to make your fears known to your instructor, rather than conceal them. Only then can you get help.

TOP TIP

Headshy
If your horse is headshy, making bridling a problem, look for the possible causes and act appropriately. Causes can be:

● Sore ears due to fly bites, mites or a badly fitting browband.

● A sore mouth.
● Roughness in handling and/or being hit about the head at some time.
● A cold bit – or one that causes discomfort.The short term measure to make bridling easier for you both is to put the bridle on in pieces.

Encouraging 'honesty'

question

For 95% of the time we have no problem with my daughter's mare. However, if she has to stand around having been warmed up, e.g. at a competition, she then plays up when asked to work. For instance, she refused the first two fences and then flew around the rest of a hunter trial course.

How can we make her more 'honest'? She is more than capable of all we ask and has a very varied life, with hacks, schooling and jumping.

answer

It sounds as though your mare is not being 'dishonest', rather that she goes 'off the boil' very quickly. When at competitions, your daughter should work her in to loosen her up and try to avoid allowing her to stand around idling and assuming her job is done immediately prior to starting her class.

If there is a delay for some reason and your daughter is anxious not to tire her she can be walked on a long rein, but she must insist that the mare moves forwards actively whilst doing this.

As soon as the preceding competitor starts their round (or earlier if necessary) your daughter should take up the contact again and get her moving briskly and obediently forwards once more; rapid transitions will help to get her moving off the leg and get her attention back again, when she can quickly pop over one or two practice fences before going straight into the competition area.

Whilst waiting for a signal to start your daughter should keep her trotting or cantering, ready to begin. This is not an uncommon problem, but one easily remedied; standing around the entrance to a collecting ring is asking for trouble, including nappiness!

Prances and pulls

question

My seven-year-old gelding is fine until we turn for home and then he prances around and keeps putting his head down, pulling at the same time.

answer

Firstly, try to avoid turning directly back towards home: try to work out circular routes instead so as to minimise such difficulties and prevent other problems arising such as nappiness.

When this habit does occur, use half halts as frequently as necessary, raising both hands at the same time but not pulling.

By lifting your hands you will make it more difficult for your horse to rake downwards at the bit; once your hands have dropped and you have collapsed forwards you are no longer in a position of authority – you also make it easier for him to set his jaw against you and pull.

If your horse pulls you forward then it has the upper hand

Looking the part

How should I turn out a cob for showing? What should I wear?

Your cob should be trimmed up – legs, edges of ears and jawline – and hogged. You can plait the tail if you prefer, but this needs to be done really well to look good; most professionals pull tails rather than plaiting as it is quicker and does not weaken tail hair as frequent plaiting would.

The end of the tail should be cut straight across at the bottom so that it hangs at a length of two to four inches below the point of hocks when moving.

Recommendations for dress and turnout by the British Show Hack, Cob and Riding Horse Association at County level are as follows:
• bowler hat
• tweed coat
• plain fawn or buff coloured breeches
• plain black or brown boots with garter straps
• spurs
• any form of leather or string gloves
• plain malacca or leather cane not exceeding 22 inches
• ordinary shirt with collar, tie (must be pinned down)

In classes where jumping is required, a skull cap with navy blue or black cover should be worn for the jumping phase, or a BS 6473 velvet cap.

As regards saddlery, a plain bridle in proportion to the horse's head with a plain browband is correct, with either a double or pelham bit. A snaffle may be worn in Novice classes. Saddles should be reasonably straight cut and without a numnah.

There are plenty of good books available on showing, including useful sections on turnout and presentation which you might find helpful – try *Showing to Win* by Carolyn Henderson and Lynn Russell.

Efficient locomotion

I compete in long distance riding with my seven-year-old Arab, Durmush. After a successful novice year he has been brought on slowly and has now started 40-milers. My problem is that he is not tracking up very well. Any help would be welcome.

Congratulations on your success with Durmush so far. Assuming your horse is not suffering from any physical problems you will need to concentrate on controlled, free forward movement, straightness, rhythm and relaxation, which involves schooling to improve strength and suppleness.

Time spent on school work is never wasted – establishing correct locomotion is as important as achieving fitness, and will allow the horse to utilise its energy efficiently and with less stress and strain all round.

It is important, however, not to become so obsessed by forward movement whilst schooling that your horse becomes overbalanced and runs on to the forehand – this results in poor use of the back muscles and quarters.

This may well be a part of your problem – that in your anxiety to send your horse forward on to a longer stride you have actually ended up with him running forward instead.

Use transitions from walk to trot and back to walk again, use half halts and use your legs and seat to help maintain rhythm and impulsion.

Shortened and lengthened strides can be introduced as part of your schooling once you can obtain and maintain the above mentioned criteria.

As schooling is a huge topic to cover, it would be worth your while investing in some lessons with your horse to develop his athletic potential more fully and help overcome your problems.

Bridle-riding holiday

question

My friend and I are interested in taking our horses on holiday, riding off-road, e.g. in Dorset. Any ideas on how we could plan our route?

answer

One way which takes all the worry out of your holiday is to book a break via Bridle Rides. They've been designing routes and finding places to stay for riders like you for almost 10 years. They have many networks and they've actually ridden the 2000 plus miles of bridleways they recommend!

Basically, you tell them where you want to go (they cover 10 areas from the North York Moors to the South Coast) and for how long (2 – 8days). They design you a route, arrange your overnight stops and send you a very easy to follow description of the ride plus a highlighted map. You also get lists of vets and farriers and notes about the countryside you're riding through. You make up your own group of two to four riders (lone riders are discouraged for safety reasons). There's a luggage ferry too.

You can ride 15 – 20 miles a day, stopping at a different place each time, or do different rides from one base. The cost is £40 – 45 per day for which you get the fruits of Bridle Rides' research, a huge evening meal, bed and breakfast, grazing and unlimited coarse mix for your horse. Your accommodation is in comfortable farmhouses.

If you hack out regularly you should be fit enough – but fitness tips are also provided as part of your package. The routes are planned to include lunch stops at pubs. Many riders have found that they have a new, improved relationship with their horse after enjoying one of these holidays. The horses love exploring new territory and soon settle into the routine. Contact Bridle Rides, Elms Cottages, 16 Queens Lane, Eynsham, Oxford.

Youngster takes off

question

My three-year-old gelding has recently been backed. He is fine at the start of a ride but then starts to tank off at every opportunity. He is being fed well as he is underweight. Do you have any ideas on how I should deal with this problem?

answer

I think you are expecting a great deal from your youngster in a very short space of time; he has after all, just been backed, but this does not mean 'schooled'!

He has to learn to be obedient to both your hand and leg, so that if something unexpected happens you can control him. This is down to education – and he also has to learn not just discipline and obedience, but to be confident in and trust you.

This all takes time and experience and you would probably find it helpful to have some regular lessons with him from an experienced instructor. It might also be helpful if, until he is a little more settled in his ways, you lunge

Lungeing takes the 'edge' off youngsters before you ride them

him briefly before riding, to give him a chance to settle down and relax.

Take care with your feeding programme too; if he is underweight it would be better to ensure a regular worming programme and plenty of bulk, rather than stuffing him with concentrates – if you continue to be worrried about his condition, consult a vet.

RIDING

question

Bucks after work

My new horse has started to buck very badly, usually towards the end of his exercise and for no obvious reason. Two very competent riders have been bucked off. We toned down his food to compensate for his reduced work (he was a hunter and is now mainly doing school work) and his saddle has been fitted and checked by a competent saddler.

He has never bucked with me and I would welcome any ideas or suggestions to help please.

answer

The fact that your horse tends to buck towards the end of a work session rather than at the beginning would seem to indicate either a physical or psychological problem (or possibly a combination of the two) rather than freshness.

Do get him checked out by your vet even if he was vetted prior to purchase it is possible that he may have sustained some kind of injury since you have owned him, unknown to you.

Whilst with some physical problems the horse feels more comfortable after a period of work, in other conditions discomfort may be aggravated with exercise. In particular, get his teeth and back checked.

Next, consider the sort of work he is doing:

if he has gone from hunting to school work it will be a big change for him. You say that he has never bucked with you, just with the more experienced riders who exercise him; it could well be that they are more demanding of him whilst riding than you are, and he may resent this, become psychologically frustrated, or find it difficult to cope physically with such unaccustomed exertion for long periods.

Shorter, perhaps less intensive periods of schooling (which can gradually be increased over a period of time) might suit him better, with hacking out afterwards as a reward and to help relax him, as well as to keep him fit and prevent boredom from setting in.

You can even incorporate some schooling into your hacking, if it comes to that; schooling needn't be confined solely to exercises in a marked-out area!

It would probably also be helpful if you could try to turn him out each day, even if this was only for a couple of hours. This would give him the opportunity to kick up his heels and have a buck and a gallop if he feels like it, without risk to yourself.

If you are worried about him injuring himself, put boots on all round, secured with tape, before turning him out, and put him out with a quiet, steady companion.

TOP TIPS

Pause for Thought....

Remember that you and your horse are a partnership – so if things go wrong don't just blame the horse!

Your role as rider/owner of a horse also includes another function – that of trainer. So if your horse does not do as he is asked consider whether he has been properly prepared

for the task, i.e. have you carried out your job properly?

Horses are usually very genuine creatures – if your horse starts to misbehave try to discover the real reason for his actions instead of automatically punishing him.

If you want to understand horses then learn to think and reason as they do, for they cannot act like humans.

Wobbly 'shoulder-in'

question

When I ride shoulder-in I can produce a few good steps but then the horse 'wobbles' and comes in, off the track. I use my inside leg as strongly as possible and try to keep hold of the outside rein but it still happens.

answer

There are a number of reasons why you may be experiencing this problem in shoulder-in. Points which you might consider (and bearing in mind there may be several contributory causes rather than just a single one) and which you should discuss with your instructor during your next lesson include:

1. Check that you are not attempting to ride your horse forward too fast, as this will cause loss of balance and manoeuvrability – whilst impulsion is desirable, speed isn't!

2. Check your own position; when starting to perform lateral work it is all too easy to become crooked, and this leads to problems and confusion on the horse's part. Large mirrors at the ends of the school can help you to be aware of and correct this problem, but are really only feasible if you can work in an indoor arena. You will need help from someone on the ground to check on this.

3. Make sure you do not have too strong a contact on the inside rein.

4. Check that you are not being over ambitious and asking for too much position too soon. It is better to start off with a more shallow shoulder-in and gradually increase the position as your horse becomes more familiar, confident and supple. Asking for too much position too soon will be difficult for him – he will resist and try to evade.

5. Make sure that your horse is accepting your aids correctly; it may be that you would find it beneficial to work a little more on circles before returning to the shoulder-in. If he is resistant on a circle you will never achieve a satisfactory shoulder-in.

6. Make sure your outside leg is not being used over strongly; it should act as necessary, but not unnecessarily.

7. Don't expect too many steps initially; shoulder-in is one of the most beneficial movements, but also a demanding one. Build up the number of steps gradually; a good exercise is to ride a few steps, halt in your shoulder-in, move off in the position for a few more steps, halt again.

Whilst these points may give you a few ideas to work on, do ask the advice of your instructor, who has the benefit of being able to observe the problem as it is happening!

Using Market Harboroughs

question

I have a problem with my pony as she shakes her head before a fence. I have had a few knocks on my face as a result. I was advised to ride her in a Market Harborough and she's much better, but is it okay to ride in these devices?

answer

If both of you are happy with the Market Harborough then continue using it. You might want to investigate further – check for saddle, back, teeth problems, allergies, sinus and ear infections.

TOP TIP

Warm Up

Warming up is a vital part of your horse's exercise – in effect it prepares the horse's bodily systems, ensuring, for example, that enough blood is sent to the muscles. Without this the chance of premature tiredness and possible injury is increased.

question

answer

Excitable in company

My TB gelding easily gets excited in company. He jogs and pulls all the time. I have only had him for a few months. He is fine when ridden out alone.

If your horse is temperamentally inclined to be highly strung and excitable, then you should try to gear your work, and the way in which you ride him, accordingly.

You will need to be tactful, and encourage him to accept the hand and leg at all times, albeit possibly with soft aids. Although his temperament should not be allowed to become an excuse for disobedience, you will have to be careful in dealing with problems.

It is very easy with this sort of horse to try to ride it from the front; that is to say, become very reliant on the rein contact, and this can lead to further problems such as bit resistances, jogging, rearing, bucking etc.

You have not had him for very long, and may not have had a great deal of opportunity to school him, but this is a course you should embark on as soon as possible so you can sort out your relationship with him more satisfactorily – preferably with the help initially of a good instructor.

It takes time to establish a partnership, and this is more difficult to achieve if you can only hack out; try to hire an all-weather surface or indoor school in which to do some work – if you club together with a few friends it is usually cheaper. Working with a few other horses present will certainly help with your hacking problems, provided you are patient, consistent and don't end up following tails.

When you do hack out, for the moment try to keep rides quiet, and position your horse at the front of the group where you will not be inclined to restrict his stride (which may be longer than that of your friends' horses) as this will encourage jogging.

question

answer

Ready to bolt

My seven-year-old gelding is well behaved on the roads but when out in open spaces he pulls constantly and is ready to bolt. His previous owner used to gallop him in company but I have managed to calm him down a little. He is fine when out on his own – I ride him in a Dr. Bristol for extra brakes. My daughter has been riding him and we are able to canter and get him to calm down afterwards.

We have just started going out with other horses but he has started to get fizzy and silly again. I would like some company when hacking but do not want to undo all my good work. What do you advise?

For the moment hack out on your own so you do not make matters worse, and use the stronger bit, as apart from giving you more control, it will increase your confidence in your ability to control him, which is also an important factor. If you want company, why not take it in turns with your daughter to cycle and ride?

Try a slightly different tactic by having lessons on him with a group of other horses at a riding school – or see if others in your yard would like to form a group and hire a freelance instructor.

This will give you the opportunity to ride your horse in company, in a controlled environment. Although he may get excited at first, after a few sessions he should begin to settle down. A good instructor will also help to boost your confidence so you will be less inclined to be anxious when hacking.

When you do decide that the time is ripe for hacking out in company again, be selective in your choice of hacking companion. Start off with just one steady escort who won't mind you going in front so there is less inclination to want to race or jog to keep up, and who won't mind if, to start with, you only walk or have the occasional slow trot.

Although old habits die hard, you should at least be able to contain his fizziness with ease and without anxiety.

Low head carriage

question

My horse has a very low head carriage. He works slightly on his forehand and I use draw reins as otherwise he tends to poke his nose. Is there anything I can do about his head carriage?

answer

It sounds as though much of your problem stems from the fact that your horse is not using himself sufficiently well behind; this can be an easy trap to fall into, particularly when using draw or running reins.

I would suggest that you abandon them for the moment at any rate and concentrate on encouraging him to work forwards into your contact instead.

Use transitions and frequent half halts to encourage better activity and balance, and to discourage any tendency to run on to the forehand; you might also find it helpful to try riding with a slightly higher hand position where it will be more difficult for him to drop on to the forehand and bear down on the bit.

Once his balance and activity has improved, you can start to work more on asking him to accept the bit and come into an improved outline, but it would probably be best to achieve this by more conventional means.

Do have some lessons on the flat with him from an experienced instructor, as this will help you to achieve your ultimate goals more quickly.

Draw reins may disguise some problems so use them with care

Riding school advice

question

I am interested in setting up a small riding school. Can you advise on any helpful publications?

answer

Riding Establishments Acts 1964 and 1970

(HMSO), *Running a Stables as a Business* by Janet MacDonald and *Horse Business Management* by J. Houghton-Brown and V. Powell-Smith, will give you an idea of what's involved.

question

Short striding

On the lunge my gelding trots well but on hacks he takes short strides which I find impossible to rise to. At times it's like he's cantering with his hind legs. If I try to steady him he fights against me and then continues to hurry along.

Other riders get the same reaction from him. His teeth and back have been checked.

answer

Presumably this problem happens whenever you ride him. Although you have sensibly had his teeth and back checked there are a couple of other avenues worth investigating.

Get his saddle looked at by a competent saddler who can see it fitted on him to make sure this isn't a cause of the problem – although you may lunge him in it and he is fine, don't forget that once you are sitting on top it can alter the situation considerably!

Next, you also need a good instructor to come and look at your riding to see if the problem lies there to some extent; if you are a little behind the movement, urging him on too strongly with your legs or similar, it will also create this sort of problem, but this is something which can only be assessed at first hand.

In addition, do consider his length of stride. It may look nice on the lunge, but sometimes when you are riding it can feel short (especially if you have been used to riding horses in the past which have a longer stride and cover more ground) and this might be causing you to over-ride him, resulting in his steps becoming very short and hurried.

Having a lesson will help you to feel what is right. When you are schooling try not to hurry him – if anything, encourage him to trot as slowly as possible initially so that he has a better chance of beginning to balance and lengthen his stride a little: he cannot do this if you are continually pushing him out of his natural rhythm in your enthusiasm to make him go forward.

Work over poles on the ground too, spaced initially at around four feet apart and gradually lengthening the distances between them (in steps of three inches at a time) but without allowing him to speed up as he negotiates the poles.

This should all help to improve him – when out hacking try to place him at the front if you ride in company so that he is less inclined to want to hurry.

question

Taking advantage

I have just started riding a friend's elderly but fit horse. The problem is that when hacking along bridleways the mare suddenly decides she's had enough and promptly takes us home!

My riding is a bit rusty and I don't want to get too firm with her, but at the moment it's very annoying to have the ride cut short.

answer

This horse really is taking advantage of you – she's discovered that you are not going to insist she carries on so she does as she pleases!

As you are 'rusty' it's likely that not only are you not as effective as you could be, but you lack confidence in your own ability to get your own way.

It would be beneficial to have some lessons

on the horse so that you can polish up your skills and begin to develop your authority and confidence over the mare. You will be surprised how this will help your problem when out hacking.

TOP TIPS

Canter Clues
If your young horse goes disunited in canter try cantering with your weight out of the saddle.

Frequent half halts can be used to encourage a horse to carry itself and not lean on you.

Too laid back

My first horse is an ideal family mount and has given me lots of confidence – but I do have difficulty in getting him to go at all! He is reluctant to canter and often trips. I asked my farrier to check the horse's feet and was told they were fine but that the problem could be rider-related.

I feel that my riding position suffers from my attempts to get him going but I'm also worried that the constant 'nagging' at his sides will make matters worse. Do you think he will ever be more responsive? What can I do to try to improve him?

Don't worry – your problem is not an uncommon one! Your horse is obviously a laid back sort of person who believes in economising on energy expenditure, and whilst this has given you a lot of confidence, it isn't expecting too much for him to be just a little more responsive and to have a little more respect for your authority instead of just ignoring you!

It sounds very much as though laziness is also the cause of his stumbling, although it might be wise to ask your vet to check him over just in case there is a physical problem present.

Whilst your position may basically be fine, you also need to learn to economise on your energy expenditure, otherwise you will end up too exhausted to be firm when it's really needed – and by becoming a bit too acrobatic in your attempts to get him going forward, it may actually make it more difficult for him to move with impulsion, as well as putting you off-balance and losing you the ability to be effective.

In addition, using very strong leg aids can often achieve exactly the opposite of the effect you want, creating resistance, and ultimately a 'deadening' of the sides to all leg aids.

Try to set aside some time for schooling each day; this needn't be a long period – how long depends on your enthusiasm and the horse's fitness – and you certainly don't want to bore him.

If you achieve what you want after ten minutes, leave it at that and go out for a ride. Your main aim is to encourage your gelding to respond more quickly and obediently to the leg aids and to move with impulsion; until you can achieve this, don't ride too many consecutive circles, which may end up inhibiting his desire to go forwards.

Send him on down the long sides of your schooling area, and diagonally across it to change the rein. Start off working in walk; ask for an active halt with his hocks beneath him, and having established this, then ask him to walk on, using the lightest of leg aids. Don't grip inwards with your legs or resort to kicking, just nudge with the lower leg. If he fails to respond instantly, is hesitant or sluggish, give him a sharp smack with your stick close behind your leg immediately.

He may be surprised and jog forwards rather than walking – be ready for this so you don't get left behind and accidentally 'punish' him by snatching at the reins. Gently re-establish the walk, ask for halt and go through the whole procedure again, repeating it until he walks forwards briskly the instant you ask and without recourse to the whip.

You may find that it is best to carry a schooling whip rather than a short one, so you can keep hold of the reins in both hands when using it – some horses will anticipate the stick if you carry a short one, and will shoot forwards the moment they feel you putting the reins in one hand. With a long whip, your response can also be far quicker if he ignores your leg.

It should not take long to establish this, when you can progress to transitions from walk to trot in the same way, and ultimately trot to canter, and then non-progressive transitions.

Once you have started to work him in trot, also incorporate some pole work to encourage activity and 'push' from his back end; vary the length of stride of trot too, shortening it slightly for a few steps, then sending

answer
from p 75

him on into a longer stride.

When you hack out, you must be prepared to follow this work through, and not allow either of yourselves to lapse back into old habits; he must be as quick to obey you when out hacking as when schooling!

As your horse becomes more active in his work, you should find that he will become fitter and more athletic, which should generally help improve his attitude to working, and make him a more co-operative person.

Heavy in the hand

question

What sort of bit should I use on my Highland pony? I cannot get a collected canter from her – she is very strong and will go on to the forehand, becoming very heavy.

I also have problems controlling the speed or turning her when galloping. I ride her in a French snaffle and drop noseband.

answer

When you know you are going to be doing some faster work it sounds as though it would be a good idea to use a severer bit so you can stay in control: it is ultimately far kinder than sticking religiously to a mild one which you then may have to use very strongly and roughly in order to be able to stop – this will only bruise and perhaps cut the mouth. With a stronger bit which your pony has more respect for, you will not need to use it as strongly, and this will be appreciated!

Generally, it does sound as though you also need to work on your pony's schooling in order for you to get her to be more responsive and to accept the hand and leg better. If

she is stiff, gets unbalanced and runs on to her forehand, she won't be able to 'collect' her canter anyway and will end up leaning on your hands for support all the while.

What you need to do is ride plenty of transitions, both progressive and non-progressive ones, and lots of half halts, particularly in the canter to help rebalance and reactivate her. Until you can achieve a good, balanced, working canter you shouldn't be thinking about collection.

Bear in mind that when riding transitions and half halts you must engage your legs as well, not just rely on your hands, otherwise she will only lean on the bit more and will never start to lighten her forehand.

Think about the position of your hands too: if they are very low or your arms are stiff or shoulders tense, (or you are tipping forwards), it will only make matters worse. Try to keep your upper body upright, and carry your hands a little higher so that your forearms are parallel to the ground.

Schooling youngsters

question

I ride a five-year-old horse who hasn't done any work. When I ride her in the paddock she pulls on the bit and tries to lower her head. She's driving me mad! What can I do?

answer

It sounds as though the mare is simply very green – it isn't so much that she doesn't want to do what she is asked, as she doesn't understand.

Added to this, she is probably still unbalanced, hence the low head – carriage, and

will feel stiff until you have been able to put in further work on her schooling.

Presumably you haven't had the opportunity to help bring on a young horse before, so you may feel a bit at sea initially as the 'feel' and reactions of a youngster are very different to those of a schooled horse. Have lessons from a good instructor who can explain the type of work you should be doing with the mare.

Coloured poles phobia

question

I have recently purchased an ex-hunter who is super over natural-looking fences but goes mad when we try to showjump. At present I am trying to walk her up to the jump and then at the last minute go into a trot. However, she throws her head up, stops and then cat leaps. Any ideas?

answer

Rather than persevering with your current approach over coloured fences, go right back to basics with her, working her first over single coloured poles on the ground in walk, then trot and finally canter.

Be patient and wait until she is relaxed and confident. Then start to introduce more poles in a line, spaced about nine feet apart, building up to a line of four to six poles. Continue to work quietly and steadily over these and, once she is happy about it, introduce a small crosspole, as low as possible.

Work steadily over this, then begin to introduce other different coloured fences, keeping them sufficiently small that height is not a problem but she can get used to lots of different types of obstacles.

Do try to allow her plenty of freedom with her head in the air and maintain a nice steady, regular rhythm with the minimum of interference.

Approaching fences as you are doing now is not a particularly good method, and if anything is going to frighten her more, until you won't be able to get near them, never mind over them.

Try to find an experienced instructor to help you but do be prepared to be very patient, and if at any time you have a problem, go back a few steps.

Some of the best hunters are terrified of coloured fences and it may be that although you do achieve an improvement, she will never really be a competent or confident showjumper.

Many horses will jump natural-looking obstacles, but dislike coloured fences

question

answer

Correct leads

I have a five-year-old mare who finds canter-ing on the correct lead difficult. On her stiff rein, the left, she finds it impossible to strike off on the correct lead. I've tried asking her over a pole on a circle, over small jumps, in the corner of the arena and just after chang-ing the rein, all to no avail.

This is a common problem with youngsters. Work in walk and trot will help to make her more supple which will be beneficial, provided it is along the correct lines.

The methods you have tried generally work but if she is not terribly supple or well bal-anced she may find it hard to cope with such approaches. However, there is another method you could try.

Walk her on a 20m circle, then begin trot-ting on an accurate 10m diameter circle in towards the centre of the larger circle. As you leave the track of the larger circle and begin to trot, maintain contact on both reins and gently but firmly lift the inside rein up (with-out pulling back) approximately six inches, to lighten the action of the inside shoulder and foreleg.

Maintaining the contact and position on both reins, as you are halfway round the 10m circle and returning to the 20m circle, ask for canter. When you obtain the correct lead, keeping the inside hand higher than the outside one, keep the canter going for one or two 20m circles before returning to trot and walk.

Make a fuss of her and when the walk is settled and established, try again. When you have established the correct leads on each rein for four or five days you can gradually begin to start lowering the position of the inside hand about an inch each day until it is level with the outside hand.

TOP TIPS

Overwork
Be careful not to overdo a young horse's work – signs of fatigue include a low head carriage, tripping, a slower gait, the horse appearing to be more unbalanced than normal and the horse brushing.

Split up a youngster's work periods, e.g. two 20-minute sessions are preferable.

Lateral frustration

question

answer

When I attempt lateral work the horse usually has too much neck bend and escapes through the shoulders, or, having got the correct amount of flexion, I lose the forward move-ment. I find this very frustrating and would appreciate any help you can offer.

It sounds as though the majority of your prob-lems are because the horses are not always correctly between hand and leg; in your anxi-ety to achieve a movement you probably com-pensate for this by becoming a little too domi-nant with your hands – which would explain why you end up with an excessive amount of neck bend or losing the forward movement.

It is a case of getting the basics right first; if the horse is accepting, and on the aids to start with and you are applying them correct-ly, you will find things much easier, so concen-trate on this for a while.

It is also advisable to try to get the correct feel from a really good schoolmaster horse before trying to tackle the same work on a horse which is lacking in education.

Have a chat about this with your instructor – if you are particularly keen on dressage you might find it worth your while going to some-one who specialises in this field.

Overcoming fear

question

answer

I am wary of working without stirrups as I have had a couple of bad experiences. I feel that I am going to fall off – how can I overcome my fear?

The good news is that with a good instructor sympathetic to your fears you should eventually be able to overcome your worries and regain your confidence. The bad news is that even with the best instructor in the world, it can take an awful lot of time!

Fears are sometimes irrational, which can make it frustrating, but in your case it sounds as though you have plenty of reason for being a little worried! If you are imaginative and sensitive (very desirable qualities in a rider) it can work against you.

Try to think less about what might happen, and more about ways of preventing the worst from occurring – if you feel a bit wobbly or insecure for example, put your imagination to good use visualising your legs becoming longer, and your feet heavier, helping to draw your seat down deeply into the saddle so you can't fall off.

Training your mind is as much a part of learning to ride as training your muscles or developing your co-ordination, but takes infinitely longer to achieve; and what's more, your brain and body have to learn to work together in mutual co-operation.

In a panic situation, where you feel that you have lost your balance slightly, instinct tells you to protect yourself by gripping on with hands and legs, even though your brain may be telling you that it is the worst possible thing to do, as it is likely to upset the horse as well as often unbalancing you further.

When riding you have to learn to overcome incorrect instinctive responses which may serve you well in other circumstances, but not when mounted, and learn a whole new set of reactions which may go against the grain to start with.

If you haven't already told your instructor about your past experiences, then do – or ask one of your parents to do it for you. Ask if you could stick to working in walk for the moment when doing work without stirrups, until you feel confident enough to trot.

When you do decide to try trotting, keep the pace as slow as possible so you don't get bounced about so much, and hold the reins in one hand and the front of the sadddle with the other for extra security.

Just a few steps of trot at a time will do to begin with, then walk, settle and relax yourself and try a few more steps. Gradually you can trot longer distances, and ask for more impulsion.

Only when you are quite happy working without stirrups in a more active trot for at least a couple of circuits of the school without having to hold the front of the saddle should you try cantering without stirrups.

Be prepared to stand up for yourself and to say what you are and aren't happy about trying; if your instructor isn't very sympathetic, ask for a different one, or if you can join a different group.

If you feel you are in an ambitious group of riders who are all more advanced than you, a different group lesson might be a good idea anyway, giving you the time you need to re-develop your confidence without feeling that you are under pressure to keep up.

TOP TIPS

Local Knowledge

A good way of improving your knowledge and getting to know the horsey people in your area is to take the Riding Club grade tests. Contact your local RC Secretary for details or call the RC Head Office on 0203 696697 or 696764.

Chews her bit

question

My 14-year-old mare has a sensitive mouth and wears a Nathe duo snaffle but she tends to put it between her back teeth and chew. The central, metal core is now showing and she appears to be getting through this too! How can I stop her doing this?

answer

The area where the bit lies – the bars – is a toothless space and if a bit is correctly fitted it should be virtually impossible for the horse actually to grab hold of the mouthpiece; in extreme cases, if the bit is pulled up against the molars damage may occur to mouthpieces made of softer materials, or the horse might just manage to grasp it between the back teeth, but this is not very common.

Check your horse's mouth again, with the bit fitted, to try to determine how far down along the jaw the back teeth are growing in case the problem lies here; if they extend unusually further forward than is normal so

that contact with them from the bit is unavoidable, then even a metal mouthpiece may possibly cause some irritation and it might be worth considering a bitless bridle as an alternative.

If you continue with a bit for preference, use a metal mouthpiece, choosing something such as a French link snaffle which is mild in its action. If her mouth is as sensitive as you say, there is no need to use a duo (I assume we are thinking of the same bit here, which goes under several names including continental and three-ring snaffle) which is considerably more severe in effect.

Alternatively, if you feel the cushioning effect of a softer material is desirable, you could try using a conventional snaffle covered with rubber, but will have to resign yourself to the fact that the rubber covering will ultimately suffer the same fate as the Nathe bit.

SADDLING UP

1. Fold the girth over the seat and gently place the saddle on the horse's neck, forward of the withers.

2. Slide the saddle back, so that it 'slots' into place just behind the withers, ensuring that it clears the shoulder. Never fiddle about pulling the saddle back and forwards, or from side to side, or you'll brush up the hair the wrong way and cause the animal discomfort and irritation.

3. Go around the front of the horse and let down the girth.

4. Fasten the girth up gradually, one hole at a time, using the first and third straps for added saddle stability.

5. Pull down the buckle guard to cover the girth buckles. Girth guards help prevent the buckles from damaging the saddle flap and are more comfortable for your leg position.

6. The girth should not be over-tightened. There should be enough room between it and the horse to enable you to get your hand easily between them and be able to pull the girth away from the horse's side.

7. Finally, ensure there is no wrinkled skin under the girth by gently pulling forward each of the horse's forelegs. Use a mounting block.

Rescooling hunters

My horse is an ex-hunter who has a high head carriage. She is not relaxed in her back and has dropped her nose but she has ugly muscles underneath her neck. Will this go away? She is starting to build muscle on top of her neck – I was considering using a pelham but would this just pull her into an outline? She is also resistant in downwards transitions, especially walk to halt. Any ideas?

It sounds as though you have made some progress with your mare; don't be too despondent about the musculature on the underside of her neck, as with further correct schooling she will develop a more correct top line and less pronounced muscle bulge under the neck – it will take a long time, however, before you really begin to see the results.

Remember that as an ex-hunter she has probably not had the benefit of a great deal of flatwork, so is bound to be stiff and may find the unaccustomed work difficult and demanding initially; some ex-hunters do not always take kindly to this sort of discipline, so keep your schooling sessions interesting, short and sweet so you do not overtire her too much and make her sour.

Doing some schooling whilst out hacking instead of always in the field will encourage a better disposition, and encourage her to move forwards into the contact with better impulsion.

At home, you could also try using polework and introducing some simple lateral work to help develop her suppleness and stride – but as mentioned before, bear in mind that it will take time to develop greater suppleness and co-ordination.

Stick to the snaffle whilst schooling – you will have to use one in dressage classes any-way. As you may appreciate, it is very difficult to comment on riding problems without actually being able to see both horse and rider working together; the resistance you describe in downwards transitions may be due to an unlevel contact, crookedness, stiffness, teeth problems, or too severe or rigid a contact.

Polework gives added interest to flatwork sessions

81

RIDING

question Q

Too 'fizzy'

My 17-year-old part Thoroughbred mare is always a fizzy ride, jogging and tugging the reins out of my hand. When we hack out and are approaching home she starts napping and rearing.

I no longer enjoy riding her but cannot find anything which is making her behave like this. Her tack fits well; I have lessons on her; she is not fed oats; her bit is an ordinary snaffle (pelhams etc. make her mouth bleed) and her teeth are fine.

answer A

Some horses are naturally of a more volatile disposition than others, regardless of what they are fed. Preventing them from becoming out of hand relies on good, sensible management with sufficient time out in the field plus quiet, careful but firm riding.

You are already having lessons with her, which is a step in the right direction, and it would be worth discussing your hacking problems with your instructor so that you can include some work which would benefit you on these occasions.

Don't forget that sometimes the rider can influence the horse's temperament greatly – if you tend to have a bit of a 'hot' seat or react in the wrong way when you have a problem, it can result in increasing difficulties.

It might be a good idea for you to try a slightly different approach to your hacking for a while, schooling her quietly for twenty minutes to half an hour at home before going out, so that you have established some obedience and control before you start, and taken the edge off any excessive high spirits whilst in a relatively safe environment.

Such work should be quiet, aimed at developing discipline and a relaxed attitude, rather than taking the form of cantering endlessly in an attempt to wear her out – this just doesn't work with a naturally 'fizzy'

horse, but more usually succeeds in making them even more hyped up. Flatwork can be made demanding if necessary working in slower gaits!

When you go out hacking, provided you feel it is safe to do so, go out on your own, having first told someone of the route you intend to take. If you feel it would be safest to go with company, take just one other escort horse, which should be quiet and steady and quite happy to go at the rear so that your horse will be less inclined to want to catch up all the time.

Stick to circular walking hacks to start with until she is more relaxed, and so you are not doubling back on your tracks, which will encourage nappiness.

Do not attempt cantering out on rides until you can walk and trot and slow down easily; try to keep her between hand and leg as though you were still schooling, and using half halts rather than a continuous pull to encourage her to stay balanced and steady.

When you feel the time is right to try cantering again, keep the pace very slow and again treat it as you would schooling; the moment you feel things starting to get out of hand return her to walk, until she is settled and relaxed once more.

You might also try a different bit – there are others which are stronger in action than a snaffle, but which she may find more comfortable than a pelham or kimblewick.

Your instructor or local saddler can advise you on these; be prepared to experiment, and perhaps even consider trying different nosebands too, as some of these can exert a steadying effect without the need to upgrade to a more severe mouthpiece.

As buying bits can be expensive, ask amongst friends and borrow some to try out, or ask if your saddler operates a bit hire service.

Wayward stirrups

I have been riding for five years, having a lesson every fortnight. My problem is that I cannot seem to keep my stirrups when I ride. I'm okay in walk and rising trot but in sitting trot my feet slip through the stirrups instead of staying on the balls of my feet. This gets even worse in canter and I often lose my stirrups completely.

It sounds as though you are probably gripping up with your legs because you are a little stiff and lack depth of seat – this leads to insecurity, hence the gripping in order to stay on board.

Unfortunately, the more you grip to try to keep your position, the more you lose it, as your seat is forced out of the right place in the saddle.

There are lots of exercises you can do to try to improve your suppleness, both on the ground and when riding; there are also lots of little tips, such as imagining that your feet are very heavy and are drawing your legs and seat downwards towards the ground, which might help.

Keep going for as long as you can maintain a good position, but the moment you feel it beginning to go, return to walk, sort yourself out, and start again – trying to keep going when you are struggling is pointless as you'll only revert to gripping again.

However, it does take time and practice as well as hard work and persistence – there are no short cuts! Ask your instructor for some more exercises you can try, and have a chat to him/her if you are still worried about it; but be patient, and don't expect your position to become brilliant overnight!

'Headless' horse

My problem is my newly loaned gelding who is an ex-racehorse. He is a willing ride, but he appears to be a 'headless horse' at times as he sticks his neck right out!

I've been having regular lessons since loaning him and have been told it is a problem which may not be easily rectified as it stems from his past. He is quite heavy in the hand and has tripped on occasions. Are there any remedies to this?

You have started to solve your problem already, by having regular lessons with your horse; it is going to take some time to resolve the habits of years, so try not to expect too much too soon! Do take the precaution of using knee boots when out hacking, however, just in case.

Think a little about the quality of your rein contact as well as his general balance and activity behind. Use frequent half halts to help rebalance and reactivate him, and try adopting a slightly higher hand position so he cannot bear downwards on the bit so easily.

Initially you may find this hard to achieve, and it will probably feel odd, so spend some time establishing it in walk before progressing on to trot and eventually to canter. You will be surprised at how high you can actually raise your hands if necessary (this is not the same as pulling them backwards, simply raising them!) – most people tend only to think in terms of lowering them.

Don't worry if he feels a little hollow to start with – this can be resolved easily later on. At the same time insist on activity from behind – you can use varying sizes of circle, or even poles on the ground, slightly raised if you wish, to encourage better engagement.

Don't mistake activity for speed, however, or he will simply run forward on to his forehand even more, becoming ever heavier and more reliant on your hands for support.

You might also find it helpful to start doing some pirouettes in walk with him too; do have a chat with your instructor to see if you can work out a suitable programme of different exercises which you can then work on by yourself at home.

question **Q**

Goes on 'strike'

My horse has acquired a bad habit – when being led he stops and refuses to budge. Standing by his shoulder and tapping him with a whip only makes him back away from me.

answer **A**

It sounds as though you will need some assistance initially to overcome this problem. Organise a leading lesson, obtaining some help from an experienced person, or possibly a freelance instructor.

Put a bridle on your horse for extra control, and position your briefed assistant behind him armed with a long-handled, stiff-bristled yard brush. Ask your horse to walk forward using a firm verbal command and suiting your actions to your words, although without advancing in front of his eye (or staring at him) or getting in front of him.

If he sticks his heels in and refuses to budge, your assistant can encourage him forwards from behind by 'scrubbing' his quarters with the broom; the moment he moves, you repeat your command, and the person with the broom ceases using it.

When he stops, repeat again, until you give the command and he walks forwards without any other encouragement. He may try to kick out at the broom, hence the need for it to have a long handle, and for the person wielding it to be an experienced and competent horse-person.

The other reaction you might get is for him to rush forwards abruptly, so be prepared for this, but try to avoid punishing him if he does, which will confuse him as to what you want; just firmly but gently encourage him to move more steadily. Depending on his character you may find that one lesson is sufficient, or he may need several.

Do also consider possible causes for this habit; if you only catch him to ride him, for example, he will be very reluctant to leave the field. Try to give him a reason for wanting be caught up and brought out away from the field – such as walking to his stable for a short feed instead.

Find out the cause of your horse's stubborn attitude before applying gentle persuasion

STEP BY STEP GUIDES

PUTTING ON A BRIDLE

1. It's always safer to tie your horse up first. Start bridling, on his nearside, by slipping the reins over his head. This is so that you will have him secure when you remove the headcollar. Then pop your right hand under your horse's jowl and take hold of the bridle cheekpieces, lifting the bridle up against the horse's face.

2. This leaves your left hand free to insert the bit. Ensure the noseband is outside the cheekpieces and the throatlash hangs free. Cradle the bit in the palm of your hand, leaving your thumb free to encourage the horse to open his mouth and accept the bit. Some people prefer to support the bit with their thumb and first two fingers. Either way is acceptable, providing it suits you and your horse, but the latter method makes it easier for fingers to get bitten!

3. Keeping the bit cradled in your left hand, slide your thumb in the side of his mouth at the bar (the toothless bit between the back molars/front incisors). Most horses will then open their mouths and you can gently pop the bit in whilst lifting the bridle up to keep it there. If a horse resists, gently press down on the bar with your thumb.

4. With the bit in, ease the headpiece over each ear in turn taking care not to poke straps in your horse's eyes. It's easier if you take hold of the ears and gently pull them forward, through the gap between browband and headpiece. Ease the forelock from under the browband and clear any mane from under the headpiece so it sits comfortably.

5. When the throatlash is fastened there should be four fingers' width between it and the gullet. This one is too short - even on the last hole, which isn't ideal.

6. The browband should not pinch or rub against the ears. If it does, a larger size browband is necessary.

7. Straighten the noseband by gently sliding one side up or down as required. Finally, put all ends into their keepers.

TOP TIP

Correctly fitted, the noseband should lie halfway between the bottom of the cheekbones and the corner of the lips. A snaffle bit should just wrinkle the corners of the lips. There should easily be a finger's width between each side of the mouth and the bit ring.

When left bridled, the horse should be tied up (pop a headcollar on over the bridle) and the reins caught up in the throatlash.

Always clean the bit after use.

Make it a habit to check your tack before and after use for insecure stitching, etc.

In cold weather, many horses prefer synthetic bits, e.g. rubber, Nathe, vulcanite, as they are less cold than metal bits. Warm a metal bit between your hands before asking your horse to accept it. Ensure that a synthetic bit has a safety chain running through it before you buy, and check the bit after use for any signs of cracking. Discard if damaged in any way.

question

Too tense?

My 11-year-old gelding sets against the bit and tenses up so he goes hollow in the back and has a high head carriage. He is quite exhausting to ride as he pulls a lot – I have tried various bits and nosebands to no avail.

His teeth have been rasped recently and I have had his back and tack checked. His tenseness and head carriage results in me becoming tense and we fight each other. I do try to relax but it is not easy.

answer

You have taken the right initial steps in checking for saddlery and physical problems, although you do not mention whether you have had your horse's mouth checked; discomfort in this area will cause problems, so if you haven't already done so, ask your vet to take a look.

Even though he is 11 years old, it sounds as though it would be a good idea to return to basics for a while and forget about competing for the moment.

If you can afford to have some lessons from an experienced instructor do; start by improving the flatwork and trying to obtain a better outline, with him being more relaxed and accepting the hand and leg rather than fighting the former and running from the latter.

Once you can keep him between hand and leg with less difficulty you can introduce pole-work exercises and eventually small fences using placing poles. Keep your approaches slow to start with, preferably out of trot, so that he has to use himself more correctly and is less inclined to rush.

Don't overlook the benefit of returning to walk between each jumping effort and doing a little steady flatwork schooling to restore balance, discipline and a relaxed attitude each time.

This is going to take some time and will involve a lot of hard work and patience on your part, but it will be worth spending time on the basics.

If he has not been well ridden by the previous owner, this reschooling will be essential if you are going to really enjoy him and his ability. Putting in some work on him will also give you a chance to work on yourself, and you may find a distinct improvement in your effectiveness as time goes on.

You might also take him occasionally to shows, but without competing, whilst you are in the process of re-educating him; find a corner and do a little schooling, so he learns to go to competitions and relax.

You do not say what bits and nosebands you have tried so far, but there is an enormous range available nowadays, and it is likely that you haven't exhausted all combinations yet.

Many saddlers offer a bit hire service, or you may be able to borrow some from friends, but be prepared to experiment a little more – it is better for both of you if you can find something you can hold him in more easily, rather than having continually to take hard pulls which will bruise his mouth. A good saddler should be able to offer you advice, as should a competent instructor.

question

Slippery road

How can we stop our pony sliding when we walk downhill on a tarmac road and there is no verge to ride on?

answer

Very often the surface of tarmac can be so smooth (these areas are often shiny in appearance) that it is unwise to venture out for a

walk. Take the precaution of using knee boots on your pony, have a chat with your farrier about fitting road studs for extra grip, and try to ride at the very edge of the road where it may still be 'roughed up'. Try to keep the walk steady and balanced, as if your pony hurries she will be more likely to slip.

Bridleways monster

My horse is perfect on the road but once on bridlepaths and fields he becomes a monster and I cannot hold him. Could you suggest any bits which I might try? I've also heard there is a supplement which might help.

Although many people claim to have had some degree of success using various supplements, I don't think this is the solution in your case since your problems only occur when on bridlepaths and fields, not in other situations.

The feed you are giving him is also unlikely to be responsible for his behaviour; it is more likely that in the past he has been cantered or galloped when on suitable going, and has thus come to associate doing this with every time he sees an expanse of grass or bridlepath ahead.

It would be a good idea if you could encourage him to walk (although this may be a jog to start with) when hacking out, only trotting when on tarmac.

Gradually you can dispel the idea in his mind that off-road riding means fast work, although it may take some time. A quiet hacking companion may or may not help – you will need to try this to find out.

Initially, at any rate, it sounds as though a stronger bit would give you more control so that you can go at the speed of your choice, but again, this is something you have to experiment with. Whilst one bit may suit one horse, it doesn't follow that it suits all horses!

To save yourself the expense of buying a lot of different bits which may not be the right ones for you, you could try hiring out different bits. Depending on the reaction you get (some horses don't like curb chains for example, and will simply tuck their noses in to avoid the action), you can then discuss it with the saddler you have hired from and try something likely to be more appropriate!

Alexander Technique benefits

I would be interested to hear your views on the Alexander Technique as I have heard conflicting reports on the matter. Does it really help a rider as much as some people claim, and if so, why?

The Alexander Technique can be useful not just for riders, but for people in all walks of life! It is not just a method of relieving tensions caused through body 'misuse' but a whole philosophy of movement and co-ordination.

It is difficult actually to explain it in so many words – it is more easily understood by experiencing it than by talking about it; it is a subtle experience, always taught individually and different for everyone.

It addresses the fundamental causes of many medical conditions such as back pain, neck and shoulder tension (common to a lot of riders!), breathing disorders, stress related illnesses and general fatigue where misuse and a loss of poise are contributory factors.

Alexander can also improve co-ordination, performance and well being – all vital in improving riding skills. Some instructors find that it is very much easier to teach riders who have experience of the Technique than those who do not!

You can find out more about the Alexander Technique and obtain a list of qualified teachers by sending a sae to: The Society of Teachers of The Alexander Technique, 20 London House, 266 Fulham Road, London,

Grips up in canter

question Q

I can only ride every month or so. My problem is with the transition to canter as I tend to bring my knees up when I give the aids. Once in canter, the horse I usually ride requires constant leg contact so that he doesn't fall back into trot, but I seem unable to return my legs to the correct position. Can you help?

answer A

Gripping up with your legs during a transition is a fairly common problem, especially in the case of more novice riders on horses which are perhaps a little lazy. With time and practice, as your co-ordination and suppleness improves and you become more effective the problem will diminish; it is good, however, that you are aware of it, and anxious to sort it out!

You would find it most beneficial to have a couple of private lessons which would enable you to work more intensively on this – although you might only have half an hour as opposed to an hour group lesson, the improvement is usually much faster when sorting out specific difficulties.

A lunge lesson would be particularly useful, on a well-balanced horse capable of working on the lunge in canter, as it would leave you free to work on lengthening your leg and deepening your seat in this gait without having to worry about either asking for, or maintaining the canter, until your position is more effective.

Working on improving the horse's response to your aids through transitions to halt, walk and trot will also assist you considerably when it comes to cantering, and could be concentrated on during a private lesson. Generally, exercises which can be done dismounted at home might be of help, although this problem is really one which can only be solved satisfactorily in the saddle!

Talk to your instructor about this problem so you can be given more help with it, and ask him/her for some exercises you can do at home to help with any specific postural problems you have. See also the Alexander Technique question and answer on page 87.

Gripping up can be solved – ask your instructor for some lunge lessons

Checking diagonals and canter strike-offs

question **Q**

When I canter I can't tell if the horse is on the correct leg without looking down. Does it matter if I look down to check this? In trot, on one rein, I can't set off or come back to the correct diagonal. My instructress says this will come with time and I will be able to 'feel' that it is wrong but I am starting to get a complex about it. Any tips?

answer **A**

Don't get too obsessed with this – as your instructor says, it comes with time and practice! Ask for canter without looking down, and try to feel which leg your horse is on – having made a decision, then glance down to check and see if you were right.

This will help you to begin to develop your feel for when it is right or wrong more quickly than when you are looking down all the time to check, since you will start to have to rely more on sensory input and less on your vision! The same applies when sorting out your trotting diagonals.

Don't worry too much about whether you are able to set off immediately on the correct diagonal in trot; most horses will tend to throw you to their more comfortable diagonal anyway. What is

Try to learn to 'feel' whether you are on the correct diagonal or not

more important is that you can feel when it is wrong and do something about it within a few strides, rather than being blissfully unaware of it!

Try not to look down as such when checking which diagonal or canter lead you are on – simply lower your eyes to glance down instead, so that your posture is not affected. Moving your head to look down can make you tip forwards and become ineffective, unbalanced and crooked!

89

Less efficient leg aids

question **Q**

If I've been jumping or riding for an hour my ankles become very painful. To overcome this I ride with my stirrups short but this means I tend to lose balance. Any ideas?

answer **A**

Riding with very short stirrups may well aggravate your ankle problem, particularly if you force your heels down or have them too deep; it will also affect the efficiency of your leg aids.

Without actually seeing you ride it is difficult

to comment on your position, however. Have a chat with your instructor about this, checking on the depth of your heels, stirrup length, amount of weight you are putting into your heels etc., and try a little bit of experimentation.

If your instructor feels unable to help you with this, it might be worth booking a lesson with someone who is perhaps a little more experienced or able to cast a fresh eye over the problem.

Correct diagonals

I have my own horse but it's a long time since I had a lesson. I have forgotten how to check if I'm on the correct diagonal in trot and my horse and I are beginning to become stiff on one side.

answer

When hacking, change your trotting diagonal regularly, rather than staying on the same one all the time; you can do this by sitting for an extra beat of the trot, and then rising again.

When schooling at home, you should sit as the outside shoulder moves back towards you – to start with, you may need to check you have got it right by briefly glancing down.

Whenever you change the rein you should change trotting diagonals, in the way described. Don't forget that other factors

than sitting on the wrong diagonal can cause one sidedness, including physical problems, a one-sided or crooked rider, and spending too much time on one rein.

Regular lessons are important to help prevent bad habits creeping in, as well as to enable you to continue to improve both you and your horse.

Don't forget that it is very difficult to tell exactly what you are doing and whether it is correct or not, since you cannot see exactly what you are doing (an instructor can!) and whilst something may feel right to you, it isn't necessarily! See if you can get some lessons with a good instructor, and you'll find it will help a lot.

Skill not strength

I have recently been riding a strong, 15.3hh gelding. I can control him well but I am only 5ft 2ins and weigh seven stone. I would like your advice as to whether I am suited to this horse. I have been told that weight keeps a horse's back down which supposedly means you can control them better, although I feel control is due to skill and not strength in the rider.

answer

Weight is not an essential requirement to ride bigger horses well, although in some circumstances strength may be required with certain animals – usually the ones who have not had the benefit of correct schooling, or which are likely to become difficult to hold whilst taking part in particular activities.

Often schooling plus the use of a stronger bit can be the solution to the latter, although it has to be said that it doesn't always work and a stronger rider may be necessary (not necessarily a heavy one!).

When riding larger horses, problems are more often created by lack of height than lack of weight, which can lead to loss of effectiveness and ultimately, of control.

Presumably you are enquiring about this as you are experiencing some degree of difficulty with the gelding you ride, although this may still be fairly minor at the moment. If this is the case, do seek some expert assistance from a good instructor before things escalate!

Riding skill, not strength or weight, will determine how successful a rider you are

Speed king

I have recently acquired a 14-year-old 16.1hh TB gelding, whose past career includes steeplechasing and eventing. My problem is basically his strength. When either hacking or schooling, he gets very bored walking and trotting, and when trotting he gets very excited and throws his head up in the air.

Canter usually means gallop as he is very hard to hold, although I am very strong in both my legs and arms and try to hold him back, which usually ends in half rears and him throwing his head up and down.

I wouldn't usually mind galloping, but he gets so engrossed that he often doesn't think to stop and has frequently galloped straight into fences and hedges, which is frightening. He gets very excited if he even sees a jump and refuses to walk and warm up.

When we do get round to jumping he canters with his head held very high up to the jump, then at the last minute rushes it, gets too close and flattens over, making it hard to stay on without the aid of a large handful of mane! He then gallops off in a manner such as above, unless there is another jump in the way.

He is ridden in a vulcanite pelham with a cavesson noseband and a running martingale. I ride with quite long stirrups as I find this is the only way to stop myself getting ejected out of the saddle. Is there anything I can do to gain the upper hand and get him to work properly without so much unbridled speed, or is he just too old and has such a past that he will never learn?

My other problem is that I want to get him freeze branded due to a recent spate of horse thefts but he is grey and I cannot afford to pay out continually for hoof branding. Is there any cheap and painless alternative for him?

There is no reason why you cannot get your horse freezemarked, even though he is grey. The chilled markers are simply left on for longer, so that a patch of hair is killed; if you

contact a freezemarking company, you can obtain further details about this.

The other alternative is to have a microchip inserted in his neck; you should contact your vet, who will carry out the insertion, if you are interested in this. The chip is about the size of a grain of rice, causes no discomfort, and the information carried on it can be picked up by using a special scanner.

As regards your horse's problems under saddle, it sounds as though you would both benefit from having some lessons from an experienced instructor.

Fighting him is not the solution, and is more likely to lead to more resistance, as well as not being pleasant for either of you; and at the end of the day he is always going to be stronger than you are.

You may need to rethink your tactics with him and use more subtle ploys rather than relying on sheer brute strength; there are a number of different exercises and techniques you can use instead.

If you are imaginative and constructive in your schooling and the exercises you use, there is no reason why either of you should be bored.

Having said that, there are some horses who tend to be more of a man's ride than a lady's ride, and if, after seeking some expert help, you feel you are not really making progress, it might be better to sell him on and buy something you find more enjoyable and easier to ride.

TOP TIP

Lazy Bones

If your horse is lazy, e.g. when trying to work in an arena, then a change of environment can help, i.e. doing school exercises out on hacks.

Highland showing

question

Could you tell me the best way to show, at local level, a 29-year-old purebred Highland and an Exmoor cross?

answer

How you turn your ponies out depends upon what sort of classes you want to do with them: presumably you will want to do native classes as well as veteran, condition and turnout, so it would be best to leave them in their natural state. For classes where they should really be plaited you can overcome the problem of a full tail and long mane by plaiting the tail and doing a long running plait along the crest.

As regards tack and your own clothing, this varies a little from class to class. Your local library should have some books on showing and correct turnout – alternatively, try a specialist equestrian bookshop. If you go along to a show as a spectator you can pick up a lot of useful tips.

Balance and canter

question

I am schooling a friend's four-year-old ex-racehorse. He is very responsive but anything faster than trot obviously brings back memories! So far I have been encouraging him to stretch his neck down and long by keeping a fairly long rein and light contact, maintaining an active walk and trot with my legs and seat.

Am I doing things correctly so far and how long will I need to keep up this type of work? Will it be obvious to me when he's balanced enough to ask him to canter? How do I ask for canter without letting him throw his head up and 'dive' at it?

answer

It sounds as though you are doing well with the horse you are riding, and as though he is improving considerably. As with all things, how long it will take you to make further progress or reach particular goals depends entirely on the individual as much as on the experience and competence of the rider – you might as well ask how long a piece of string is!

Once you feel he is calm and relaxed in his attitude, try introducing canter again – although you want to achieve a degree of balance, there is no point in waiting until his walk and trot is perfect, otherwise you will never get around to it!

Get the walk as balanced as possible on a 20m circle, ask for a few steps of trot and then for the canter so you lose balance as little as possible through the transition.

Try to keep a firm contact – if you anticipate him diving downwards at the bit, carry your hands slightly higher rather than lower to discourage it. With good riding and co-ordination, this can be done without becoming a backwards tug.

Canter for as long as you feel appropriate – this might be a quarter of a circle, less, or maybe a half or a whole circle, depending on how he is going. Return to trot and walk, get him settled and relaxed and when you are ready try again.

Don't feel you have to keep on asking for canter, simply work on it when things feel right; but you can't keep on avoiding the situation forever. Doing lots of work in walk and trot will improve those gaits, but not the canter itself!

Try to keep your circle accurate – mark it out with cones if possible, as it is easy to allow it to start to wander. Although he isn't your horse, you would probably find it helpful to have the occasional lesson on him from a good instructor who can help you with specific problems; look on it as being a useful learning experience which could stand you in good stead in the future!

Wary of water

question

answer

I have a lovely horse but there is one problem – if presented at water on a hack he digs in his heels and refuses to move, even though he will go through water when out hunting. His habit is infuriating – I have tried running a hosepipe over his feet daily.

Many horses are extremely wary of going through water, although they may be braver when participating in activities such as hunting – the same may be said for the riders, who will often do things in the heat of the moment which they would never dream of in cold blood!

Your chap sounds absolutely perfect except for this one problem; as he is so ideal for you in every other way, you might feel able to overlook it and simply avoid doing any water work with him.

If you feel this is unacceptable and that you really must have a horse which will go through water, then you will simply have to work at it, building up his confidence and ensuring that he is always obedient to you – even when he is a little dubious about something (which is where trust and confidence in you will swing the balance in your favour on most occasions).

Every time it rains, go out and look for puddles you can ride through; and find a shallow area of water you can also practise riding through on a regular basis – not just occasionally. Bear in mind that fast running water can obscure the bottom, as can muddy water, so try to find somewhere which is not too swift or deep (if he unexpectedly finds himself out of his depth before he is happier about water generally, you will only reinforce his fears).

Find somewhere which also has a sound surface, so that he does not slip either on entry, exit, or whilst in the water – avoid potholes or sudden dips in the water, even if it means you have to wade in yourself first to check it out.

Take a friend with a reliable horse and follow as closely as possible (without getting kicked) in walk. Don't try to use speed to get him in, otherwise even if you succeed, he will become unbalanced and anxious – think of how difficult it is for you to run from dry land into water without falling over.

Be patient but positive, using voice as well as legs; you may even need some help from someone prepared to don wellies and walk in front of him offering some food (or you could do this yourself, leading him, provided you can control him adequately from the ground).

If he is genuinely anxious about things, try to avoid using force as this will only confirm his suspicions that there really is something to be frightened of – and neither do you want going through water to be associated with unpleasant experiences.

Once he is in, stand him, praise him and possibly even offer him a titbit as a reward. Walk up and down in the water for a while, stand him again and make a fuss, then quietly walk him out and repeat all over again – you will need to leave plenty of time free for this.

Repeat until he is walking in and out following his escort confidently, when you can call it a day. Do this again on successive days; when you feel he is confident, you can then try it on his own – first of all going through the water to join his companion on the other side, and then going through on his own without the inducement of following another horse.

TOP TIP
Warm up
When schooling your horse remember that you must allow time for warming up before you start serious work and for cooling down after work. School work can be strenuous for your horse and if not prepared properly, injury may occur.

question **Q**

Value of schooling

My new horse has not been particularly well schooled and I cannot get her on the bit. Draw reins and a balancing rein have been suggested but I have never used either of these. Can you advise?

answer **A**

I think you should spend a little time investigating the cause of her evading the bit, rather than merely treating the symptoms. First ask your vet to check out her mouth thoroughly. Her back also needs checking as any discomfort in this region will affect head carriage.

Then consider her conformation as this may make it difficult for her to accept the bit correctly – your vet should also be able to offer advice about this.

You must also consider your own style of riding: encouraging a correct head carriage is a combination of hand and leg, applied with tact and co-ordination, rather than forcing her to draw her nose inwards.

Her bit must also be at the right height and of the correct width for her so it is comfortable in her mouth. Often, evasion of the bit is symptomatic of discomfort – the horse tries to escape the discomfort by adopting an incorrect head carriage and opening its mouth. If she is stiff and unschooled she will either be ignorant of what you are asking, or find it physically very difficult, and will seek to escape the discomfort.

Learning how to ride a horse correctly into a contact and to accept the bit is something which is best learnt at first hand with the help of a good instructor who can correct any positional problems you have.

The use of 'gadgets' should really be looked upon as being a last resort, and for the best results should be left in the hands of experts who fully understand their uses and what they are trying to achieve.

You will find that you will gain far more from learning how to do it properly without the assistance of artificial aids and it will be far more beneficial to your mare. From the horse's point of view, a correct head carriage is not just to do with carrying the head in the right place, but the result of correct overall locomotion and co-ordination – in other words, correct schooling.

question **Q**

Lost confidence

After I had been riding for two years my parents bought me a pony. She was young and green and I have lost my confidence on her. We have decided to sell her but no-one seems interested.

I have ridden some other ponies which my instructor says are just what I need but I still feel very nervous. Will I feel like this on all ponies? Should I give in to my fear and give up altogether?

answer

What a shame that your first pony didn't work out for you, although buying something which is green and in need of schooling is rarely ideal if you are a novice yourself.

It sounds as though you have taken the right course of action in deciding to sell her; have a word with your riding instructor about the adverts you have placed for her, as this might be one of the reasons why you have not had much interest.

By wording the advert differently you might get a better response; ask her also whether you are asking a realistic price. If you still cannot find a buyer for her you could try approaching a reputable dealer instead – your instructor should know of someone in your area.

In the meantime, since you have lost your confidence somewhat, it might be best if you went back to having regular lessons at your riding school – build up your confidence and improve your riding to the point where you feel you can cope with the odd little hiccup before you look for another pony to buy.

Rather than give up something you enjoy, ensure you prepare yourself a bit better for the next time!

First lessons

q u e s t i o n

a n s w e r

My mum has decided that she'd quite like to try riding but is worried about having a lesson as my school just seems to cater for children. How can I convince her that it's worth her at least trying a lesson?

It would be a good idea for your mum to have a word with the owner of your riding school – first lessons are often private ones and if she arranged for this during the day in term time then your mum need not worry about being watched by children.

Lots of riding schools also run special 'Mums or Housewives' rides during quieter times in the week – if your riding school doesn't, perhaps it would be worth suggesting such a venture to the owner! You never know, your mum might start a trend! If she is still wary perhaps she should try to find a school which already has adult lessons.

Riders' weights

q u e s t i o n

a n s w e r

I am worried that I am too heavy for some of the horses my friends ask me to ride. Can you give me an idea of how to assess weight carrying capacity?

Many thoughtful people worry unnecessarily – see the table opposite for a guide to weights of horse and rider. Bear in mind that other factors are involved in weight-bearing capacity, besides the mere size of the horse.

For example, a short-coupled horse is always a better weightcarrier than a long-backed one. A horse with good 'bone' (the circumference of the leg just below the knee) is stronger than one with less bone.

Thoroughbreds and Arabs tend to have denser bone than other breeds and are thus up to more weight than one might expect.

Weights of horse and rider

Horse (kgs)	Rider (kgs)	Rider (stones/lbs)
300	50	7st 12lb
350	58	9st 2lb
400	67	10st 7lb
450	75	11st 12lb
500	83	13st 2lb
550	92	14st 7lb
600	100	15st 12lb
650	108	17st 2lb
700	116	18st 7lb

Youngster stumbles

q u e s t i o n

a n s w e r

My 5-year-old mare tends to trip when I ride her downhill and occasionally she stumbles on the flat. Why does this happen?

Your mare's stumbling may simply be a factor of over-long or unbalanced hooves, causing her to catch her toe or it to dig into the ground as she brings her limb through. Therefore you must first check with your farrier as to whether this could be a possibility. If so, remedial foot trimming to keep the toes short, leaving the heels long and fitting a shoe with a rolled toe and slightly raised heels are all that is necessary.

It is true that some horses and ponies stumble because of stiffness in their forelimbs, due to various conditions in the limb. You should ask your vet to check her over to see whether he thinks a trial course of painkillers may be beneficial in alleviating the stiffness. However, this problem is less likely in a young mare.

The other possibility may be that your mare is exhibiting some unco-ordination in her forelimbs, although this is again less likely than the other explanations. Your vet could also check out this possibility at the same time.

Nose to the sky!

question

I have a young Arab who keeps evading the bit by lifting his nose in the air. I ride him in an eggbutt snaffle and keep my hands still so that I don't interfere with his mouth. Am I doing something wrong to cause this problem?

answer

Your description of your Arab's head carriage is a typical Arab trait; this does not mean that you will be unable to achieve a more correct outline and better acceptance of the bit, however. Encouraging this may take patience, good riding skills and perseverance – plus an understanding of the Arab psyche; being forceful to obtain your ends can lead to them becoming stubborn and unco-operative.

Encouraging him to accept the hand better will not be achieved by adopting a rigidly still hand; although you should not saw at his mouth, gentle squeezes and eases of alternate reins will encourage your horse to mouth the bit and salivate, and to relax his jaw rather than set it against the pressure of the contact.

You can practise this in halt (take care not to pull backwards with your hands) and in walk initially; once you have mastered it you can then progress to the same in trot and then canter.

Offering a peppermint at intervals may help a little initially – some people may view it as a cheat and it certainly isn't a long term proposition, but in the early stages with a very resistant horse, it can be a useful tip since mastication and the flavour (particularly if it is the extra-strong variety) will encourage movement of the lower jaw and production of saliva.

You should also check that he is comfortable in his bit and that his teeth are not causing any discomfort.

A better head carriage isn't the only point to consider when talking about a correct 'outline', which really involves the whole of the horse's body, not just the eating end! Achieving an improved outline is not always as easy and straightforward and you will probably find that you will make the quickest progress by investing in a few lessons with him from an experienced instructor – although for preference, try to find someone who likes this type of horse.

Riding donkeys

question

I am hoping to have a donkey to ride – I am 5ft 5in and weigh almost nine stone. Would it be possible for me to ride one? Also, do they have the same needs as horses in terms of care?

answer

Donkeys need every bit as much care and attention as horses or ponies. You would be too heavy to ride one (and too tall as well) but have you considered driving one instead?

I would suggest that you obtain a book on donkeys, such as *Looking After a Donkey* by D Morris which will answer most of your questions. You might also find it helpful to contact the Donkey Breed Society, Manor Cottage, South Thoresby, Nr Alford, Lincs LN13 OAS if you have any specific queries.

Driving donkeys is a popular pastime

Veterinary

Lymphangitis

question

About two months ago I discovered swellings on my horse's hind legs and face. Lymphangitis was diagnosed and a five-day injection course of a diuretic called Lasix and antibiotics was prescribed.

The vet has now left the practice so I cannot speak to him. However, my horse still has the swellings. On his face they are above his nasal passages, his legs are swollen in front of the hock and from the hock upwards. He has also developed 'windgall'-like swellings above his fetlocks.

Some people say this problem is like a virus and will have to run its course. Is my horse likely to have this for a long time? Will it recur? He is overweight – will this have an effect?

answer

The type of localised chronic swelling that has developed in your horse's legs is what we generally term 'lymphangitis', which your vet has already initially diagnosed. This problem usually follows a traumatic injury, or a diffuse infection of the soft tissues of the limbs, or quite commonly a combination of the two.

In this type of condition, where swelling has not appeared to resolve over several weeks, a more aggressive approach may be needed.

Firm bandaging of the limb from coronary band up to the lower part of the hock will help reduce some of the swelling gravitating down the limb. Various anti-inflammatory painkilling medications will help reduce swelling and inflammation, and broad spectrum antibiotics may be necessary if exudation of material has started to occur through the skin. Enforced walking exercise, perhaps 30 minutes three times daily, will also help reduce swelling.

Changes in diet and overfeeding can be an initiating factor in the development of this type of problem and obesity may reduce your horse's ability to remove any excess fluid through the circulation.

The peculiar factor in your gelding's problem is his head swelling, which may indicate the swelling is due to 'waterlogging' of the tissues, which is termed oedema.

Despite the fact that your initial vet is no longer available, it would be wise to ask the practice to re-examine your gelding and assess the current status of his condition.

With prolonged swelling, fibrosis in the subcutaneous tissues can occur, so some of the swelling may remain over a long period and only very gradually disappear despite adequate treatment of the initiating cause.

Heavy-metal levels

question

I recently had to have my horse destroyed. He was found to have 11mg per kg of cadmium in his kidneys. This was not the reason the horse was destroyed but could you tell me what damage this could do, if any, and what problems and symptoms it would show?

I have a youngster who lives in the same field as my old boy and wondered whether he was at risk.

answer

Cadmium is one of three heavy metals, along with lead and zinc, that has been associated with toxicity due to its potential for accumulation in body tissues. High intakes of cadmium due to environmental contamination result in cadmium accumulation in the liver and kidneys.

Horses have been reported to have suffered from a probable toxic condition affecting the kidneys, due to accumulation of cadmium there; horses seem to accumulate cadmium to a greater degree in the kidney compared to other animals in the same circumstances.

However, because cadmium is often present in addition to lead and/or zinc it is sometimes difficult to be sure if signs of toxicity are due to the other heavy metals rather than to the cadmium.

Therefore it may be worth having cadmium, lead and zinc levels measured in the soil of the field in question to assess any chance of possible toxicity. If the kidney tissue has been preserved, microscopic examination of the tissue would be able to check for evidence of the type of kidney damage associated with the presence of cadmium.

Check ligament injury

My mare strained a muscle in her leg just below her knee. On the vet's instructions she was given three months off, then brought back to fitness and was fine – competing successfully in hunter trials etc.

Some months later she went lame again, with the swelling in the same place but not as bad.

She was rested again but this time she is a little short in walk and there is some thickening in the leg.

My vet and farrier have suggested retiring her and breeding from her but I feel I am not experienced enough to cope with a foal. No-one can tell me whether more time off will help or whether she'd be capable of any work in the future. If it's only hacking she could do, that would be okay. Would sports medicine boots help? What do you think?

From the diagram you supplied and description it would appear that your mare suffered an injury to her inferior check ligament. This ligament, otherwise known as the accessory ligament of the deep digital flexor tendon, is a supporting structure with attachments from the back of the carpus to the middle of the deep digital flexor tendon, halfway down the cannon bone. Its function is to provide stability to the extended carpus.

A recent study of horses suffering from desmitis or 'strain' of the check ligament has shown that box rest, with a controlled walking exercise programme, has provided a favourable outcome in a majority of horses.

For example, an initial period of 15 minutes walking exercise twice daily would build up to 30 minutes twice daily over the next three months.

The period of time before work can be begun depends on the severity of the initial injury; in milder cases this can start after the three-month walking programme, whilst in more severe cases a more prolonged period of convalescence is needed, of up to six further months of walking exercise.

Sports medicine boots will certainly help support the fetlock joints, but if the injury has not healed adequately they will not prevent further problems from this injury.

One way to monitor when healing is satisfactory is to have an ultrasound scan of the affected limb performed, before work is resumed; this will indicate whether sufficient time has elapsed for repair to occur.

The above is a useful guide to long term outlook and potential future activities; if the injury has finally resolved well then work can be resumed, whilst if the ligament shows signs of chronic injury then retirement from competitive work may in the end be the only option.

Acupuncture

Do you have any information on acupuncture for horses with allergy problems?

At present there are only a handful of veterinary surgeons in the UK who practise equine acupuncture, but this number is increasing gradually in response to requests from the horse-owning public.

To contact a vet specialising in equines and acupuncture get in touch with the Royal College of Veterinary Surgeons, 32 Belgrave Square, London, SW1X 8QP. Tel 071 235 4971.

question Q

Nitrate levels

Analysis of our river water revealed that it was high in nitrates. Can you tell us what the implications of this are for our horses?

Nitrates are extremely water-soluble and move easily with water coming into contact with the soil. The most common source of contamination of horses' water supplies is surface water run-off from soil containing a high quantity of organic matter, or those that have been heavily fertilised.

Nitrates are not significantly toxic to horses, since horses lack the ability to convert nitrates to the more toxic nitrites as occurs more commonly in the cow. However, if the water supply contains high levels of nitrites then this can cause serious poisoning, with severe acute anaemias and possible collapse.

There is some evidence that levels of nitrates may affect a mare's fertility and her ability to maintain a pregnancy and also the foal's ability to grow and fight off opportunist infections.

Is your natural water supply free from contamination?

Palomino odds

If I put a palomino mare to a palomino stallion would I be certain of a palomino foal? Is there any other colour that can be mated to a palomino mare to make certain of a palomino foal?

Your mare would have a 75% chance of producing a palomino foal if she were mated with a palomino stallion, this being the greatest chance of getting such a foal. Mating a palomino mare with stallions of other colours only lessens the chance of getting a palomino foal.

Sesamoidities worry

question

My daughter's pony, a six-year-old 11hh Dartmoor X Welsh, has developed sesamoiditis in her left foreleg. She has not been doing any strenuous work but is overweight. She is having one sachet of bute a day and appears sound at walk and trot, but the swelling at the back of the fetlock is still very evident even though she has been off work for three weeks.

Regarding her weight, I am using an electric fence to control the available area of grazing, while my vet says keeping her on bare ground and feeding hay would be the answer. Your help would be appreciated.

answer

Sesamoiditis is a difficult injury to manage successfully and veterinary opinions do differ slightly as to whether rest or continued exercise should be instigated. Some vets would suggest a prolonged period of rest gives the maximum chance for satisfactory healing, as hastiness increases the possibility of recurrence. The changes within the bones reflect tearing of the fibres of the suspensory liga-

ment as it attaches onto the sesamoid bones, which must have occurred at some time to cause an initial injury of the suspensory ligament. Your vet's cautious approach in suggesting a period of rest will offer the best chance for satisfactory healing. Prolonged periods of flat work following rest may be helpful before returning to previous levels of performance.

The prognosis for sesamoiditis is quite often not good for a complete recovery in the long term, so it may be best to keep the horse in work under the influence of anti-inflammatory painkilling medications such as phenylbutazone. You must be guided by your vet, who is familiar with the specific features of your pony's problem and can therefore advise you best.

With regard to restriction of grazing to reduce obesity, a Dartmoor X Welsh pony is designed to survive on fresh air and water: therefore the use of electric fencing in restricting her grazing is the best medicine in the long run.

Sweaty marks

question

Our aged gelding has developed an almost perpetual sweat on the right-hand side of his neck. This has been happening for three months and is most prominent first thing in the morning. The vet can find no reason for this condition but there must be an explanation.

answer

The commonest reason for the appearance of an area of patchy sweating on the neck is following a reaction to an intramuscular injection in that area. This would appear to be due to a disruption of the local nerve supply to the skin which upsets the normal sweating mechanism.

The other possibility is that this area of

sweating reflects a problem with the nerve supply to the skin as it actually exits from the spinal cord within the vertebrae of the neck. However, this clinical sign is usually associated with other symptoms suggestive of a more generalised problem of the nervous system; it is likely that you would have noticed other obvious symptoms if they were present.

Hopefully the above is of some help in explaining your horse's problem, although it is not an exact answer to your question. If the sweating persists it would be advisable to ask your vet to repeat his examination of your horse to reveal any other possible associated signs.

VETERINARY

White line disease

question

My mare has developed 'white line disease' which my farrier thinks is because she is bedded on shavings. What do you think?

answer

I can see no link between the type of bedding you use and the development of any problems affecting the white line, being the union between the wall and the sole of the hoof.

The conditions that affect the white line in various ways, namely laminitis, seedy toe and gravel, are not problems which have a foundation in the type of bedding a horse stands on in the stable.

I would stick to shavings. Obviously hygiene is important in the stable, so continue to remove all wet shavings and replace them with fresh, but I see no reasoned explanation for you to need to change the type of bedding.

Eruption cysts

question

My yearling came in from the field with a very noticeable swelling on his face, just above the nostrils and even on both sides of the face. My vet cannot find a reason for it and the swelling is still there after several days.

answer

The most likely explanation for the development of equally sized, firm, painless swellings in the region underlying where the noseband fits, is that they have formed in reaction to impaction of the permanent cheek teeth in the upper jaw.

This is a condition usually seen in pony breeds when their cheek teeth start to erupt from the jaw and push out the deciduous 'milk' teeth. Due to obstruction of their passage 'eruption cysts' form, which cause bulging of the overlying bone of the upper jaw and thus the swellings that you can see. The good news is that these swellings usually regress spontaneously over 12 months, without any treatment being necessary.

Young ponies may have problems with impacted teeth

Copper alert

question

We have a 14.2hh, 13-year-old mare who competed until a year ago when she started showing unsoundness in the form of imbalance in her quarters. We tried all kinds of things, then eventually a young vet did a blood test and diagnosed copper deficiency.

For a year we have kept her on Super Copper Supplement and her copper levels have swung from 16.2 to 13, then 11.6, 18.1, 15.3 and now 17.3. If we stop the copper she becomes stiff in her quarters.

We would like to put her in foal before we retire her and need to know if her present copper level is too low. Also, will she need copper during the whole of her pregnancy?

answer

Two types of copper deficiency are recognised, the first being primary copper deficiency, which arises due to inadequate intake of copper in the diet. However, secondary copper deficiency is the more common form in the UK, and occurs where absorption and storage of copper are adversely affected by a light molybdenum or sulphate intake, even though there is adequate copper present in the diet. Cattle and sheep are more susceptible to excess dietary molybdenum than horses and therefore some pastures which cause severe disease in cattle can leave horses unaffected. However, if excess molybdenum is a problem on your pastures, this may explain your difficulties.

Copper deficiency has been implicated in causing developmental orthopaedic disease of the bones and joints in foals and young horses. In the adult horse it is said to cause thinning of the bones and swelling of the joints, with some limb deformities having been reported. Good feed sources of copper include molasses, linseed and soybean meal.

Indiscriminate dressing of pastures with copper salts is liable to cause poisoning and is therefore not advisable.

Blood levels of copper tend to lag behind changes in dietary levels of copper, which may explain some of your problems in getting adequate blood levels. The normal range for blood copper concentrations in horses I have found set out in reference material is 16.4 - 27.9 mol/L and therefore your mare's current level of 17.3 should be adequate for a brood mare.

It would probably be wise to maintain supplementation throughout pregnancy, although it appears the mare preferentially provides adequate copper to the foal.

Carnivorous Shetland

question

I seem to own a Shetland that is partial to the occasional meal of meat! He has been seen to eat a young bird and a young rabbit. Is this flesh eating another sign of dietary deficiency?

answer

Your pony's exhibition of carnivorous activity, although an unusual manifestation, would certainly fall into the category of wood chewing, coprophagia etc. This evidence of a depraved appetite we often term 'pica', which is classed as the ingestion of material not normally considered to be food. Mineral and trace-element deficiencies can result in this type of activity so the provision of a multi-vitamin/mineral mix may be beneficial.

Boredom and lack of exercise can also cause behavioural vices and pica, so improving this side of things may also help your pony.

Navicular options

question

Several months ago my horse was found to have navicular. He has had a course of treatment which has now finished. Every morning when I go to feed him he is pointing a foreleg and he is rather stiff but with exercise he loosens up.

Could you tell me whether he is likely to be in pain? Am I doing more harm than good by exercising him? Would something like MSM or bute help? How long could he stay on bute?

Would turn out help him as well as exercise? What about herbal help for him? As a last resort, what about denerving him? Vets in my area seem against this.

answer

I think it fair to say that the jury is still out regarding the efficacy of methyl-sulphonyl-methane (MSM) as a dietary supplement. As a metabolic end product of a substance called dimethyl sulfoxide (DMSO), a substance well recognised and used by the veterinary profession, it definitely has possibilities. There is certainly no harm in trying it.

Pain alleviation using drugs such as phenylbutazone for navicular disease is common, with the dose being that which is sufficient to abolish the lameness. It may be necessary to increase the dose periodically as the disease, which itself is not treated by the medication, may worsen. Long term use of sensible doses of this drug is frequent, with few side effects.

If the disease is going to progress, it will do so no matter what you do, and as long as your horse remains sound there is no harm in continuing his present level of exercise, or turning him out for a period of time. Pointing of the limb is a symptom of his condition and nothing to do with the exercise he has done. Phenylbutazone only acts by giving pain relief and reducing inflammation, this being part of the degenerative process.

There is certainly no harm in trying herbal remedies or acupuncture; I have no first-hand experience of these treatments.

Surgical treatment consists of:

a) Neurectomy is the earliest form of surgery used for navicular syndrome. Here the nerves running along the underside of the pastern, which give sensation to the back half of the foot, are severed. This is sometimes considered when other methods of treatment have failed, but there are several possible complications following the procedure. Prices vary a great deal between practices, but the operation would probably cost at least £500.

b) Severance of the navicular suspensory ligaments, as they attach on to the long pastern bone, has been introduced as a surgical technique in recent years. Its long term efficacy is not known as yet, but very promising initial results have been achieved in a fair proportion of horses treated.

Melanoma

question

I have a 13-year-old 13.2hh Eriskay mare with an awful lump on her side and I don't know what it is. Over the last two years it has grown very quickly and it is now the size of a golfball. I have taken advice and received two different answers: a) it is a wart; b) it is cancerous. When I groom over the lump she stamps her legs and moves around so I am concerned that it hurts her. What should I do?

answer

From your description of the growth I think it most likely that this is melanoma. Melanoma are one of the most common skin tumours found in horses. They are almost exclusive to greys, usually when they are 10-years-old or more and the tumours tend to appear around the anus. The tumours can be divided into two groups: the vast majority are benign and will not change significantly with time; a small percentage are malignant, showing a rapid increase in size and spreading to other parts of the body. Treatment is not usually necessary for tumours which fall into the first category unless they become sore or injured so that they bleed repeatedly. If, however, your mare's tumour is increasing rapidly in size you should consult your vet. It is well worth considering surgical removal of the tumour.

Spreading spots

question

My gelding has round spots on his skin. My vet said it was Canadian pox and gave me some lotion to apply and powders to feed. These had no effect. The spots have now increased – as my horse's summer coat came through so did white spots all over his body, spreading down his legs and even on to his hooves.

He has always seemed fine in himself but my vet is intrigued by all this. Can you help?

answer

The name of your gelding's condition is 'acquired leukotrichia and leukoderma' or sometimes it is termed 'vitiligo' – well you did ask!

This can be caused by a variety of initiating factors whose effect is to cause loss of pigmentation of the skin and hairs growing in that area of skin.

It is impossible for me to say what was the initiating factor with your horse but the migration of miniature worms, called onchocerca, under the skin can set up such an inflammatory reaction with consequent loss of pigment. Cases such as yours have been reported following infestation with this miniature worm.

Whatever was the cause, it is likely that it is now long gone and you are just left with the white areas as evidence of a previous problem. It is therefore unlikely that they will progress to any problem that should warrant undue concern.

Poor condition and gelding

question

I have just bought a 15.1hh piebald stallion aged three. He was in very poor condition and exhausted. I am trying to put condition on him but I wondered whether he ought to be gelded first? How soon can I give him a double dose of Strongid-P? What should I feed him to put condition on? He has been broken to ride – when should I start riding him?

answer

With regard to your exhausted stallion I think it unwise to consider castration whilst he is in such poor condition, as not only will he lose further condition immediately following the castration, but his poor state may well have had a deleterious effect on his ability to fight infection and leave him open to it post-castration.

Once he has regained some condition he will be more able to cope with the strain of castration. There is no reason why he should not be gelded at his age, but at the time of surgery your vet will be more aware of a slightly increased risk of haemorrhage.

It is difficult to assess clearly the degree of damage that parasites have caused to his bowel, but there is no reason why he cannot have double-dose Strongid-P now to treat any potential worm burden. Micronised barley would probably be a good addition to his diet, for something to put condition on him relatively quickly without making him difficult to handle. Please follow the guidelines on the bag as to quantities he should require for his present weight.

I would consider riding him after he has been castrated and when he is in adequate condition; this could be started while he is still three years old rather than waiting until he is four, if you so desire.

> ### TOP TIP
>
> **Lame Alert**
> **If a horse is lame in a front leg he will nod his head down as the sound foreleg goes to the ground and raise his head as the lame leg goes down.**
> **It's easier to detect lameness if a) you see the horse coming towards you or b) watch as it goes past you, i.e. sideways on.**

question

Circulon prospects

My mare has been diagnosed as having navicular disease in her near fore. The vet recommended she has a six-week course of Circulon and then a withdrawal dosage. She is currently on the withdrawal dosage.

From his initial assessment the vet has been very optimistic about the outcome of this treatment. So far it does seem to have been effective and she has been 100% sound for the past seven weeks. Once cured, the vet reassures me that the symptoms of navicular disease will not return.

As soon as we have finished the Circulon I hope to begin a fittening programme and resume our competitive work where we left off. However:

a) What are the realistic chances of my mare remaining sound?

b) What amount of work will I be able to subject her to in the future?

c) What has been the outcome of similar cases which have been treated with Circulon?

d) If I bred from her would her offspring be prone to navicular?

answer

I am sorry to hear that your mare has developed navicular syndrome, which is best described as an osteoarthrosis, which involves degenerative changes occurring within the navicular bone and its surrounding structures. The degree and speed in development of these changes varies dramatically from horse to horse.

What you can expect in the future depends to a large extent on the severity of the lesions within the navicular bones. If only one is affected and the changes in the bones are not advanced then this is of some comfort, and your mare may well be able to return to her previous activities.

Circulon contains isoxuprine, which affects the blood supply by dilating blood vessels within the navicular bone and hoof and reducing blood viscosity. This has been shown to be very beneficial in a proportion of horses; however, in my experience the time a horse remains sound following a course of treatment is very variable.

Whatever treatment she has, the bony changes within her navicular bones are there to stay; the possibility of the lameness returning, after a period of soundness following treatment, cannot be ruled out. Circulon can be tried again if this occurs but it can sometimes not work as effectively second time around.

The chances of your mare producing foals that are prone to navicular syndrome are very difficult to judge as the condition is multifactorial in origin, with the importance of inheritability still by no means properly understood.

question

Spavins explained

My mare has a lower-joint bone spavin and the vet has recommended nine to 12 months off, during which time the spavin will hopefully fuse and the mare will then be able to return to hacking and possibly some jumping. She has been off for over three months and is no longer lame. Some people have said I should now ride her gently. What do you think? What are the chances of her being hacked and jumped again?

answer

First of all, to lessen confusion I will define exactly what 'bone spavin' is: it is the development of arthritic or degenerative changes within the three, relatively immobile, lower joints of the hock. It is a condition of gradual onset which affects all types of horse and pony and at any adult age. Its incidence seems to bear little relation to the type or amount of work done.

The three joints in the hock that are affected comprise the articulation of the cannon bone with the hock joint and with the bones within the lower part of the hock joint itself. The

types of changes that can occur are cartilage degeneration, bone destruction and proliferation, and changes within the joint capsules around the bones of these joints.

The degree to which these changes can occur varies dramatically from horse to horse. Some have small spurs of bone that form along the joint edges, whilst others have large destructive lesions that affect all three lower joints of the hock. The rate of progression of these changes can also vary, with some horses having virtually static arthritic changes within their joints whilst others suffer rapid degeneration with severe joint changes. Only your vet will have the best idea of the degree of changes that have occurred.

The common medical treatment with bone spavin involves allowing the horse to carry on working under the influence of anti-inflammatory painkilling drugs, such as phenylbutazone, provided that they abolish or significantly reduce the degree of lameness.

Workload and/or previous expectations may have to be reduced to allow this method to succeed, but quite often horses respond extremely well to this treatment and can certainly become sound enough to resume work.

If she comes sound on medication there is no reason why you should not keep your mare in gentle, steady work. However, if she remains unsound then turning away to pasture would be the better option; it is true that a proportion of horses suffering from bone spavin never come sound despite prolonged periods of rest.

107

Soaking bed

My 16.3hh 14-year-old gelding is bedded on shavings and every morning his stable floor is soaking wet. He has free access to a stream in his field from 7.30am to 5pm every day. Could I therefore ration his intake of water at night?

At the moment he has four to five gallons and the container is almost empty in the morning. His hay is soaked and his feed is dampened. Do you think he prefers to stale in his stable rather than the field or could he have a problem?

I think it would be unwise to restrict your gelding's water intake until you know the underlying reason for his excessive drinking and urination; five gallons intake overnight may indicate a possible metabolic imbalance stimulating this reaction.

Whilst it is true that horses often stale on entering a freshly bedded stable, continued excess urine production through the night may be of significance. Possible causes are numerous, including kidney problems, hormonal or electrolyte imbalance, chronic infection or psychological upset.

A check-up by your vet would be in order to investigate this problem and confirm or deny any of the possible causes. This may involve blood and urine samples – catching a urine sample and taking this to your vet for analysis may be a good first step

TOP TIP

Foal Needs
Use a weanling or yearling mix for your foal. Foals need good quality protein as well as more vitamins and minerals than adult horses. Remember too that you can actually cause bone problems by feeding too much protein and energy that hasn't been balanced properly with vitamins and minerals.

VETERINARY

Capped hocks

question

My four-year-old hunter has a capped hock which has ended his career as a show hunter. However, what, if any, damage can it do to the strength of the hock?

answer

A capped hock refers to the presence of a floppy ball-like swelling which forms over the point of the hock due to the accumulation of excessive inflammatory fluid in a membrane-lined cavity called a bursa.

This bursa is present in the tissues between the flexor tendon and the skin as the tendon runs over the point of the hock. The wall of the bursa may thicken with the formation of fibrous tissue due to the low-grade inflammatory reaction present.

These swellings are invariably cold and pain-less and do not interfere with the function of the hock joint. Horses are rarely lame as a result of the swelling. Neither does the swelling represent any appreciable weakness in the hock joint. Therefore I would suggest that you regard this purely as a cosmetic blemish rather than any real problem.

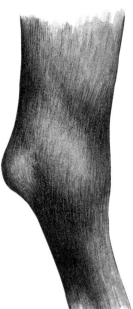

Older mums

question

I am considering putting my 14-year-old mare in foal. She is extremely fit and healthy but has never had a foal. Is she now too old to breed from? What is the difference between the terms quoted on various stud cards ie NFNF, NFFR and October 1st terms? Would June be the correct time to cover the mare?

answer

When considering breeding from an older horse or pony there are certainly more things to think about and more to be aware of: a general health check by your vet is advisable to examine her heart and lungs, for example, to see whether they can withstand the extra load of supporting a life of a foal as well as maintaining her own well-being.

Also, more specifically, a physical examination of her external and internal genitalia is recommended as, with advancing years, ageing changes can occur within these structures that may make her less likely to conceive and to maintain a pregnancy to term; there is a gradual decline in a mare's chance of conceiving with increasing age, and also more chance of losing the foal if she actually becomes pregnant.

Overall there is roughly a 60% chance of conceiving and carrying a foal to term with your mare, whereas a four-year-old mare would have more like a 75% chance.

A suggested fertility check with a mare of her age would involve a visual examination of her external genitals. Also routinely a swab is taken from her clitoris, and it is sensible to have a swab and smear taken from her cervix/uterus whilst she is in season. This will tell you whether there are any undesirable bacterias present and also a microscopic examination of the smear would give information on the healthiness of her womb.

No Foal No Fee (NFNF) means that you will only have to pay if you get a foal; No Foal Free Return (NFFR) means you pay the stud fee and get a free return to the stallion the following season if you do not get a foal from your mare that season.

'October 1st terms' means that the success of the stallion is gauged by pregnancy determination on or before October 1st.

With a non-thoroughbred mare it is less important and usually easier to get the mare to conceive in June rather than earlier in the year.

Blocked tear ducts

question

My horse has had a blocked tear duct for several years. Two vets have tried to unblock it but without success. the horse's eye is infected and there is pus and watery blood coming out constantly. A course of penicillin injections did temporarily alleviate the infection but now it is as bad as before.

Can you suggest any course of action? I live in Guatemala but any special equipment needed could probably be obtained in the States and used by vets here.

answer

The nasolacrimal, or tear, duct is contained within a bony canal in the skull and upper jaw. It runs from the corner of the eye in a roughly straight line down the face towards the nostril, where it exits on the floor of the nostril. This opening, or ostium, can be seen by lifting the flap of the nostril and looking on the lower surface.

There is a commercially available indwelling catheter which can be left in place for several days, with regular flushing of the duct being possible. However this is a more involved procedure that in some cases necessitates a general anaesthetic.

It is also a technique that is used to flush the duct continually, where the catheter is left in place for several weeks to try to prevent re-blockage following removal.

It would appear that this is not possible in your horse. In these circumstances a useful technique to investigate the site and cause of the obstruction in the tear duct is contrast radiography, with radiopaque contrast agents being flushed from the top and/or bottom of the eye and X-rays taken of the skull to ascertain the cause of the problem. Anaesthesia may also be necessary to get adequate views of the affected area.

Bony changes in the canal through which the duct runs can completely occlude the duct, making drainage and flushing impossible no matter how hard the force, so it may be that resolution of the blockage may be impossible.

Ligament strain

question

My five-year-old mare strained the annular ligament in her hind leg. She has been rested and I am now due to bring her back into work. As she is high spirited, should I attempt to lunge her before riding her again?

How many weeks should I walk her for? I can do roadwork three times a week and the rest of the time she will be ridden in an arena. Can I school her at walk or will circling etc. put extra strain on the leg?

answer

Inflamation of the annular ligament of the fetlock can occur if either the ligament itself, or the structures lying within it, or both, are injured. Therefore you must ensure that the healing process is complete and your mare is sound before you begin exercising her.

I would suggest you ask your vet to re-examine your mare before you start work to ensure that she exhibits no lameness and there is no sign of chronic inflammation of the ligament, which is likely to cause a return of lameness should she return to work too soon.

When your horse can work I think it would be a sensible idea to lunge her before you begin ridden exercise. I would suggest a minimum of six weeks in which to bring her gradually back into full work, with the first two weeks being exclusively of increased periods of walking exercise. Working on a circle will put extra strain on the leg if you have this leg on the inside of the circle; therefore do most of the manage work with the injured leg on the outside of the circle.

Hobday operation

My eight-year-old mare has recently been diagnosed as having a mild degree of left-sided laryngeal hemiplegia confirmed by endoscopy. The vet has recommended a 'Hobday' operation.

My mare had been getting very short of breath when exerted, even walking uphill. The classic whistling and roaring was not really noticeable. I understand that the operation helps to reduce the noise but am unsure to what extent her performance will be improved.

The aim of the Hobday operation, otherwise known as a ventriculectomy, is to remove a small pouch present on the side of the larynx that is partially collapsed; it is this collapse that occurs in laryngeal hemiplegia, when the horse is commonly known as a 'roarer'. Removing the pouch reduces narrowing of the larynx and may fix part of the collapsed larynx so that it is held out of the airway. There is a significant improvement in 60 – 70% of horses that have the surgery, but with only complete alleviation in 10 – 20%.

There should be improvement in the degree of noise and performance, and if your mare is only mildly affected then this should be all that is necessary.

The operation involves having the horse anaesthesised and laid on its back, with its neck stretched straight out. An incision is made over the larynx, just level with the angle of the jaw. The tissues below are separated to enter the larynx itself, following which a 'burr' is inserted into the pouch to be removed. This grasps the pouch, which is then surgically excised.

The surgical wound is left open intentionally, and any discharge must be cleaned daily along with the application of Vaseline to prevent wound soreness. The horse is rested for one month, with a gradual return to work thereafter.

During a pre-purchase vetting examination, the vet will listen for unusual breathing sounds

Frogs away!

question

My gelding recently shed his frogs. Within a week they all came away from the hoof in huge chunks. Underneath the frog looks quite normal and healthy but I've never encountered this occurence before. Is it normal?

Also, whilst rolling on hard ground he wounded his hocks, leaving a small abrasion on the outer bony part of the hock. Every few days these wounds open up, causing a little bleeding. I'm worried about them becoming infected (although he has had all his jabs). Is there anything I can do?

answer

The frog is a wedge-shaped mass of soft elastic horn, this feature being due to the higher moisture content compared to the rest of the hoof horn. In unshod horses, excessive growth of the frog is controlled by it being worn away by friction with the ground and by flakes of it becoming separated away from the underlying body of the frog.

When the frog is lifted away from the ground, by the placement of a shoe, this process is somewhat prevented, with frogs becoming fleshier and flakes becoming more extensive. Therefore, occasionally large pieces

of frog can become detached, where they would otherwise normally be worn away. This would appear to be the case with your horse.

The other less likely possibility would be the appearance of white, spongy frog and sole with a foul-smelling cheesy exudate which is typical of a condition called canker. This is caused by a bacterial infection of the horn-producing layer of the frog, which causes the production of the abnormal horn. I'm sure you would have noticed the stink if this were the problem!

Remedies for your gelding's hock abrasions are more tricky; ideally one would prevent the chronic irritation to the injured areas in the first place, but trying to stop him rolling is somewhat difficult.

The abrasions will only be superficial and therefore introduction of infection is unlikely. However, topical anti-inflammatory applications such as a mixture of DMSO and corticosteroid may well help to reduce the chronic thickening. This will only be available from your vet so ask him/her whether this would be advisable.

Clicking joints

question

I have noticed that after my pony has been standing for a while her joints click when she moves off. The clicks appear to be in her fetlocks and are quite loud. She does not appear to be in any pain and after a few minutes the noise disappears. Would a feed supplement help?

answer

Audible clicks emanating from joints are a relatively common finding on examining horses' limbs, this being most commonly found in the stifle joint. In your pony's case the fact that the clicks are emanating from the fetlock joints does not warrant any undue concern.

As your mare appears sound and unaffected by the clicking it is unlikely to be of any concern. However, if you want to be completely

sure, you could ask your vet to check it the next time he/she is at your premises. A food supplement is unlikely to have any beneficial effect on resolution of the clicking.

TOP TIP

Leg Check
Check your horse's legs after work for signs of heat, and any new lumps or puffiness. It's better to catch a problem early than let it develop simply because you were not sufficiently observant.

Sarcoid treatment

question

My friend's 12-year-old part bred Arab has had two operations for sarcoids, neither of which has been successful. The lumps are spreading and my vet has suggested trying something which I believe is used for TB. Have you any information on this?

answer

Firstly, it is important to make you aware that there is a possibility of regrowth of the sarcoids no matter what method is used, as in some cases they can be very troublesome to remove completely. Success I'm afraid is far from 100% with regard to complete cure with all the possible treatments.

Following your failures in surgical removal, your vet has suggested the use of the human BCG vaccine, used for vaccination against TB, as a type of immunotherapy. Here the growths are injected with the vaccine, with the treatments repeated at three-week intervals, usually requiring approximately four lots of injections. The vaccine causes gradual death of the sarcoid over the treatment period. This type of treatment appears to be particularly useful for sarcoids around eyes.

As for other possible lines of treatment: Removal with a carbon dioxide laser has recently been introduced as a treatment for sarcoids, initial results being very encouraging. Another option is cryosurgery, which involves freezing these growths using liquid nitrogen, whilst the horse is under sedation or a general anaesthetic. The preparation of an autogenous vaccine can be undertaken, produced from a sample of tissue taken from the growth.

The implantation of radioactive wires into the growths has also been used with good results, this being one of the more expensive options. Also, the horse would have to be hospitalised at a Veterinary School for some time whilst the wires were in place.

Another recent development in treatment has been the use of a special ointment, only available at the Liverpool University Large Animal Hospital, which is applied to the growths. The composition of the ointment is a closely guarded secret and the treatment can only be done at the University, but the results have been very good.

Splint-bone fractures

question

My young mare was badly kicked on the hind leg. The vet initially thought it was just badly bruised, but after four weeks' box rest and no improvement X-rays were taken. These showed the splint bone to be badly fractured and it had to be surgically removed. However, the damage to the bone was more extensive than first believed. The amount of bone left was not enough to pin to the cannon bone but the vet said this should not cause a problem as the operation and treatment are quite common.

Could you please advise if this is so?

answer

Fractured splint bones, as a result of kick injuries, are the commonest bone fracture we see at our clinic. You do not say which splint bone has been fractured; there are two – one on the outside of the cannon bone and one on the inside. However, as the injury is as a result of a kick, I would guess that it is the bone on the outside that is involved.

If so, then this is good news for your horse and yourself as these fractures are more likely to heal without further complications or long term lameness.

Despite the fact that stabilisation of the remaining portion of the splint bone was not possible I would not be despondent, as we find this procedure very rarely necessary in providing adequate stabilisation of the bone.

The long term outlook for return to full work following this injury is usually good, so I would be hopeful that this will be the case with your young mare.

Overcoming over reaches

question

My 17hh hunter type can't keep his shoes on for more than about four days. He has not been broken in for very long but when I asked the person who broke him in about this she told me it was just because he was clumsy. The farrier says he has good feet and his work only consists of about an hour's slow hacking.

answer

I presume that your horse is pulling off his shoes by over-reaching with his hind feet and standing on the protruding branches of the front shoes. To remedy over-reaching, shoes must be fitted to the front feet to hasten their breakover and to delay the breakover in the hind feet. This can often be achieved by rolling the toes and raising the heels of the front feet. In addition, the hind feet should be fitted with a shoe that has a squared-off and rolled toe and lowered heels, with slightly extended branches of the shoe so that they are fitted a little long. This shoe should be set well back and the protruding wall rounded off. I hope this combination will do the trick.

Injuries caused by kicks happen in a flash: the consequences may be long term

Twists her hind limb

question

When I bought my horse she twisted her hind leg in walk but a knowledgeable person told me this would be okay. Just lately she has seemed odd in her back – my vet says she has some tension there which is due to her twisting her legs, putting pressure on her back. Is she likely to get worse as she gets older?

answer

In my experience of horses that twist a hind limb at the walk this can sometimes reflect a previous injury to the limb which has caused some disruption in the supportive structures of a joint or joints. This can lead to long term degenerative changes and consequent lameness.

If your mare has continued to twist the limb following your vet's course of anti-inflammatory painkilling sachets, I would suggest it may be wise to ask him to re-examine her to ascertain the long term outlook for her condition. You should hopefully then be able to come to a reasoned decision as to her future.

Foal's limited sight

question

My mare's first foal has microphthalmia in her left eye and therefore has no sight on this side. She is very well put together and I would really like to break and ride her as one would a full sighted horse.

Could you explain the cause of this condition? Is there any treatment? Would my mare's next foal be likely to suffer from the same condition? Is it possible to fit a false eye? Could I compete normally on her or should special measures be taken?

answer

I am sorry to hear that your mare's first foal was born with the congenital abnormality of microphthalmia affecting her left eye.

The cause of microphthalmia is unknown, but it is thought unlikely to be an inherited defect and thus your mare's next foal is only as likely to be similarly affected as any other foal from any other mare.

There is unfortunately no treatment available and I am unaware of any work that has been done on the fitting of a glass eye.

The good news is that there are many horses that have lost an eye for various reasons who are competing, and with great success. So do not be disheartened, as she will adapt remarkably well to having only one functioning eye over a period of time; she may well learn to alter her head carriage, when working, to accommodate the fact that she only has vision on one side.

There are no special measures needed other than trying not to approach her on her blind side.

Weedkiller danger?

question

Could you please tell me if the use of 'Roundup' is harmful to horses and what symptoms would arise if they eat any of the grass or hedgerow which has been treated with this weedkiller?

answer

'Roundup' contains a substance called glyphosate which is a safe, effective herbicide and weedkiller. The substance is not poisonous per se, but it is recommended that animals are not allowed to graze the area for five days after application; however, this is more to make sure that the substance is absorbed into the plants and has the desired effect, than for the horses' sake. Any glyphosate that falls on the soil is rapidly broken down into harmless by-products.

However, there are two situations where its

a n s w e r
f r o m p 1 1 4

use may be dangerous; firstly, if it is mixed and used in conjunction with another weed-killer, and secondly, where the plants that it kills are themselves poisonous. The dead plant can often be more palatable to the horse and therefore more of a danger as a poison.

Parasites

q u e s t i o n

I have an aged but fit donkey who is a companion to my mare. She is always rubbing under her chin, tail and flanks – she is worse when her coat grows. There also appear to be warts under her chin.

My vet is not sure what it is. We have tried louse powder, benzyl benzoate and others – all to no avail.

a n s w e r

The symptoms your donkey is exhibiting are not totally specific for one particular condition, but they are suggestive of a parasitic infestation of some sort.

Possible infestations include lice and mange or forage mites. Lice tend to give more generalised irritation and the time of year and lesions you describe suggest that this is the most likely problem. If you are getting no joy with the louse powder then treatment involves the use of anti-parasitic shampoos or washes used at 7 – 10 day intervals. Your vet will be able to supply this.

Mange mites often affect the lower limb, but can just affect the face and neck. Forage mites, if she is fed hay from a rack, can give irritation on the face and neck only; however, one would expect your other mare to be affected similarly if she is fed hay from the same source.

The treatments you are using, except the louse powder, are designed for use in sweet itch, and one thing that I can safely say is that this is not her problem, so save your money. Occasionally chronic liver disease can cause skin irritation, which is possible considering her age, but one would expect this to occur all year round rather than in winter only; a blood test could check this out for you.

Helping arthritics

q u e s t i o n

My 23-year-old mare has been stiff and lame for a few months – two vets have told me it is severe arthritis. I have added cider vinegar and a herbal mix to her feed but she is still lame.

She is stabled at night and out during the day. When in the stable she can barely walk, but once she's been in the field for a while she appears less stiff and hardly lame. How do I know if she is really suffering? She runs over for her feed and still manages to attack other horses! Do you think she is better off stabled or turned out?

a n s w e r

Arthritis is a condition that it is very difficult actually to cure, but what we can do is try to relieve the pain and inflammation that can occur in an arthritic joint. Drugs like phenylbutazone act as anti-inflammatory painkillers; like all treatments, one expects a better response with only moderate signs of arthritis. If the arthritis is severe then it is often difficult to get a good response.

Phenylbutazone, and drugs like it, can be used very successfully for long term, low grade pain alleviation, so it may be worth considering their use on a permanent basis if you find that your horse's arthritis is becoming more and more of a problem. I would strongly suggest that you keep your mare out rather than in as she is very likely to 'seize up' if left to stand around in the stable. The joint movement that occurs with the exercise that she gets walking around in the fields will help considerably in keeping those joints from stiffening up.

Recurrent 'choke'

question

I have a 22-year-old TB gelding who over the last year has developed what I understand is called 'choke'. It manifests itself by a gradual blockage in his throat.

He eats a feed and develops a sleepy attitude, which is followed by gurgling and much salivating and retching. Eventually after much rolling and retching he regurgitates his feed through his nose and mouth. This is extremely distressing for him and I don't know how to deal with it. It happens on a regular basis.

He is unable to eat any hay or fibrous matter and is fed short feeds at three-hour intervals of nuts and sugar beet almost down to a gruel consistency. Summer is not as much of a problem as winter because he is at grass, but I am loathe to keep him out at night during cold wet nights.

My vet says it is a rare condition in horses. We have 'scoped' him but cannot find where the trouble lies. We suspect he may have scar tissue (from strangles in his youth) but no immediate solution presents itself.

answer

Your gelding's distressing bouts of recurrent choke strongly suggest that there is a physical or physiological obstruction to the passage of food material down into his stomach, which is thus regurgitated as green matter coming out of his mouth or down his nose.

As such, it's wise to rule out the possibility of an abnormality in the actual process of him swallowing and also to check out his oesophagus for any physical reason why it should obstruct the passage of food.

The endoscopic examination of your gelding's oesophagus by your vet will certainly have checked out any of the causes of recurrent choke in the upper half of the oesophagus.

The presence of scar tissue from a previous strangles infection may have some bearing on his problems, but one would have hoped to see this on the endoscopic examination as this usually occurs in the throat region.

Other conditions of the oesophagus can mimic choke in their presentation, such as when a stricture forms in the oesophagus due to the presence of scar tissue which inhibits the passage of food down the oesophagus.

Herniation of the oesophageal wall can also

'Scoping' a horse

occur in association with scarring following an injury; here food gets trapped in the out-pouching of the wall. If this is the problem in your horse then it is presumably in the lower part of the oesophagus, beyond the limit of your vet's endoscope.

The oesophagus can also dilate abnormally in what is known as megaoesophagus, where there is loss of the normal contractions of the muscular wall due to loss of nervous impulses. This can be investigated with X-rays taken of him swallowing food mixed with barium, which is highlighted on the X-ray films.

Radiography overall is a good method of investigating cases of recurrent choke; the passage of a normal stomach tube can sometimes be used to localise the area of the blockage, which can then be concentrated on by the taking of X-rays.

Another complication of the oesophageal choke is the inhalation of food material from the oesophagus into the windpipe, leading to a chest infection, so it may be worth having his chest checked out at the same time.

I would suggest you discuss this further with your vet as he has all the clinical details of your gelding's problem and can advise you with regard to the possibilities I have suggested.

Hoof falling away

I have a nine-year-old Shetland which my children ride in Pony Club activities. Over the last two years I have noticed that the outside wall of the hoof has been coming away from the sole, leaving a gap about a quarter of an inch deep on each hoof (outside edge only).

Daily dressing with Cornucrescine has improved the hoof condition but not the cracks. My farrier sugggested cleaning and packing the cracks with paper to prevent any stones wedging inside. I check this daily and replace as necessary but there has been no improvement. Can you suggest anything else?

The separation of the horn away from the sole to form a cavity at the white line in your pony's feet is akin to a condition which we call seedy toe, apart from the fact that the outside wall of the hoof appears more affected than the toe; however, the principles of treatment remain the same.

In simple cases any degenerate horn should be scooped out and the cavity packed with Stockholm tar. In more extensive cases the wall of the hoof over the whole of the cavity has to be removed. The cavity can then be filled with a synthetic hoof material or packed with cotton wool and Stockholm tar. It is then ideal to fit a wide-webbed shoe, possibly with a large clip, to protect the exposed sole and to retain any packing.

The problem with your pony's feet cracking is most likely to be due to a vitamin imbalance. This can lead to a fault in the horn-growing cells present at the coronary band, which leads to a failure in production of normal strong horn at this point. Weak bonds between the horn, and the normal stresses which act at this point, cause this weakened horn to split and crack.

Biotin has certainly been shown to aid the production of good-quality horn and it exerts a beneficial effect on weak, flaking hoof horn. Methionine also has a theoretical role to play in horn production; these substances together seem to have a synergistic beneficial effect on weak, splitting or flaking equine hoof horn.

Therefore a biotin combination supplement rather than biotin alone may well be worth trying. There are several products available such as Biometh-Z, Kera-Fac and Farrier's Formula which are available from your vet or can be sent for by direct mail.

These should be added to your pony's rations on a long term basis; it will take several months for you to see the benefits, but it is worth persevering.

Regular trimming also reduces the chance of splitting and cracking of the new horn.

question **Q**

Tilts his head

I have owned my horse for 15 years. Over the past four months he has started to tilt his head to the left. This only seems to happen when he is being ridden and is jogging. It does not happen at walk or canter.

His teeth have been checked and are okay. He is ridden in a snaffle – I wondered if it was his saddle but when ridden bareback he still does it. Do you think having his back checked would be a next step? Where would I find a suitably qualified person?

answer **A**

The appearance of a head tilt that is apparent during ridden exercise is certainly suggestive firstly of a mouth problem. It may not be your gelding's teeth per se, but possibly another part of his mouth causing discomfort. It would probably be wise to ask your vet to check your gelding's mouth thoroughly to examine all possible causes of the head tilt.

Secondly, it may be that the signs he is showing are suggestive of a nerve problem, as damage to some nerves can induce the presence of a head tilt; however, this type of problem usually presents as a permanent head tilt, rather than one only during ridden exercise. Again, your vet would be able to check for any neurological abnormality.

It is not my experience that back problems can induce a head tilt, but it is not impossible. If your vet, following an examination of your gelding, believes a back condition to explain the symptoms, then I would suggest you ask him/her to recommend someone in your local area, as it is usually local knowledge which recommends a qualified, experienced person.

Mouth problems can lead to head tilting or bit resistances

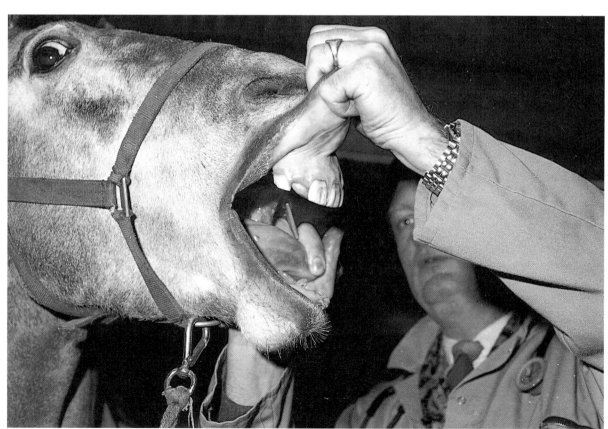

Sweet itch advice

I am worried that my cob will suffer from sweet itch as he has flaky 'dandruff' all over him and big clumps of it in his mane and tail. I have read about browbands which are impregnated with an insect repellent but I don't know where to get hold of these. Do you have any advice on this matter?

Prevention is certainly better than cure with sweet itch. You do not say in what type of environment your cob is kept, but a windy, exposed open field is much better than a field with lots of hedges or next to a pond or stream.

Midge activity occurs between April and November and during this time you should stable your cob when the midges are most active; i.e. between dawn and 8am and also from 4pm until dusk. In practice it is often better to stable affected horses from 4pm until 8am.

Medications to treat the condition are nothing revolutionary I'm afraid; tar and sulphur shampoos help remove the crusty exudate and possibly do reduce the itchiness. Benzyl benzoate is useful as a repellent and anti-inflammatory medication.

Steroid tablets or injections certainly can be of help, but be careful if your cob suffers from laminitis or you suspect that he might. Steroids can also be used as preventative medication by using the long-acting compounds at strategic points in the early part of the season.

Pyrethrin-based fly repellents are the most useful and can be used at one- and two-week intervals. These substances are also contained in the bands you require, which are called Equivite Flybands and should be available from your vet.

However, a more recent development in treatment involves the use of a fly repellent containing permethrin, called Switch. It was previously used in cattle, but has now been developed for use on horses and ponies suffering from sweet itch.

It appears to reduce symptoms markedly and acts as a good fly and midge repellent in horses and ponies when applied initially two to three times weekly at the beginning of the sweet itch season; this can usually be reduced to once weekly for long term use throughout the season.

Switch is poured along the backline - ensure you include the mane and tail. Occasionally fine-skinned horses, such as the Arab, find the treatment initially irritating, but this is usually short lived.

Oldies at grass

My pony has been in our family for years – he is now around 32! He is generally out at grass in the summer but as his teeth are now rather long I wondered whether he would be able to graze or if I should give him a supplement?

What sort of age is it 'kind' to keep a pony to? He appears perfectly happy at present but I do not want him to deteriorate and suffer.

Your ageing pony is more likely to be able to cope with grass than anything else in the summer months. Therefore I would save your multi-vitamin and mineral supplement for the winter months, when he is eating preserved forage rather than fresh grass.

With regard to keeping him in a stable condition, no specific age can be used as a guide; your best guide is how he behaves and the condition he maintains. As long as he appears fit and well and maintains a good body condition despite being a bit 'long in the tooth', then there is no reason why he should not enjoy a perfectly happy life.

120

What height will he make?

My gelding is rising three, stands 14hh at the withers and almost 14.2hh at the rump. Will he level off? If so, when, and what height can I expect him to make when, he has matured?

He has eight inches of bone so how much weight will he be able to carry, including the saddle?

Would it be okay to start riding him gently? I have been told that he was broken and ridden before I bought him – but I have done nothing so far as I thought he was too young.

We are commonly asked about expected heights at maturity and suitable weights a horse can be expected to carry. It is always extremely difficult to answer with assurance without actually seeing the horse or pony in question. Therefore I would suggest you ask your riding instructor or saddler to advise you more accurately as to the expected weight he will be able to carry when mature.

Your gelding's withers will 'catch up' over the next 18 months to two years and his final height may approach 15hh. I would agree with you that he is probably too young to be ridden, with most horses not being broken until they are a minimum of three years old

Runny nose

I am about to buy a mare who, after exercise, has a white nasal discharge. Her owner says she has always been like this and it doesn't affect her. What causes this? Is it something to be cautious of?

Could you also advise on 'big bale' haylage? The owners of the yard I plan to keep my horse at feed haylage only, no hard feed. Is this enough for a horse who is just hacking?

The commonest cause of a white nasal discharge following exercise is allergic lung disease caused by an allergy to stable dust; this is otherwise known as chronic obstructive pulmonary disease (COPD). I would suggest that a problem such as this be examined by your vet before you consider purchase.

Haylage-type products, as long as they are well preserved, are usually advantageous in managing conditions such as COPD and therefore a useful and suitable source of food for the horse.

It may well be the case that the amount of hard feed can be reduced or stopped completely when feeding haylage to horses that are only used for hacking

Thoroughpins

My four-year-old mare has a thoroughpin on each leg. I cannot understand why as she has never done any hard work. What can I do?

A 'thoroughpin', by definition, is a distension of the tarsal sheath which encloses the deep digital flexor tendon of the hind limb, as it runs in a groove down the inside of the hock. The distension forms due to inflammation of the membrane lining the sheath, which reacts by secreting fluid.

The initiating cause of the inflammation is probably long gone, but the fluid distension remains. Treatments that have met with some success include drainage and injection with corticosteroid, followed by bandaging, ideally with a hock Pressage boot.

You should contact your vet for examination of the swellings to see whether he thinks that this should be considered – although it is by no means 100% successful, with the effect sometimes being temporary. Surgical removal of the secretory membrane of the sheath has been tried but my personal experience of this is that you end up with a bigger lump than you started with – not recommended!

Fired tendons

q u e s t i o n

Two years ago I rescued a TB gelding from slaughter. He was a former racehorse who had injured his near fore tendon. This has been fired but the racing yard decided not to keep him. He has been living as a companion to my horse and his tendon has not caused any problems.

He was then brought into work and has been fine – he's very enthusiastic and I would like to jump him. Would this put too much strain on the tendon? What happens during the firing process? Would he be placed down in showing classes because of his enlarged tendon?

a n s w e r

The technique of firing consists of either burning the skin over and around the area of damage to a tendon or, more radically, the localised burning of the affected tendon itself, which is termed pin firing.

The firing is done with specially constructed firing irons which are applied, in varying patterns, to the surface of the skin. This procedure has recently been outlawed by the Royal College of Veterinary Surgeons and therefore your gelding must have been fired just before this came into effect.

The firing itself, unless it was pin firing (which causes more damage to the tendon), will not limit the work your horse can do; it is the degree of severity of the initial tendon injury itself which will limit this.

If you need a more accurate assessment of the tendon damage and likely occurrence of future problems, then I suggest that you contact your vet to ask if he/she can perform an ultrasound scan of the damaged tendon and therefore give you a more accurate outlook on future capabilities.

It is possible that the enlarged tendon and scars from the firing will go against your gelding in show classes.

Painless lumps

q u e s t i o n

My horse has developed a hard lump about an inch in diameter under the saddle area. There is no hair loss and he does not mind the lump being touched. My vet has said to carry on working the horse but I'm not convinced about this.

a n s w e r

From your description of the history and appearance I would suggest that collagen necrosis or nodular skin disease is the most likely diagnosis; it is characterised by the appearance of one or more firm, painless skin nodules which sometimes seem to appear overnight.

They are usually found along the back, especially in the saddle region but are sometimes found over other areas. Once established, the hair overlaying them can sometimes get rubbed off but other than this their appearance remains unchanged.

Their formation is thought to be due to an allergic reaction; however, what the horse's skin is reacting to is not well understood.

Fly bites and migrating immature parasites have been postulated but do not explain the whole problem. It is quite likely that the lump will now always be present but it may well reduce in size with time.

Occasionally they do become sore and cause discomfort; if this should happen your vet must be consulted as topical corticosteroid medications are of use in this situation.

It is not usually necessary or feasible to have the whole lump removed. Prevention of the problem of soreness can usually be achieved by the use of a pad or thick numnah.

If you want to be sure that our suggested diagnosis is correct, consult your veterinary surgeon; he/she may suggest that a skin biopsy could be taken using a biopsy punch. This is like a miniature apple corer, taking a tiny plug of tissue from the lesion. This can be examined under the microscope to give you a diagnosis.

question

122

Stifle locks

I bought my gelding, now rising six, a year ago. His owner explained that the horse's near-side hind leg often locked at the stifle joint when he was brought out of the stable. I had him vetted, he was examined thoroughly and the vet said fitness and maturity would help the joint problem.

So far his leg has been okay but I'd like to know more about this condition. Also, could you advise on a problem with him carrying his head to the right? He does this even when relaxed in the field.

answer

Upward fixation of the patella, more commonly known as patella or stifle locking, is a well recognised condition. It is seen more commonly in a young or unfit horse.

There are several theories to explain the phenomenon which involve poor muscular co-ordination of the stifle joint along with the relative leanness of the individual, and that it may be tied up with rapid growth. This can be explained by the presence of a 'fat pad' which normally lubricates the movement of the patella in the stifle joint; in the rapidly growing horse fat reserves are low and thus the 'lubrication' of the joint is at a minimum.

There is the possibility of the young horse growing out of it, due to some of the factors I have outlined above. Young healthy horses exhibiting this condition may well improve to normality when a fitness training programme is initiated. This improves muscle co-ordination and reduces the likelihood of occurrence.

However, the frequency with which he

locks his patella does reduce the likelihood of this succeeding. In addition, once the growth rate slows then the fat reserves increase and thus the stifle pad increases in size. Therefore, improving his condition may help the problem.

However, if this uncomfortable problem persists an operation can be performed which has a good chance of success. This involves surgical sectioning of the innermost of the three ligaments that attach to the patella.

This can often be done whilst the horse is heavily sedated in the standing position, although a general anaesthetic is sometimes necessary.

After the operation a period of rest of approximately one month is necessary before work can be resumed, and as long as this regime is adhered to, the long term outlook is very favourable and surgery well worth considering.

It is unlikely that there is a connection between your horse's head tilt and the upward fixation of his patella. This is more likely to be connected to a problem directly associated with the bones of his skull and upper part of his neck and/or some disturbance of the parts of his brain which affect balance and head position. This is commonly termed vestibular disease and may be due to a previous injury.

I think it would be wise to ask your vet to examine your horse's head, neck and nervous system to ascertain whether his problem is associated with any disease connected to these systems which might explain this

What are windgalls?

question

My horse has windgalls. They do not appear to bother him but could you explain why they occur?

answer

Windgalls are caused by distensions of the fetlock joint or its tendon sheath and are

thought to form either due to a previous injury or concussion to the joints during exercise.

Navicular facts

question

answer

My horse has navicular. Could you explain this?

Navicular syndrome is best described as an osteoarthrosis, which involves degenerative changes occurring within the navicular bone and its surrounding structures. The degree and speed of development of these changes varies dramatically from horse to horse.

It is true that navicular syndrome is a cause of chronic lameness in the horse, and as such the treatments and medications available are to a large extent designed to affect the symptoms rather than the cause. This is because the actual cause of navicular syndrome is not fully understood; it is quite likely that several factors are involved. Therefore the symptoms and radiographic changes are well understood, but the cause is still a matter of opinion.

Isoxuprine affects the blood supply by dilating blood vessels and reducing blood viscosity. This has been very beneficial in a proportion of horses and works quite rapidly; however, the time a horse remains sound post-treatment is variable.

Hoof trimming and corrective shoeing are also of importance in navicular disease, with trimming designed to maintain a correct hoof/pastern axis and a surgical shoe such as an eggbar shoe with a rolled toe being advocated to spread the concussion and weight around the foot more evenly, and also to encourage heel expansion.

Riggish behaviour

question

answer

My gelding is well mannered except during spring, when he pesters the mares and manages to serve them. Apparently he is not a rig. Is there anything which can be administered to curb this behaviour?

It can be proven whether your horse is a rig by the taking of a single blood sample which undergoes hormonal analysis. If this proves to be negative then your horse is what we term a false rig, which is a horse that has been correctly castrated but still exhibits sexual behaviour towards mares and possibly aggressive behaviour towards geldings or people.

If you do not have the facilities to separate mares and geldings in separate paddocks then you may be recommended injections with substances which suppress male behaviour can be tried – however, these are not licensed for use in the horse. Therefore I would persevere with establishing segregated paddocks.

TOP TIPS

Poulticing

Use a poultice to clean wounds and draw out any pus, to soothe bruising, and to reduce inflammation. Change the poultice every four hours or less. Remove bandages and rub the legs to promote circulation. Ensure wounds are cleaned of any bran, lint or gauze before re-poulticing. Poultice until the bruising has cleared, or until open wounds have been thoroughly drawn of pus - usually three or four days.

Crib-biter or windsucker?

question

I have a pony on loan. He chews his stable – I thought this was crib-biting but the owner says it is windsucking. Could you please explain both terms?

answer

Crib-biting and windsucking can occur due to inactivity and boredom, stress and excitement, develop as a habit or be copied from other horses.

They are in fact different varieties of the same vice, as in each case the horse swallows air.

A horse that crib-bites grasps a stable fitting or other convenient fixture between its incisors and, depressing its tongue, swallows air; this can eventually lead to undue wear of

Crib-biting leads to undue wear on the incisors and may predispose the horse to colic

answer
from p124

the incisors.

The use of a crib-biting strap is often effective in early cases. As the horse arches his neck, the metal plate of the strap presses on his throat, making swallowing difficult and unpleasant. When the horse is swallowing normally the plate hangs loosely, causing no interference.

Windsuckers achieve the same end in that air is swallowed, but it does not require a resting place for the teeth.

Air is swallowed by closing the mouth, firmly arching the neck and forcing the air down the oesophagus, accompanied by a gulping noise.

Some horses which have been crib-biters learn to windsuck when remedial measures are taken, and there are some windsuckers that learn to crib-bite.

Horses that crib-bite and windsuck are said to be more prone to tympanitic colic, as the air they swallow can cause discomfort due to gaseous distension of the stomach and intestine.

Reaction to the bit

question

A few days after I backed my four-year-old he was unhappy with his mouth and I noticed red marks on the gums well to the front of where the bit sits. I bought a nylon snaffle but by this time his mouth was very red and he would not tolerate a bit, actually trying to spit it out.

My vet gave him long-acting penicillin and told me not to try a bit again for a while. I have since tried a nylon snaffle but my horse's mouth was again extremely red. He is fine in a hackamore but our local shows are run under Pony Club rules so I am not going to be able to compete with him if I do not get this problem sorted out.

answer

Your young gelding's sore mouth may or may not be directly related to the *presence* of the bit. Some horses are allergic to nylon, plastic or vulcanite bits and if your snaffle bits were not stainless steel this may explain the problem.

Strong or undiluted disinfectants can also cause a generalised inflammation of the mouth, so if you have been washing the bits in such a solution and they have not been thoroughly rinsed then this may have some bearing on the soreness.

However, the presence of a soreness with red ulcers on the gums may be a part of a generalised mouth inflammation, or stomatitis, due to an infection of the oral cavity which unfortunately happened to coincide with your breaking of the pony. If the mouth now appears normal then this would suggest the infection has now resolved and should cause no further problem.

I therefore suggest you try a clean stainless steel snaffle again, after a suitable time period from the last bout of problems, and see if the problem recurs. If you have no further problems this would suggest one of the possibilities I have outlined above. If the inflammation and ulcers return then I would suggest you contact your vet for further advice.

Violent head throwing

question

My horse is very violent with her head throwing. Changing the bit has no effect. When jumping she is very resistant, insisting on going very fast and then knocking poles flying etc.

answer

The evasion of the bit and rushing at fences are suggestive of mouth pain. I would suggest you ask your vet to examine your horse's mouth, possibly whilst your mare is sedated, so that he can check out all possible causes of her behaviour thoroughly. It may also be necessary to X-ray her head to check out the bony structures of the jaws as well as what can be seen by looking in the mouth.

Tetanus reaction

I have three horses aged 19 months, two years and 14 years. They were recently vaccinated for tetanus and when the second jab was given, two of them, the youngest and the oldest, reacted badly to it. Neither could stand properly and both had a huge bulge where they had been injected.

My vet had to give both horses painkillers and put them on antibiotics. I had to poultice them three times daily. Yet more medication followed for the youngest horse and the end result was an additional bill of over £200.

My vet said reactions of this nature were not common and she is going to speak to the drug company. Do you think I could have any redress against the company?

It seems clear from your description that two of your horses had a severe inflammatory reaction to the administration of the vaccine. It is very uncommon for horses to suffer a reaction as severe as you describe and for two horses owned by the same person to react in this way is almost unheard of.

As the two horses were vaccinated one after the other it is likely that both vials of vaccine were from the same batch made by the manufacturer. Therefore it is certainly worth asking your vet to check if the drug company have had similar problems with other horses vaccinated from the same batch of vaccine.

If they have, then it may be feasible to attempt to get some compensation from the drug company; if they have had no such problems with other horses vaccinated with that vaccine batch, then it would be more difficult to prove that the vaccine was at fault and it could be argued that some other factor may be involved.

Overall we have very few problems with tetanus vaccination such as you describe, with many thousands of doses being given every year without problem.

Recurring swellings

For the past three years my gelding has had a swollen gland, just below his throat in between his cheek bones. It appears at the same time each year, he does not run a temperature, there is no nasal discharge and he is not interested in his hard feed. Over a week the swelling gets larger and comes over the cheek bone, up to the ear.

Each year the vet has told me to hot foment and poultice the swelling. In the past injections of penicillin have been used and the swelling has reduced and lain dormant. Have you any ideas, as I dread it recurring each year?

You may be relieved to know that you are not alone in having a horse with recurring swellings in the angle of the jaw. I have come across numerous cases in the past 12 months, the majority of which seem to occur in the spring.

As in your case, all the horses appeared well in every other respect apart from having these persistent swellings. I have blood sampled, biopsied and endoscoped them, all with very little of significance to find.

The general consensus is that it appears to reflect excessive activity within the salivary glands, which are present in the tissues of the affected swollen area. There is no sign of infection or inflammation of the area, just exuberant activity.

This seemed to coincide with flushes of grass growth on pastures and the problem would appear to be connected with this as the swellings tend to go down when the horse is stabled, but come up when out at grass. As such the swellings cause no pain or discomfort and can frequently be ignored.

question

Poor feet

I have a homebred three-year-old filly with four white socks and very pale feet. I simply cannot get her hooves growing properly, especially the hind feet. Over the last four months I have tried Farrier's Formula and one can see a distinct line where this has taken effect. The front feet are now reasonable but the hind feet, although not splitting, have grown very little.

She also has a problem with mud fever – it started with one small bramble scratch and soon spread to the other legs. Any help would be great.

answer

Feed supplements are only really of benefit in treating weak, flaking horn that easily splits or cracks and do not make horn grow faster as such: they produce stronger, harder horn which is less prone to cracking.

Vitamin imbalance can lead to a fault in the horn-growing cells present at the coronary band, which leads to a failure in production of normal strong horn at this point. Weak bonds between the horn, and the normal stresses which act at this point, cause this weakened horn to split and crack.

Biotin has certainly been shown to aid the production of good-quality horn and it exerts a beneficial effect on weak, flaking hoof horn (see 'Hoof falling away' on page 117).

You are seeing the benefits in the front feet but I think it is still worth persevering in the hindfeet.

Hoof oils can also be of help by acting as a waterproof coating for the hoof horn. They retain the moisture already present in the horn but do not add to it. It can be beneficial to soak the feet in water first before applying the hoof oils as this seals in the maximum amount of water within the feet.

With regard to prevention of mud fever, a barrier cream is a good idea as this provides protection from infection and also acts as a waterproofing agent. You should also aim to try to prevent prolonged wetness of the potentially affected areas, attend promptly to abrasions and small wounds, and rule out the possibility of external parasites, such as mites, contributing to the problem.

You should consider stabling your filly on dry bedding for part of the day, reducing the contact with rain and wet pastures. When you bring her in from the field, hose down her limbs to wash off any mud and then thoroughly dry the lower limbs, even resorting to a hairdryer to ensure they are bone dry.

Clipping of the hair of the lower limbs will further remove the areas in which mud can collect and also, should the worse come to the worst, make it easier for you to treat any areas that erupt.

TOP TIPS

Weigh-in
Weigh your horse regularly, at least once every week – a weight tape is the easiest method – so that you know whether or not he is losing or gaining condition. Keep a regular check on his temperature, pulse and respiration rates too, then if anything untoward is brewing you will catch it in the early stages.

VETERINARY

question Q

Drags her toes

In trot my mare drags both her hind toes, although she is worse with her right one. She is not super fit but in recent weeks we have been increasing her work and she has seemed lifeless. She is on a high performance mix but this has had no effect.

One friend said my mare looked stiff in her back legs but she does not look lame. Could you offer any advice?

answer A

There are two reasons, amongst others, that spring to mind as to the cause of your mare dragging her toes:

1) She may be equally lame in both hind limbs, which would explain why you haven't noticed an obvious lameness. This would be backed up by her apparent hind-limb stiffness.

2) She may be dragging her toes due to fatigue, this being supported by her apparent lifelessness in the last few weeks.

I suggest you ask your vet to check out these possibilities, along with any others that are apparent from his investigation of her problem.

Ask your vet's advice if you notice any change in your horse's way of going

Headshaking

Last year my mare started to nod her head and then try to scratch her nose. She does this whether ridden or lunged and even out in the field I have noticed that she flicks her head. After a while swellings appeared on either side of her nose, about four inches up from her nostrils.

Three vets have seen her and we are no wiser, although one thinks it could be an allergy.

answer

Your mare's symptoms seem to be typical of a horse suffering from the syndrome of head-shaking, which can have many possible causes. This is characterised by an involuntary vertical 'flick' of the head up and down, usually when ridden. You are not alone in suffering from this problem and I'm afraid response to treatment is often somewhat disappointing. However, you may get a good response to some of my suggestions, so try them and see.

An allergic nasal irritation, due to inhalation of various pollens, has been postulated as an underlying cause in recent years. Your description of evidence of nasal irritation, as manifested by her desire to rub her face after she has started headshaking and the presence of some swelling about her nostrils, would fit perfectly with this scenario.

Possible remedies are to try attaching a piece of stiff netting, muslin or fly fringe to the noseband of her headcollar or bridle so

that it partially covers the nostrils and acts as a primitive air filter when she is being ridden. This may not effect a complete cure and only works in a proportion of horses, but is often a good first line of attack.

If this does not suffice, a thorough investigation of all the possible causes may be worth considering.

A white or creamy nasal discharge may suggest a sinus irritation/infection, which has been associated with headshaking in the past. It may be necessary for X-rays to be taken of your mare's skull and sinuses to check for any evidence of such a problem, which can then be treated accordingly.

If nasal allergy/irritation is found to be the cause a surgical technique called an infra-orbital neurectomy can be performed in an attempt to alleviate the headshaking. Here the nerves which supply the upper lip, cheek, nostrils and lower parts of the face are surgically sectioned under general anaesthesia. This gives them permanent loss of sensation over this area, but is only effective in approximately 30-40% of headshaking cases; however, when it does work it usually works very well.

Potential success of the procedure can be tested by desensitizing the nerves with local anaesthetic prior to surgery; if a favourable response is achieved then surgery is a much better proposition.

Caring for wounds

My new loan horse was kicked and although the wound in itself isn't serious I am worried about it becoming infected. It is red, slightly swollen and hot. How should I care for it? She also has cracked heels.

The wound should be kept clean, dry and free from contamination from sources of infection. Therefore I would advise that you keep your mare stabled, out of the mud, and do not bandage the area as this may establish an environment which could encourage a wound

infection to occur.

Your description of swelling and reddening of the wound suggests that the area is generally inflamed and thus open to infection. The presence of cracked heels is a potential source of wound infection, so you should attend to this problem to prevent spread of infection from this area.

If the leg becomes generally swollen, inflamed or painful then I would strongly suggest that you ask your vet to examine your mare immediately and treat her accordingly.

question

answer

Hernia options

My 15 month old gelding has an umbilical hernia. Two vets have looked at it and said to leave it until he gets older. However they have suggested different methods of treatment - one said surgery, the other suggested a tight band to stop the blood flow. Could you advise?

The umbilical hernia is probably the commonest type of hernia seen in the horse. The bulging sac protruding through the hernia is formed by the lining of the abdomen and the skin itself. The contents of the sac vary from fat to loops of intestine or both. The complication of the presence of a hernia is when a piece of bowel becomes trapped in the sac, causing severe colic.

The two suggested methods of treatment will both quite possibly effect a cure. The choice of technique depends to an extent on the vet's experience and preference, but also on the size of the actual hernial defect in the abdominal wall ie the diameter of the hole that can be felt in the abdominal wall - this is not the same as the size of the bulging sac,

which usually appears bigger.

If the diameter of the ring is greater than eight centimetres, then this generally means a surgical repair under general anaesthesia will be necessary. This involves removal of excess skin over the hernia and then the return of the sac to the abdomen and repair of the abdominal wall defect with sutures, or in very large hernias a synthetic mesh is used to repair the defect.

Smaller hernias can be treated in the same fashion but are also more amenable to the use of elastic rings which are used to push back the contents of the hernia in to the abdomen, thus allowing the defect in the abdominal wall to heal. This technique can be performed under sedation, but is usually performed on the younger foal before weaning. This technique has the potential to lead to complications such as the trapping of a piece of bowel in the elastic ring.

Whichever technique is used, once the hernia has healed the horse can return to full work and be treated as normal.

question

answer

Sandcracks

My horse has a sandcrack which has now reached the coronary band. My farrier has managed to keep it from widening any more but the band itself is damaged. Will the band heal properly? It feels as if there is actually a lump across the split.

Hoof cracks, depending on their position, arise from slightly different causes: cracks which start at the coronary band form because of a fault in the horn growing cells present at the coronary band which leads to a failure in production of normal strong horn at this point. A crack that begins further down the wall and extends to the bearing surface of the hoof arises due to weak bonds between the horn at this point, and the normal stresses which act at this point cause the weak horn to split.

If there is a lump present on the coronary

band and the crack extends all the way down to the bearing surface, this is most likely to indicate that this is the site of a previous injury to the area. This has interfered with normal hoof growth at this point and caused a crack to form.

One has to ascertain whether the crack penetrates to the deeper, sensitive parts of the hoof or is more superficial. Simple superficial cracks should be treated to limit movement between the sides of the crack by cutting two parallel grooves, one on each side of the crack from the coronet to the ground surface; the ground surface is also 'eased' to prevent pressure from the shoe applying forces to the crack itself. The shoe should have toe clips on either side of the crack to provide support.

The same applies for complicated deep sandcracks but more radical treatment may be needed to effect a cure: here a full thickness section of hoof horn is removed from coronet to ground surface and the edges stabilised by wire sutures or metal staples. The defect is then filled and packed with epoxy resin or acrylic fillers. It will take six to nine months for the new horn to grow down and hopefully bridge the deficit of the original sandcrack.

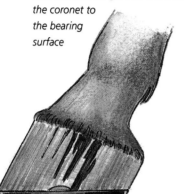

A simple sandcrack may be treated with two parallel grooves cut from the coronet to the bearing surface

A wide crack may be stabilised by a wire suture

Bridge a crack with staples and fill the gap with resign paste

Mud fever defence

q u e s t i o n

Last winter my mare suffered from mud fever on her hind legs. When she was in at night her legs filled so I tried keeping her outdoors but she jumps out of the field. How can I prevent mud fever this year without keeping her in too much?

a n s w e r

Preventative measures for the control of mud fever include stabling your mare on dry bedding for part of the day, reducing the contact with rain and wet pastures.

However, to finally beat the problem it may well be advisable to stable her permanently for period of time so that one can prevent re-infection from the copious mud and aggressively treat the problem.

Clipping of hair and the removal of loose crusts and scabs, with the help of a medicated antiseptic wash, will remove material in which the bacteria can be harboured.

The removal of this potential source of infection, followed by the application of antibiotic/steroid creams are necessary to aid healing.

The use of boots and bandages must be very carefully monitored as there is the possibility of exacerbating the infection causing further spread of the lesions, due to the development of a damp and/or sweaty environment.

In the treatment of considerable swelling in the limbs, in association with this type of problem, I often find that a course of in-feed antibiotics and anti-inflammatory painkillers to be of considerable help; this along with enforced walking exercise on dry tracks or roads usually significantly reduces stiffness and swelling.

With regard to the prevention of mud fever, caused by the bacteria infection of Dermatophilus, it can certainly be easier said than done.

You should aim to try and prevent prolonged wetness of the potentially affected areas, attend promptly to abrasions and small wounds and rule out the possibility of external parasites, such as mites, contributing to the problem.

A barrier cream is a good idea as this provides protection from infection and also acts as a waterproofing agent.

Ringbone explained

My four-year-old was recently diagnosed as having non-articular ringbone on both front feet. What does this mean? He is on 'bute and I have been told to work him for a month even though he is lame. Will he ever be sound again?

'Ringbone' is a collective term for arthritis and degenerative joint disease around the pastern joint. This causes lameness which is usually gradual in onset, and the arthritic changes may be relatively advanced before it is noticed or diagnosed.

High Ringbone
(non-articular)

Low Ringbone
(articular)

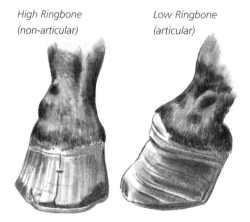

The lameness is associated with the laying down of new bone around the joint margins, which can sometimes be palpated above the coronary band or in the pastern region.

'Non-articular ringbone' is caused by excessive strain on the tendons, ligaments and joint capsule attachments around the joints which disturbs the attachments of these structures. This can be caused by a variety of factors including the type and speed of work done, injuries to the area, inherited and developmental abnormalities and poor conformation.

The degree of severity and progression of symptoms can vary dramatically from horse to horse, and only your vet can tell you how mild or severe your gelding's problem is.

It is possible that your horse will no longer be lame after a prolonged period, this depending on the severity of the radiographic changes.

Treatment involves the use of anti-inflammatory painkilling medications; these treat the symptoms, i.e. pain and lameness, and not the cause. However, it has to be said that a lot of horses can be put on this type of medication and become sound enough to undertake some work. Again, the amount possible varies a great deal.

Phenylbutazone is often the first line of therapy in equine arthritis. It often has a very good effect in alleviating any lameness or soreness from this condition. Occasionally the effect of phenylbutazone is not sufficient to alleviate the symptoms and abolish the lameness; in this case more potent anti-inflammatory painkillers can be used.

Severe shock

My pony was not her normal self: she refused her feed, was sweating, kept trying to lie down and was kicking at her belly. I called the vet out imediately. He examined her and said there was nothing wrong. He gave my pony a painkilling injection and told us not to worry.

My pony died the following day.

Please give me your opinion as to what caused my pony's death.

The symptoms your pony exhibited were suggestive of colicky abdominal pain. The fact that she succumbed within the following 24 hours suggests that the condition, causing your pony abdominal pain, progressed to such a degree that she went into severe shock and consequently died.

There is a multitude of various specific conditions that could initially present with the non-specific symptoms of abdominal pain. A diagnosis could only be made after a full post-mortem had been performed.

What is the sacroiliac joint?

Could you please provide some information on the sacroiliac joint of a horse's back? The horse I ride retired from point-to-pointing as he fell and injured this joint. His owners have been told he will never be able to gallop or jump again.

I have galloped him with no apparent ill effects and would like to jump him – only small show jumps, nothing like point-to-point fences. Would this be okay?

How might his injury affect him using his back and coming on the bit, as this is the major problem I have when schooling him. I'm not sure whether it's his lack of schooling or his back problem.

If you press him around the sacroiliac joint he twitches and occasionally if he has his hind-leg off the floor for some time, e.g. when being shod, he likes to stretch it right out behind him, as if it becomes stiff.

The sacroiliac joint is a slit-like joint between the sacrum and the ilium, which one should not visualise as a joint in the usual sense of the word; this is because it is relatively immobile, has roughened surfaces and is crossed by bands of tough fibrous tissue and ligaments which provide stability to the joint. The ideal is that the joint is virtually immobile in the adult horse.

Sacroiliac subluxation, caused by a traumatic injury, causes partial displacement and instability of this joint leading to chronic pain and thus lameness.

Since subluxation means that some of the ligamentous attachments have been damaged, time must be allowed for healing to occur.

There is commonly an asymmetrical prominence of the bones of the sacrum when the area is palpated or the horse viewed from behind.

You may notice that there is a lump on his croup, which is an abnormal prominence of part of his pelvis at this point called the tuber sacrale. It is this prominence that indicates there has been a subluxation of his sacroiliac joint.

The long term outlook for return to work is fair overall, but depends on the degree of initial injury to the joint, and its early management. Many horses show improvement after rest, but may not stand up to hard work.

In an uncomplicated case of sacroiliac subluxation, three months' rest is usually considered to be sufficient for healing scar tissue to form in the joint that has become partially dislocated, and thus the horse becomes sound and free from pain. However, in horses where there has been repeated injury and weakening to the joint, healing can sometimes take considerably longer.

I could not recommend that you start jumping him myself, but would recommend that you ask your vet to examine him for any evidence of low-grade chronic problems from his initial injury; this may have some bearing on his reluctance to accept the bit and explain his leg stretching following shoeing.

There are unfortunately some cases that, due to the severity of the damage, never heal and in these circumstances the horse will never regain its previous level of performance.

Kicks his stable

My gelding constantly kicks the back of his stable, causing considerable damage. He has also been very stiff in his hocks lately. Could there be some connection and can you suggest how to get round the problem?

With regard to your gelding's box kicking, it is likely that his hock stiffness is a symptom of the kicking rather than the fact that he is kicking because his hocks are stiff. So they are connected, but the stiffness is likely to be a result of the kicking.

This type of behaviour usually occurs as a result of attempted aggression against

answer-
from p133

another horse. You do not say whether he is stabled alone or in a yard with other horses, but if it is the latter then it may be time to move stables, away from the horse your gelding has fallen out with.

If he is stabled alone it may be a symptom of boredom or frustration due to the length of time spent in the stable; if this is the case, turning him out for longer or more exercise may improve the situation.

Advancing age

question

I look after a 24-year-old gelding who no longer works as he has arthritis. He is turned out for about 40 minutes each day and is then stabled. He seems fine apart from the problem that his sheath swells and his feet split.

answer

Your gelding's sheath swelling may be due to several factors. Older geldings do suffer from the development of lumps and bumps in their sheath or on the penis which can stimulate inflammation or secondary infection. The use of a sedative to relax your gelding's sheath and penis may be beneficial to examine the area completely.

The other factor on which his age may have a bearing is that his circulation may not be as good as it used to be. A consequence of this may be the formation of oedema and therefore swelling around his prepuce; this swelling is due to the waterlogging of the tissues by the presence of excess fluid in the area. A check-up of your gelding's circulation would confirm or deny this possibility.

From your description of the hoof splitting I gather that this split always occurs in the same place, which would suggest that he has previously injured his coronary band, where the hoof horn is produced, and this scar has left a weakness in the hoof horn, encouraging it to split easily. As he doesn't wear shoes any more this makes it difficult for your farrier to try to prevent forces bearing on the hoof wall. He may be able to 'ease' the bearing surface to try to reduce the distracting forces, which may help.

If your horse's feet splitting is a more generalised problem the most likely underlying cause is a vitamin imbalance. This can lead to a fault in the horn-growing cells present at the coronary band, which leads to a failure in production of the normal strong horn at this point. Weak bonds between the horn, and the normal stresses which act at this point, cause this weakened horn to split and crack. (See 'Hoof Falling Away' on page 117.)

Is bran safe?

question

Is it still safe to feed bran? I have always fed it without any problems, mixing it with chaff, pony nuts and cooked flaked barley. Although I have tried various complete mixes my horse goes 'nutty' on them.

answer

Bran is mainly the husk of wheat. It is about 8-10% fibre and 14-16% protein. It is a rich source of phosphorus and very low in calcium. The milling processes today are very sophisticated and most of the goodness is removed.

It is very difficult to buy good broad bran and

much of the product available is very fine. Bran can absorb much more than its weight in water and therefore has a laxative effect. This is a disadvantage as it wipes out the fibre digesting bacteria upon which the horse relies.

If you feed bran with a cereal and hay you are feeding your horse a low calcium and high phosphorus diet which is not advisable. You are as well to add chaff and pony nuts (which incidentally contain similar ingredients to a mix) however I would not go so far as to say bran is unsafe.

Sesamoid fractures

My horse fractured one of his sesamoid bones and tore his ligaments when he struck his hindleg on a concrete slab when cantering. He has been rested for several weeks but there is no improvement to the lameness.

My vet has suggested a year's rest but thinks the horse may only be suitable for light hacking in the future. Can you shed any light on this problem and possible treatment?

Management of fractures of the proximal sesamoid bones varies considerably with the type of fracture involved; there are three more common types of sesamoid fracture:

* those which involve the tip of the bone (apical)
* those occupying the main body of the bone (mid-body) and
* those affecting the base of the bone (basilar).

Apical fractures carry a favourable prognosis and the fragments can often be removed surgically. However, healing can take place without surgery if the fragments are not separated apart.

Mid-body fractures are best repaired by inserting a bone screw through the two fragments of the sesamoid bone, uniting them together.

Basilar fractures do not heal well as the fragments tend to be pulled apart. Therefore they do not heal by bone formation and tend to re-fracture at a later date. More rarely, the fracture can become more complicated with several fragments fracturing in more than one direction; this reduces the prognosis considerably.

All these types of fracture leave the fetlock joint open to the development of arthritis and disruption of the suspensory ligament and/or distal sesamoiodean ligaments, which further affect the prognosis adversely.

I would suggest you ask your vet to advise you regarding the exact type of fracture and ligament disruption that has occurred and therefore the likely future prognosis.

Suspensory ligament injury

My 5-year-old 16.3hh thoroughbred gelding has just sustained a suspensory ligament injury in training. The trainer assures me that with rest he will recover and be able to endure most diciplines so, as he is a sensible and affectionate chap, I have decided to keep him. Any more information on his specific injury and its rehabilitation would be greatly appreciated.

The suspensory ligament is part of the supporting structures on the back of the cannon bone; it's structure divides above the fetlock joint into two branches which attach on to the sesamoid bones on the back of the fetlock joint. Injury to the ligament usually occurs at the site of the division of the ligament and may involve one of the branches.

Rest is the major factor in successful treatment and nine to twelve months may be required in some cases. Ultrasonographic examination of the suspensory ligament can be performed providing the most accurate assessment of the severity of the injury and bear in mind that resolution of lameness and an improved external appearance of the ligament can give a false impression. Premature return to work will often result in a recurrence of the injury.

Following the period of rest your gelding will need a graded exercise programme. Usually this involves ten minutes twice daily walking exercises building up over four to six weeks to one hour twice daily. This can gradually be replaced by trotting exercises and then full work.

Your vet can give you the best guidelines about whether your horse can attain the same level of work as before as this will depend on the full extent of the injury.

question Q

Recurrent azoturia

My home-bred mare has had attacks of azoturia and I have been unable to work her as I would wish. She has had a foal – will her offspring also be liable to these attacks? Is there anything I can do with my mare, as I would like her to have an active life rather than just be a brood mare?

answer A

Azoturia or equine rhabdomyolysis is a well recognised but poorly understood condition affecting the locomotor muscles of the horse. In recent years, with the increase in competitive riding, it has become more common in performance horses. Its association with irregular exercise and excessive feeding is well known.

Recurrent azoturia can be a very frustrating condition both to treat and manage successfully. If your mare continues to have attacks despite your careful management, then more intensive investigation and laboratory tests may be required by your vet to aid successful management.

Obviously this involves further expense on your part, but this might outline an underlying problem which may be rectified following advice taken on the laboratory results.

It may be worth asking your vet's opinion regarding a referral appointment to see the Animal Health Trust where further investigations, involving muscle biopsies and electrical muscle activity recordings can be performed to help in elucidating your mare's problems.

It is unlikely that your mare's offspring will be similarly affected, as this is only a very rare occurrence.

A predisposition to azoturia is not normally passed on to the next generation

Inflamed coronary band

Two months ago I saw sudden changes in the coronary bands on all four feet of my eight-year-old gelding. The bands were overgrowing and had gone white and dry. My vet took samples of horn growth which were sent for analysis but no-one has yet positively identified the complaint.

Coronitis has now been suggested and he is currently receiving daily penicillin infections. Otherwise his general health is fine.

a n s w e r

Your gelding would appear to be suffering from a proliferative coronitis which is a chronic inflammation of the coronary band. The inflammation of the skin/horn junction causes the proliferation of horn growth at the coronary band and the loss of the chestnuts.

As to the cause of the coronitis, further investigation will be needed to get to the bottom of this: I would suggest the taking of skin biopsies of the affected areas of the coronary bands. This involves the taking of a tiny skin sample, using a device like a miniature apple corer; this is then sent off for analysis, probably with further hair samples and skin scrapings.

It is to be hoped that skin biopsies will give information on the nature of the inflammation and whether an auto-immune problem is involved. Treatment of such conditions involves the use of high dose corticosteroids, but the response can sometimes be disappointing.

The other less likely possibility is that he is suffering from toxicity of the mineral Selenium; however it is usual that skin and coat changes accompany this disease affecting the coronary bands and as these areas are not affected this is unlikely. Check with your vet as to his local knowledge of Selenium status in your area.

137

TOP TIPS

A Little, a lot!
A scoop of feed, once diluted by saliva and stomach juices, will almost half fill the stomach of a 500kg horse! So your horse's daily ration should be split into several smaller feeds rather than two larger ones. Little and often is the rule!

Over-reach scars

My new horse has old over-reach scars where the hair has not grown back. The rims of her boots sit on these scars and cause rubbing. How should I best cope with the problem? Is there anything my farrier could do? What should I do to keep the scarred skin in the best possible condition?

a n s w e r

I would go to your farrier first to try to prevent over-reaching. To remedy over-reaching, shoes must be fitted to the front feet to hasten their breakover, and to delay the breakover in the hind feet. This can often be achieved by rolling the toes and raising the heels of the front feet. (See the question on page 113 for more about this.)

A hypo-allergenic skin moisturising cream may well be worth trying to soften and keep the previously scarred skin in good condition.

'Cold back' syndrome

My mare suffers from a 'cold back'. What can be done about this? Will it get worse with her increasing age? Would the weight of the rider affect her?

Some horses which suffer from 'cold-back syndrome' fall over when their girth is tightened. Others simply crumple and cave in until they are crouching with their belly near the ground. A few will then explosively launch into the air and throw themselves about. On other occasions the affected horse will just appear unsteady on his feet for a few paces.

There are several theories which attempt to explain the phenomenon, none of which appear entirely satisfactory. It is possible that the horse suffers a sudden drop in blood pressure due to a problem with the heart and circulation induced by pressure on the chest. Although this is often offered as an explanation, I am not aware of any convincing proof to qualify this explanation.

A physiotherapist has suggested that the root of the problem may lie at the joint on the rib cage where the ribs hinge on to the spine; pain here might worsen by squeezing the rib cage with a girth.

From my experience I am more of the opinion that the collapse is due to some sort of initial panic reaction. We commonly see horses which learn to blow out their chests as the girth is being tightened and I believe that the sensation of restriction may induce panic in some horses. Clearly the problem will be self perpetuating; once the horse has suffered one such attack he will be conditioned to fear the tightening of the girth and therefore will panic again on subsequent occasions.

The secret of success in these cases is to leave the girth fairly loose until you are mounted and then walk a few paces before you tighten it up a bit, move on and then tighten it up once more.

In this way it will be possible to condition the horse not to 'panic', although this may not effect a complete cure. It is difficult to predict if your horse will get better, worse or stay the same with age, but it is likely that a heavier rider would make symptoms more obvious.

Contamination details

Is there any printed scientific information/research available to the general public with regard to heavy-metal environmental contamination? Do you know how I could get my soil tested?

Your local Ministry of Agriculture, Fisheries and Food (MAFF) office may well be able to help you; their address and number will be in the phone book.

The other option, which the Ministry may suggest, is that you contact your local Agricultural Development and Advisory Service [ADAS] office, who now run an equine consultancy as a complimentary service for veterinary surgeons, which includes the chemical analysis of soil samples. MAFF, your vet or the phone book will give you the number of your nearest ADAS office.

Other sources of scientific information/research will most easily come from the scientific library of the nearest University; their librarian should be able to point you in the right direction.

TOP TIPS

Cleaning Wounds
When cleaning a wound, work from the middle outwards, taking care that you do not cause any foreign objects – e.g. bits of grit – to work further into the wound. Always work with clean swabs. Saline solution acts as a mild antiseptic.

Skull fracture

My mare recently had an accident and fell over backwards. She fractured her skull and this will apparently take eight weeks to heal. She will then be X-rayed. At present her back is out of line but the vet has said he will recommend a specialist later. I am able to walk her around the yard. She has also torn a ligament in her neck and can only bend her head downwards a little.

Have you come across other similar injuries and if so, could you advise what problems may arise later on?

Firstly, I must say that I am very glad to hear that your mare has got this far down the road to recovery, as injuries and fractures caused by going over backwards and striking the poll on the ground are often disastrous.

The fact that she showed only signs of con-cussion and not any other nervous abnormality, including blindness, are favourable indicators of a return to normality. Also, the fact that you do not mention any evidence of head tilt or facial nerve paralysis would indicate that hopefully there has been no fracture or bleeding into the middle ear as can often occur.

If you can also walk her around the yard then this would suggest there is no gross inco-ordination or weakness, again another favourable sign. Hopefully the neck ligament injury (the ligamentum nuchae) and pain it causes will gradually resolve with time.

The appearance of any of the symptoms described should warrant immediate examination by your vet and may indicate a poorer long term prognosis.

Strange lump

About three months ago I noticed a lump just behind my gelding's chin. Sometimes it is really big and hard and then the next day it will be small and soft.

The vet has had a look at it, but has no idea what it could be. A lot of my horsey friends have also had a look at it but don't know what it is either. At first we thought that it could be a midge bite but we soon decided against that idea due to the way it has developed.

Please could you tell me what you think it could be and what I should do about it.

The fluctuating swelling on your pony's jaw is likely to behave in such a manner because it is intermittently inflamed, infected or both. This may be due to the presence of a foreign body under the skin, such as a thorn etc., or may be due to a more deep-seated problem in the bone of the jaw itself. This type of swelling usually also discharges infected pus-like material, but this is not always the case.

I would suggest you contact your vet for further investigation of the swelling, such as by the taking of X-rays of the jaw or surgical exploration of the swelling and taking of samples under sedation.

This should give considerably more information as to where the focus of the problem is, and how best to approach it with regards to successful treatment.

TOP TIPS
Poison
Remember to check fields for poisonous plants before letting your horse graze the land. Ragwort, laurel, yew, foxglove and bracken are just some of the potential hazards for horses. Check your hay thoroughly for any problem plants as they may be more readily eaten in hay.

VETERINARY

140

Grass sickness explained

My five-and-a-half-year-old pony has been destroyed after contracting grass sickness. I have many questions to ask as I was too upset to ask my vet at the time.

What is grass sickness? Why did it happen and could I have prevented it? Is it contagious and are any of my other ponies at risk? Why was it so quick? My pony was fine on the Wednesday but by Thursday evening had been destroyed. Will there ever be a cure for this disease?

Grass sickness is still somewhat the enigma of horse diseases. It is a disease of horses occurring in the UK and Europe, typically seen in horses at pasture and characterised by obstruction of the large intestine and reduced bowel motility.

There are two forms of the disease; the acute form is invariably fatal, as was unfortunately the case in your pony, with rapid deterioration in gut motility occurring over 12 – 24 hours. There is also a chronic form of the disease, of which many cases are untreatable; however, in the recent past new research results have shown that some chronic cases can be intensively treated, can recover from this condition, and remain fit and well following recuperation.

Management of the horse with chronic grass sickness involves the provision of palatable high-energy feed that is easy to swallow.

Cases that are going to recover will show significant improvement in appetite and demeanour, but not necessarily weight gain, within one month of the onset of symptoms. Obviously attempting this type of treatment was not an option with your pony.

A surge in recent interest and research into the disease has further elucidated factors that may be involved. The current thinking is that grass sickness is caused by a toxin ingested during grazing; the most likely culprit for production of this toxin may be a fungus, although the evidence to support this theory is not overwhelming.

We still do not know why this disease spontaneously appears, but it does not appear to be an infectious or contagious disease. There is some evidence that young adults are more predisposed than other horses, but any age of horse that is grazed on pasture can be affected. Suggesting that you do not allow your horses to eat grass is not really practical and therefore there is nothing you could have done to prevent it.

In answer to your final question regarding a cure, there is now some hope for treatment of the chronic grass sickness cases and there are new research results coming forward every year to help towards a better understanding and management of both the acute and chronic forms of the condition.

Deciding on dad

I have recently bought a 14.1hh skewbald mare and wish to breed from her. I am not sure whether to put her to a Trakehner or Throroughbred stallion. She is quite light herself, has a lovely temperament and has bred one foal previously. I hope to breed a good all-round horse of around 15.2hh. The two stallions are both 16.1hh.

With regard to your choice of stallion, you have made the ideal selection of either a

Thoroughbred or Trakehner to acheive a suitable horse of the size you want. Beyond this, there is little to choose between the two for achieving your goal. It is now really down to your own personal preference based on the characteristics of the two stallions.

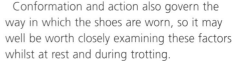

Excessive shoe wear

question

My Arab mare is used for long distance riding, travelling between 20 and 30 miles. However, she wears her hind shoes down very quickly on the outside edge of both of her hind feet.

My blacksmith has levelled her feet, welded harder metal on to the outside edge of her hind shoes and used frost nails in an attempt to lengthen the time between shoeings.

Do you have any suggestions as to how I might overcome this problem?

answer

Excessive or uneven wear of shoes can be due to many factors. Normal wear is due to the material the shoe is made from, the ground or road surfaces the horse works on and the pace of work performed.

Conformation and action also govern the way in which the shoes are worn, so it may well be worth closely examining these factors whilst at rest and during trotting.

It is considered normal for a horse to wear the hind shoes quicker than the front to a certain extent; this is commonly seen on the outside branch of the shoe as in your case. Heavier shoes are recommended in these circumstances, using a wide webbed rather than a thicker shoe. One must remember, however, that excessive weight can be counterproductive, in increasing the drag of the shoe.

The excessive uneven wear of your horse's shoes suggests that she is dragging her toes as the hoof lands on or leaves the ground. Excessively long toes or hoof imbalance are a common cause of this problem. This can be rectified by careful trimming of the hind feet by your farrier.

One other possibility is that your mare is working on her toes to alleviate discomfort or mild lameness. An examination by your vet would help rule out this possibility.

Shoeing remedies for excessive or uneven wear are a wide webbed heavier shoe, as I have mentioned, or a convex shoe where the inner edge of the shoe is thicker than the outer one; here this area is worn down first so that the nails and outer edge are saved from wear for a longer period.

Rolling the toes and raising the heels may also reduce your mare catching her toes as frequently. It would appear that the use of harder metals such as tungsten carbide welded on to the outside branch of the shoes has already been tried by your farrier.

The wear on a horse's shoes reveals how the horse moves

Ioniser benefit?

My mare is sensitive to dust. Do you think an ioniser would help? She does not share her airspace with any other horses. Could you tell me how much Horsehage would cost? What is the likelihood of her becoming broken winded?

I'm afraid I have never been convinced as to the efficacy of ionisers in the environment of a stable. Firstly, there is such a large airspace in a stable on which the ioniser must to try to have its effect.

Secondly, the composition of the stable air is constantly changing due to wind currents exchanging air through the stable door and other vents/windows etc.

Therefore any effect that the ioniser causes can only be very temporary, before the composition of the stable air changes due to continual air currents. The intake of fresh air achieved by your mare being outside has a much greater overall beneficial effect.

The distinction between when a horse has a dust allergy and when it becomes broken winded is by no means clear cut. Both terms describe varying degrees of the same condition, and when one progresses to the other depends to a large extent on how the horse is managed.

Therefore, if your environment management is very good, your mare may never progress to being broken winded. When dust allergies are well controlled the horse may perform as though it never had any problem at all, and therefore if your mare shows no symptoms she can work as normal.

Horsehage is approximately £4.45 a bale, cheaper if bought in bulk.

Disposing of muck heaps

My muck heap is around two years old. Will the horse worms have been destroyed in the rotting process? Would it be safe to spread the manure on our land?

The answer to your question is YES, with one or two provisos.

It is true that the heat produced by the composting and rotting process will kill the worm eggs and larvae carried in the droppings. So, as long as you are happy that an adequate composting process has occurred in the manure heap over the past two years then spread to your heart's content! If the more recent areas of manure have not rotted thoroughly then leave them till next year.

Dropping off

My horse has been diagnosed as having a condition called narcolepsy, which causes him to have sudden attacks of sleep. These can occur when he is being ridden, causing him to fall, or at rest and have no set pattern. I have been advised not to ride him.

I would be grateful for any further information as he is only four years old and I am uncertain of the best decision to make for his future.

Narcolepsy in the horse is a very rare condition but not unique, with cases having been reported in Shetland and Welsh ponies, Thoroughbreds, Standardbreds, Quarter Horses, Morgan, Appaloosa and Suffolk horses.

Apart from the obvious signs of collapse, one thing to really look for during an attack is evidence of rapid eye movement (REM), where the eyes quickly flicker about while the horse is recumbent and apparently asleep.

One other diagnostic test is the administration of a drug to either induce or inhibit an attack. It is probably safer to try to inhibit an attack and this can be achieved by your vet giving him an intravenous injection of atropine.

Narcolepsy is potentially treatable with the use of a human antidepressant drug called imipramine, the trade name of which is Tofranil. This is known to inhibit the onset of REM sleep and can be given by injection or in tablet form in the feed. It may be worthwhile discussing your horse's problems further with your vet to see if it may be of benefit to consider such treatments in this particular case.

Hacking cough

Sometimes, when out hacking, my mare starts to make a croaking sound, as if she is trying to cough, but then she blows out through her nose. She does this several times and then is back to normal again.

Before I had her she had 'suspected strangles'. Could this have affected her wind permanently?

Your concern over your mare's problem with 'clearing her throat' may be unjustified, as this frequently occurs in many normal horses during a period of exercise.

Strangles can occasionally cause long term problems if a so called 'cold abscess' forms a swelling in the structures surrounding the throat. This may cause an obstruction to airflow as the horse breathes during exercise, but here the problem causes continual obvious symptoms; the mild transient signs your mare suffers suggest that a complication from strangles is not the cause.

Occasionally, mild dust allergies can produce the symptoms you describe, although your mare does not appear to be suffering from any of the other common signs. However, if you wanted to be sure, an examination by your vet would rule out any low-grade underlying chest problem.

Riding in your paddock all the time can soon become boring – so think carefully about this before taking off a horse's shoes

Vaccination and shoeing plans

question

Am I right in thinking that my pony should have her 'flu and tetanus jab just once a year? Also, could I just have my pony's feet trimmed if I am doing all her fast work in her paddock?

answer

To ensure that your pony is adequately immunised against equine influenza and tetanus and is suitably vaccinated to ensure entry to any shows, events etc. the following schedule should be followed:

• Two vaccinations against influenza and tetanus approximately one month apart.

• This is followed by an influenza vaccination five to seven months after the second vaccination of the primary course.

• Thereafter a vaccination every 12 months after the influenza vaccination, which should be on or before the date you had her vaccinated the previous year; this is initially an influenza and tetanus vaccination, but then alternates between an influenza and an influenza and tetanus vaccination.

You should be guided by your farrier regarding the trimming/shoeing of your mare's feet. If her feet consist of good-quality horn which does not easily split or crack then you may well be able to get away with trimming alone, if most of your work is in the paddock. Your farrier will be able to tell you if this is the case.

Stumbles when ridden & led

question

My mare is 18 years plus. She is a lovely lively ride but over the last year she has begun tripping. At first it was when I was riding her but she now does it when being led. I have been schooling her to encourage her to pay attention, concentrate on going forward and look where she is going. I have also bought some knee boots – is there anything else I can do?

answer

Your mare's stumbling may simply be a symptom of over-long or unbalanced hooves, causing her to catch her toe or it to dig into the ground as she brings her limb through. Therefore you must first check with your farrier as to whether this could be a possibility.

If so, remedial foot trimming to keep the toes short, leaving the heels long and fitting a shoe with a rolled toe and slightly raised heels are all that is necessary.

It is true that some horses and ponies stumble because of stiffness in their forelimbs, due to various conditions in the limb. This is something to bear in mind, as at 18 years old your mare's joints may not be as supple as they used to be. If so, anti-inflammatory pain-killing medication may have a beneficial effect: you should check with your vet to see whether he thinks a trial course may be beneficial in alleviating the stiffness.

question Q

Recurring nosebleeds

My pony mare is 21 years young and has always led an active life. On three occasions recently, whilst hunting and out exerting herself, she has had nose bleeds, from both nostrils. She seems to run out of steam and have difficulty getting her wind and then the bleeding starts.

My vet has found nothing amiss but it has happened again. Opinions of horsey people seem to differ about this. What should I do?

answer A

Your old pony mare's problems with recurrent nosebleeds, or epistaxis, is certainly of significance and should be further investigated by your vet.

There are three important conditions that could give symptoms such as you describe. The confirmation of any of these conditions would require further investigation with the use of an endoscope and also taking X-rays of your mare's skull.

The first possible condition has a rather long-winded name of exercise induced pulmonary haemorrhage or EIPH for short. As in your case, it is usually associated with strenuous exercise.

The incidence of the condition increases with age and this is thought to be due to permanent ageing changes that occur within the substance of the lung. Confirmation of this condition involves examining the lower airways with an endoscope for evidence of recent haemorrhage.

The changes that occur in the chest cause a degree of obstruction to the air flow in the very fine airways of the lungs. This makes these affected parts of the lungs less elastic than they would normally be; during strenuous exercise these areas are put under tremendous stresses that they cannot withstand, and it is this that causes blood vessels to rupture with blood escaping into the lungs, which is then coughed up or comes up the trachea with continuing exercise – this can obviously cause a sudden onset of exercise intolerance.

It is only in the last couple of years that this

condition has become more fully understood; it is now suspected that it is related to chronic obstructive lung disease commonly known as 'broken wind' or 'heaves'. Therefore it is very important that your stable management is carefully observed. Bedding on shavings and soaking hay or using Horsehage are advisable.

It is possible that a course of medication such as Ventipulmin may well benefit the condition in the long run; you would need to consult your own vet to see whether he thinks this would be advisable.

The second condition is ethmoid haematoma, where an encapsulated 'haematoma' develops within the fine airways of the nasal passages; here nosebleeds can occur at rest or during exercise and can be down one or both nostrils. Coughing can also be a feature. We are not sure why these develop initially, but they can be diagnosed by examining the nasal passages with an endoscope or X-raying the skull.

Finally one must consider guttural pouch mycosis, this being a fungal infection affecting the guttural pouches, which are the termination of the eustachian tubes in the horse as they enter the back of the throat.

This can cause very severe, sometimes life-threatening, nosebleeds. Other symptoms with this condition include difficulty in eating, possibly with coughing, lethargy and sometimes a one-sided nasal discharge.

Again the cause is not clear, but it may be that the fungus attacks damaged blood vessel walls in the inside lining of the guttural pouch. Diagnosis is by examination of the interior of the guttural pouch with an endoscope.

Treatment for these last two conditions involves surgery, but success is unfortunately not guaranteed. With EIPH the long term future, after tending to stable management and following any necessary medical therapy, should be that the horse will be able to return to work.

There are other very rare conditions such as nasal polyps or fragile nasal blood vessels, but one would not expect to have the degree of bleeding that you describe with these conditions.

So, as you can see, your mare does not fit exactly into any of these categories; final diagnosis will lie in further investigation.

Greasy heels

q u e s t i o n

I think my cob may have mites. I first discovered hard flaky skin behind the back of his knees. I have treated this area as for mud fever and have tried picking off the dead skin, but the area seems to be enlarging and is not getting any better. He appears to be very itchy below the ergot but there are no cracks, as in mud fever.

I would be grateful if you could tell me how to treat mites as I understand a few of the products have been withdrawn from the market. Also, should I have the back of his legs clipped?

a n s w e r

Greasy leg or greasy heels is an exudative dermatitis caused by an underlying mange mite infestation, caused by the chorioptic mange mite, that particularly affects the lower limbs of densely feathered horses, such as yours.

The typical symptoms are due to irritation which causes stamping of the feet, and rubbing and gnawing at the affected areas. This frequently allows the areas to become secondarily infected.

Treatment for a long term cure involves complete clipping out of the feather, getting rid of as much hair as possible – so keep persevering with scissors, or borrow some clippers. Then the regular application of parasiticidal washes every 10 days for several months is the recommended regime.

'Quellada' (or other anti-parasitic shampoos containing gamma benzene hexachloride) is the easiest one to get hold of from your vet, and comes in largish bottles for economy.

You are correct in thinking that some equine anti-parasitic products have been taken off the market, which is most frustrating from our point of view, but your vet should still be able to get hold of Quellada-type shampoos.

Worming without worry

q u e s t i o n

Could you please advise on a correct worming programme and explain which wormer kills bots? I currently worm every two months, using a different make each time.

a n s w e r

New information on the use of wormers has been recently released which has affected our recommendations on worming horses and ponies.

During the grazing season you are correct in worming your horse approximately every eight weeks, but it is not necessary to alternate wormers on every occasion between a benzimidazole wormer, such as Panacur, and Strongid P and Eqvalan. It is preferable to change your wormer on an annual basis.

• Bot treatment should be carried out in December/January with a wormer such as Eqvalan.

• Tapeworm treatment should be carried out in mid- to late summer with Strongid P given at a double dose, which means twice the normal dose given on the same day.

However, new recommendations have been given for the use of a five-day course of Panacur wormer in November/December as a treatment for encysted small redworms which are 'hibernating' in the bowel wall.

Eqvalan has also been shown to reduce the number of these worms present in the bowel wall when used at this time of year.

These worms can cause severe diarrhoea, colic, weakness and weight loss when they emerge 'en masse' in the late winter/early spring. Therefore prevention of this serious problem is becoming more important.

question Q

answer A

Bone spavin options

My mare has been diagnosed as having bone spavin in the near-hind hock. Could you explain more about this condition and the options open to me? Could I breed from her or would the extra weight make the problem worse?

First of all, to lessen confusion there is a definition of exactly what 'bone spavin' is on page 107 of this book, together with an explanation of the common medical treatment.

Another possible line of medical therapy involves the intra-articular injection of various substances, such as steroids. However, recent evidence has suggested the possible use of substances based on hyaluronic acid being injected into the affected joints.

The other options are usually surgical, with fusion of the affected joints, known as surgical arthrodesis, being used to stabilise and thus remove inflammation and pain from the affected joints.

This involves drilling out the joint surfaces to destroy the cartilage that covers them. This stimulates the underlying bone to fuse together as one solid area of bone.

This may sound a bit gruesome but we know from past experience that the final results can be very good. It depends on how many joints are affected as to how good the chances are; if the lowest and/or second lowest joints are affected then there is roughly an 80% chance of return to full soundness.

If the top one of the three joints is affected then it is only a 60% chance. I'm afraid you don't mention which joint has been affected and thus I don't know which category your horse fits into; your vet will be best able to advise you regarding this matter.

There is probably no problem with your mare retiring for breeding as she is likely to be able to cope with the extra weight with little problem, unless her disease is very severe; again, your vet will be best able to advise you regarding this matter.

*Financial
and Legal*

Financial pitfalls

question

We have an old pony who is ridden by a young girl, supervised by my daughter. Occasionally my daughter gives her a lesson and takes them to shows in our lorry. The child's mother feels she ought to pay us as her daughter is having so much riding. Could you advise?

answer

If you were to charge money for giving lessons to this child on your pony, and for taking her out for hacks, you would require a licence from your local authority; the requirements you would have to meet before a licence could be applied for and issued are set out in the Riding Establishments Acts 1964 and 1970.

It might be better if you were to come to some other agreement instead, either allowing the child to take the pony on loan and drawing up a suitable written agreement between you, or else asking the mother to simply contribute towards the cost of vaccinations, shoeing, etc. – although it would probably be wise to seek legal advice on this last matter to ensure that by doing so you would not still be contravening the above mentioned Acts.

If your daughter continues to teach and escort her on hacks, it would be as well also to ensure that she has adequate insurance cover in the event of an accident occurring.

Could I be evicted?

question

I have rented a field to keep my two horses in from a local farmer for 10 years. The farmer leased all his land from a local landowner. The farmer said I could rent the field whilst he had the lease. I pay my rent monthly. There was no written agreement – just an amicable arrangement. Sadly the farmer died last year and his son has taken over the lease for the land. I am continuing to pay my rent monthly.

How would I stand if the son wanted me to get off the land? Also, how would I stand if the son gave up the lease on the land?

I have laid a small concrete yard and erected two stables plus a hay store on the land at my own expense. I have also maintained the fencing, replacing posts and wire when necessary, during the time I have used the field. If I moved off the site I could take the stables with me, but the concreted area and fencing would have to remain. Would I be entitled to any compensation from the farmer?

answer

You may well have a problem due to the fact that you have no written agreement for the rent of the land.

However, I think that if you were evicted the new farmer would have to give you notice equivalent to the time space at which you pay the rent; that is, if rental is paid weekly then one week's notice and if, as in your case, monthly, then one month's notice.

Even though you have no written contract I suspect that in equity you would have the right to claim recompense for the work you have done if it can be proved that this has enhanced or improved the land.

If the farmer gave up the lease on the land, you would be governed by the terms of the lease under which the farmer held the land. I doubt that you would have much protection against eviction, although the question of reimbursement for the enhancement or improvement of the land would still remain.

Change of use

question

I have a large building in my back garden which can be used for Light Industrial Use. I'd like to remove this building and erect a stable for my horse in its place. There would be little alteration in terms of the size and height of the building.

My property is in a Conservation Area. Can you advise me on any planning and waste disposal regulations which may apply?

answer

I would think that you would need planning permission for change of use. This could mean that your neighbours would be approached by the planning authority (either your local council or your county council) and would then have the chance to object to your plans.

First of all you need to find out from your local planning authority if consent for a change of use is required. If it is, the planning authority will tell you what plans need to be lodged with the application for change of use. You will almost certainly have to follow local building regulations.

You should also inform the planning authority of your plans to dispose of waste and prevent any nuisance by way of smell or noise.

Before you go to any expense on the planning permission/change of use side, I suggest that you have a friendly word with your neighbours in the immediate vicinity to enlist their support at an early stage or to find out if they are likely to oppose you.

On the whole, local councils and planning offices tend to be extremely helpful if you ask for advice on how to go about applying for planning permission and so forth.

151

Nasty geldings

question

I rent stabling and grazing on a DIY yard, along with 13 others. The horses are all turned out together and two of the geldings are really nasty towards the others and will 'hound' mares during the summer season. What is the legal liability of the yard owner and can we DIYs insist on a change of conditions? Who is responsible for the injuries caused to one horse by another?

answer

It is up to the yard owner to take reasonable care to ensure that horses come to no harm whilst using his facilities. This would be held to be an implied term of a contract between individual horse owners and the yard owner.

However, the owner of the yard would have to be informed that some horses are being harmed by others before he could be held responsible. It is up to each owner to tell their landlord of any problems, so that he is on notice that there is a possibility of injury to other horses.

TOP TIP

Can I Claim?
Solicitors specialising in equine litigation are:

● **Cripps, Harries, Hall & Co,**
84 Calverley Road, Tunbridge Wells, Kent,
TN1 2UP. Tel: 0892 515121.

● **Michael Segan & Co,**
39-42 New Bond Street, London, W1.
Tel: 071 491 7628.

● **Shoosmiths & Harrison,**
Russell House, 1550 Parkway, Solent
Business Park, Fareham, Hants, PO15
7AG. Tel: 0489 881010.

question Q

Do I have to pay?

I am not satisfied with the way a veterinary practice treated my pony so I'd like to know if I have to pay the bill? Also, can I claim, from the practice, the charges incurred when I asked a different vet to come out and treat my pony? After everything I have been through with my pony's illness I do not feel inclined to get embroiled in a legal battle. However, on principle, surely a person has a right to complain about what they feel is bad service and get something done about it?

answer A

If you were to resist paying the bill for veterinary treatment and/or go to the Small Claims Court to claim for the costs incurred for getting another vet to treat your pony, you would be faced with the problem of getting expert witnesses to say that your pony was negligently treated.

Would the second vet be willing to testify on your behalf against the first vet? Or could you get a vet who has no connection with your case to testify for you on the relevant evidence? I have to tell you that experience suggests that this might be difficult!

On the other hand, you could go back to your original vet and tell him that you are still not satisfied and ask if he would agree to one form of arbitration.

If arbitration doesn't work and you cannot get a vet to supply evidence for your case, you are stuck with paying the bill.

Proving that your vet was negligent is an extremely difficult thing to do

Neighbour trouble

I keep my pony in a rented field behind our house. Access to the field belongs to the landowner and runs between our house and our new neighbours. I have been keeping my horsebox in the access path, which is okay by the landowner.

Then my neighbour began to park his horsebox at the bottom of his garden. This meant that every time he wanted to get it in or out, I would have to move my box out of the way. My neighbour thought that the field access was a public, not a private, one. I told him that he would have to ask the landowner if he could use it. The landowner refused him.

Since then, my neighbour has complained to the council about my parking my horsebox in the field access. The council consider the box to be a permanent fixture and say that we should park it on the road in front of our house. There, it would cause congestion and untold other problems. Now the Council are getting an enforcement order to make us move the box. What do you suggest?

It is a rather dubious premise that the horsebox is a permanent fixture. If your local authority does get an enforcement order, then you should appeal to the Secretary of State for the Environment. The other alternative would be to move the box on to the road in front of your house – and to prove that it was not a permanent fixture, move it back into the access road after a day or two.

I would appeal to your local councillor for his support and if necessary to the Secretary of State.

I do not know what you can do about your neighbour – unless he commits assault, criminal damage or a nuisance.

However, one thing crosses my mind: if your horsebox is considered a permanent fixture in the field access, could it not be argued that your neighbour's box is also an unauthorised permanent fixture? A stupid position to take? Of course, but then isn't it arguable that, on what you say, your neighbour is behaving stupidly?

Business advice

 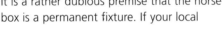

I am thinking of starting a business buying young ex-racehorses, schooling them on and reselling them. As I only intend to 'deal' in one or two horses at a time, would I have to declare my venture as a business and pay VAT, or could I sell the horses privately?

Also, my sister is considering doing pony rides. What sort of insurance would she need?

I believe that the current level of annual income necessary before having to register for VAT is in the region of £38,000. A simple enquiry to your local Customs & Excise office (you'll find this in the 'phone book) will confirm the current level.

As to whether you should declare yourself as a 'business' depends upon how much time you will devote to the venture, and whether it will be full time or not. That is a matter for you to decide, but any profit will have to be declared for tax purposes. To this end, keep all receipts for expenditure, e.g. petrol, rates, electricity, feed, etc., so that it can be deducted from any profit for tax purposes. An accountant will advise you here.

You may feel, initially, that it will pay to sell the horses privately, particularly if you have other full or part time employment.

To offer pony rides for payment your sister should take out insurance against injury to riders and third parties. She should also register with the local council as a riding school and apply to them for a licence.

Warranty worth

question

answer

I am in the process of buying a horse; however, I'm concerned about being 'caught out', i.e. if the seller lies to me about the horse having no vices, or even drugging the animal so that it appears quiet. Can you advise me on the legality of a written warranty?

In the event of a dispute, how long would a warranty be valid for?

When buying a horse, I would advise most strongly that you have a potential purchase vetted. A written warranty given by the seller should be as effective as any other guarantee, but you must ensure that all the conditions you fear may arise are covered by the warranty. This is so that it will be legally binding on the person giving it.

A warranty is of little use if it cannot be enforced effectively. By this I mean it would be no good suing a seller on the warranty, if he or she has little or no means to pay damages and costs at the end of the day.

If you think that the seller is a person of substance then a warranty should be an excellent thing to have.

Beware if a seller refuses to give a warranty.

Landowner liable?

question

I recently found my horse in his field with a badly injured foot. My vet said he'd never seen such a terrible wound; my horse required laser treatment to help heal the injury. Only £500 is allowable in my insurance policy for this alternative treatment.

It turned out that my horse had sustained his injury from a broken light fitting which had dropped off the landowner's car into the field. The landowner has admitted this is a possibility. Will I be able to claim, from the landowner, the difference between what the insurance company will pay up to and the final bill for the alternative treatment?

answer

If you can prove that the vehicle light fitting, belonging to the landowner, caused your horse's injury you could well have a cause of action against him. The landowner, by letting the field to you, owes you a duty of care to see that no harm comes to your horse. By leaving something lying on the ground which may – and apparently did – cause your horse injury, the landowner was negligent in respect of his duty of care.

I am certain that you can claim the balance of the cost of treating your horse not reimbursed by your insurance company from the landowner. This is on the grounds that he was either in breach of the contract by which he should have let your animal graze safely in the field, and/or negligent by leaving something in the field he must have realised would cause injury.

After-sales aggro

question

I sold a horse after my daughter lost interest in it. The buyer had the horse vetted and checked by her instructor before she bought him. Two weeks later the new owner rang up to say that the horse was windsucking.

I told her that the horse had not windsucked in the seven months I had owned him, and his previous owners, who had had him for four years, also vehemently denied that the horse had this vice. I advised the new owner to try altering her routine as windsucking can be caused by boredom or anxiety. I heard nothing more for a while, then received a letter demanding financial compensation of £1,750, or I could have the horse back if I returned the £2,000 purchase price.

I replied, denying liability. The only bad habit the horse displayed whilst with me was chewing the top of his door at feed times. I told the buyer about this when she viewed him.

My own vet said that horses can develop the windsucking habit if they are bored or stressed.

You say the horse was vetted and checked by the purchaser's instructor, but was it also checked by the purchaser's vet?

With your own evidence and that of the horse's previous owner, plus the fact that the horse appears not to have been inspected by a vet before purchase, you should have a valid defence to any claim.

It may also be interesting to find out if, in fact, the horse is bored at its new home.

In my view you have an answer to any claim and I should wait to see what develops before incurring any legal expense yourself.

Deposit debate

Some two months ago I advertised my two-year-old colt for sale. He's a lovely, genuine animal and the only reason I decided to sell him was that he's grown far too big for me.

I had eight or nine phone calls and the first people to see him agreed to buy him subject to vetting. They gave me a £50 deposit and asked me if I would keep him until he had been gelded. This I agreed to. My colt passed the vet as suited for riding and eventing. Then a month later, the purchaser wrote saying that as my colt had failed the vet due to sloping pasterns, and would therefore be unable to jump, they did not want to buy him and would I return their deposit.

I contacted the vet concerned. He was extremely surprised by the would-purchaser's comments and showed me the vet certificate stating that my colt was suitable for eventing and riding.

Do I have to return the deposit left by the people who decided they didn't want my horse after all even though he passed the vetting?

Presumably the contract between the would-be purchaser and yourself was that your colt would be bought subject to a satisfactory vetting examination.

What I am uncertain about is the letter you received from the purchaser some time after the successful vetting, stating that the vet had failed the horse saying that it would not be able to jump.

Was this the same vet who issued the original certificate and if not, did you receive any certificate from a vet?

My reasons for asking this are as follows:

• If the basis of the contract was that the horse would be purchased subject to a satisfactory veterinary examination and that £50 was paid as a returnable deposit if the horse failed the vet, then the £50 must be returned.

• If the £50 was paid as a deposit and the horse passed the vet – the condition of the contract – and the would-be purchaser failed to buy the horse, you are entitled to keep the money.

It appears to me that the would-be purchaser had second thoughts about buying your colt and is trying to get out of the agreement. I would certainly want more details from that person about the statement that the horse was unfit for jumping.

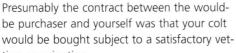

TOP TIP

Unwelcome Visitors
Keeping tresspassers off your property can be a nightmare. One of the best deterrents is to keep a dog!

Show liability

question

At a jumping show I was at as a spectator I saw a rider take a fall. Two people ran to take care of the horse, but everyone ignored the rider!

Being trained in First Aid I went to the girl's assistance; mercifully she was unhurt. When I asked the show organisers if there was an official First Aider on site, the reply given was 'There's someone about......I think?'

In my opinion this was a woefully inadequate response, given the risks involved at such an event. What is the legal position regarding First Aid at shows? Surely there is an onus on organisers to have a First Aider on hand? Would their public liability insurance be valid without them taking such a reasonable precaution?

answer

A competitor is held to know the risks involved and to accept these risks. So too is a spectator who may be injured watching equestrian events, unless the riding of a horse which causes injury is said to be grossly negligent.

On the other hand, organisers of events are expected to ensure that the course is fit for its purposes and free from unnecessary risks.

To the best of my knowledge there is no legal requirement for a First Aider to be on call. However, if the event is covered by insurance it may well be that it is policy condition that there be someone on hand to render help.

Veterinary complaint

question

I bought a horse, after having him vetted, from a dealer. The vet told me that the horse was okay apart from some melanoid tissue on the front of the lens of an eye, but that it was of no detriment to the animal.

I spoke to my own vet and asked him to contact the other vet to confirm that the horse was fine. This was done.

The week after the horse was delivered, my own vet called to vaccinate him and while he was there, checked his eyes. He found a lot more damage than the other vet had indicated; in addition to the melanoid tissue on one eye, both had cataracts, with one eye being worse than the other.

It turns out that the horse has uveitis in both eyes and this should have been spotted by the vet that vetted him fit for purchase. What is the point of going to the

trouble and expense of having a horse vetted when something like this happens?

The dealer I bought the animal from does not want to know. Where do I stand?

answer **A** On balance, it certainly appears that the vet who vetted the animal was negligent.

Unless the dealer made extravagant claims for the animal, I don't think you have a case against her at all, seeing as you did have the horse vetted.

You could sue the vet for damages for what was obviously negligence on his part, but to prove negligence you would have to

When you enter a show, it is a wise precaution to check whether there will be a vet and First Aid on the ground, or at least on call

get another vet (your own, perhaps?) to say that any competent vet should have discovered the condition on even the most cursory of examinations. You would have to claim for the reduced value of the animal as a result of the condition.

It is not easy to prove a claim of negligence, especially as the vet in question is almost certainly represented by an insurance company in any action.

158

question **Q**

Unsuitable for its purpose

Six weeks ago I bought a mare from a dealer who was recommended to me. I viewed and rode the pony and told the dealer my requirements were for a gentle hack which my five-year-old daughter could use. When I rode the mare she was quiet and well behaved in traffic.

The day after I got the pony home, I started to groom her and she tried to kick me – this behaviour has continued to date. She also behaved badly when she was shod.

I've had the mare checked by a vet, who diagnosed that she was free from any physical ailment that might cause her to kick. He said that in his opinion the mare is a 'kicker'.

As I bought the mare as being 'free from vice' I contacted the dealer. The dealer informed me that while she was at his yard she had been easy to handle and was not a kicker. I pointed out to him that he had sold the mare to me as viceless, but it is obvious now that she kicks.

I asked the dealer if he would either find a replacement or give me my money back. He said he'd do the former. Two weeks on, a replacement hasn't been found so I requested my money back. The dealer refused. When I said I would take him to court, he told me to go ahead!

Am I entitled to claim the purchase price back via court action?

answer

I think you have a good case against the dealer on two grounds. Firstly, you say that you told the dealer that you wanted the pony as a gentle hack for yourself and young daughter, and were relying on his judgement as a dealer to provide an animal for that purpose. Manifestly, the pony he sold you did not match that requirement so he is liable to you under the Sale of Goods Act.

Secondly, it appears that the animal was warranted free from vice, when it clearly wasn't. In my view you should have no difficulty in recovering your money – with interest – from the dealer, but it will be necessary for you to ask the vet who inspected the horse to give evidence on your behalf if the case has to come to court.

Really it would be better for both parties to come to an satisfactory agreement without the trouble of going to court.

I suggest you write to the dealer, by recorded delivery, saying that if your money is not returned within 14 days you will take action and he must come and collect the pony.

If he fails to return your money, take action in your local county court – by issuing a summons against him in the Small Claims Court, for recovery of your money, plus interest and costs.

> ## TOP TIP
> **Legal Advice**
> **Free legal advice can be obtained by writing to Don Cassell, the Horse Answers expert c/o *Your Horse* Magazine. Don is a journalist who specialises in equine law.**

question **Q**

Permanent loan problem

I am retiring my horse as she has ringbone. The home I've found for her seems genuine; however, I'm still worried about her long term welfare. I'm happy to let her go to the offered home providing she is: not sold on; only ridden once a week; managed in her best interests; destroyed on the premises if and when necessary. Can I legally put these conditions down on paper for the new 'owner' to sign? Would the conditions be binding?

answer

You can draw up an agreement which will allow your mare's new 'owner' to have her on permanent loan subject to the conditions you outline. This agreement would not prevent anything untoward happening to your horse, but it would give you some redress if anything did.

Product liability

I'm planning to set up in business making and selling wooden showjumps. One concern I have is whether I would face any legal liability in the event of a horse or rider suffering injury whilst using one of my jumps? Are there any product standards with which I should comply?

Does any copyright exist on showjump designs currently available? How should I go about getting copyright on my designs if necessary?

If a horse or rider were injured as a result of a defect in the design or manufacture of your jumps, and those defects were as a result of negligence on your part, you could well be held liable in law. This is known as product liability.

Copyright would exist in the design of jumps, although I admit I know of no case involving copyright infringement in respect of jumps. Copying of a building can, in some circumstances, be a breach of copyright, but I wonder if jumps could be construed as either a building or a fixture?

So although copyright would exist in the plans for the jumps, I don't know if the 'finished article' would be protected. Incidentally, copyright ends 50 years after the death of the creator of the work.

Livery liability

As a potential livery/dealing yard owner, I need some legal advice: if I asked a DIY livery owner to sign a contract which stated that they kept their animal at my premises at their own risk, would this absolve me of any blame if anything happened to the horse, or would this depend on whether I was negligent?

What type of occurrence could be counted as negligence, e.g. when I am supplying facilities, but not actually caring for the horse, e.g. if the horse was injured in the field by my or other livery horses, whose responsibility would this be? Would the situation be different if the horse was in part or full livery, rather than DIY? Would I be responsible for any injuries caused to a prospective buyer when trying out a horse?

Regarding your liability for DIY owners: if you inserted a clause saying 'horse kept at owner's risk', it could fall foul of the Unfair Contract Terms Act 1977. This would only apply though if you had the only livery business within reasonable distance of your clients and they had nowhere else to go to. If there are other livery yards in the area then clients would have a choice and then the clause you query would probably not be termed unreasonable.

It is possible that you might be held responsible, despite an exclusion clause, if death or injury was caused to an animal through your negligence, e.g. if you left the stable yard unlocked and a horse strayed on to the road.

Regarding liability for horses injured by other horses in the field: if you knew that a particular horse was nasty to others, in my view you would be negligent in allowing that animal loose with others. This rule would apply to full and DIY livery.

If a prospective buyer suffered injury when trying out your horse, your liability depends on the circumstances: if you let an inexperienced person ride your horse, and you knew that person was inexperienced, I'm sure you would be responsible if the person fell off and received injury. Under the Unfair Contract Terms Act 1977, you cannot exclude liability for death or injury to a person.

No money, no horse

question

Last year I sold my mare and agreed to let a lady have her on a three-month trial loan. If this worked out the lady would pay me for the pony. I have this agreement in writing.

Twelve months on and I still have not been paid. The buyer keeps making all sorts of excuses and I have thought about going and taking my pony back, but I have been told that I would be in breach of contract for doing this.

I am reluctant to take the buyer to the Small Claims Court as I believe that the buyer has already got two County Court judgements against her.

answer

Send a final demand for the money by recorded delivery, along with the demand that the money is paid within 14 days and if it isn't, that you will take action in the Small Claims Court. If you don't take this action, and in view of how the 'buyer' is behaving, your chances of getting paid are remote.

You could be in the wrong to take the pony back, but in any Small Claims Court action you can also ask for, as an alternative to the money being paid, the return of your pony.

Even though you have not received payment, taking your horse back from the 'buyer', without professional advice first, may land YOU in hot water!

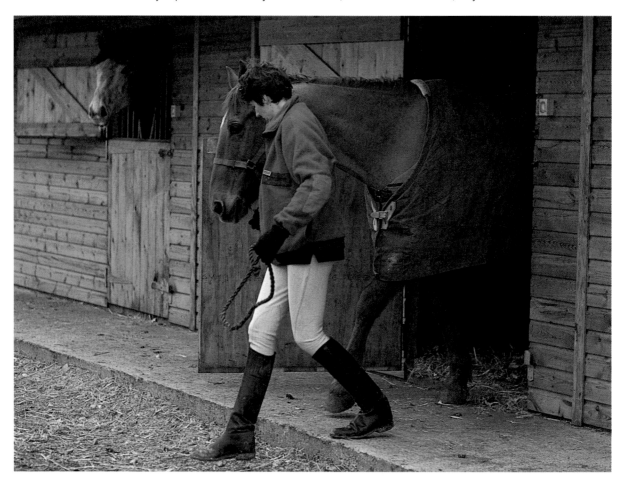

Share prices

question

My friend and I are thinking about buying a horse to share. Can you think of any problems that might arise from this partnership and advise us accordingly?

answer

I can think of many problems which might arise over sharing a horse with a friend and I suggest that you draw up an agreement between you which takes into account the following points:

- How much each will pay towards the cost of keeping the horse.
- Times when each of you has use of the horse.
- If you keep the animal on DIY, how the work will be shared between you.
- If the horse is ever sold on, what percentage of the sale price shall go to each partner.

Keeping to a written agreement will serve to lessen the chance of disagreements between you and your friend arising.

Have the horse thoroughly vetted before you buy it.

If sharing a horse, it makes sense to draw up an agreement between yourselves to state clearly who pays and does what. This saves arguments later!

161

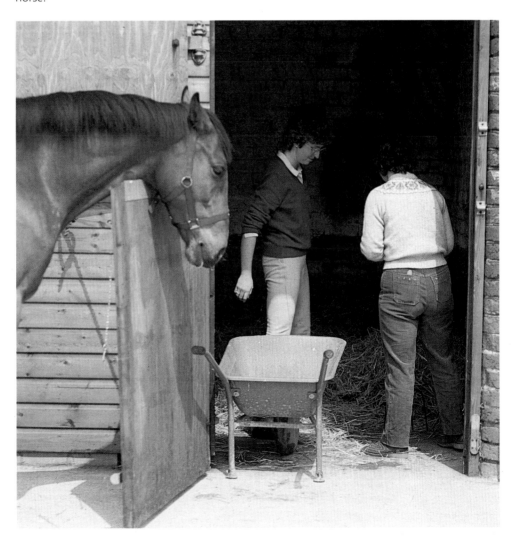

question

Can I claim?

I viewed and rode a horse I had travelled around 300 miles to see. It seemed quiet and traffic proof so I arranged for it to be vetted (in my partner's name). When this was done, I agreed the sale on the understanding that the owner would forward on all its certificates and medical documents.

Two weeks later I noticed the horse was lame when I lunged it, and then I discovered it had been pin fired. Both my vet and the yard owner confirmed this and said that the horse would only be suitable for light work, with no jumping or faster work than trot.

I informed the seller and also the vet who had vetted the horse for me. The vet said I had only asked for an examination for insurance purposes. The vet certificate stated that 'At the time of examination, there were no apparent clinical abnormalities of limb, eye, heart or action; no signs of infectious or contagious disease and in my opinion the horse is a suitable subject for insurance.'

The seller said the horse was okay when she had it and she didn't know it had been fired. She has still not supplied the horse's papers. My insurance company have said that they would not insure an animal with its condition. The horse has now been retired due to lameness. Where do I stand?

answer

When you purchased the animal, did the vendor know that you wanted it for jumping? If so you may, and I put it no higher, have a claim against her if you could prove that she knew

the horse was fired and was lame. To be honest, I think you would have difficulty in establishing a claim against the vendor as you had the animal vetted.

This leads to the second point: do you have a claim against the vet? This depends on whether or not he was informed, or had reason to know, that you wanted an animal capable of cantering and jumping.

However, there is a complication: the vet certificate states that the examination was carried out on behalf of your partner. If your partner ordered the examination, was he acting as an agent for you? If not, any complaint against the vet would have to be made by your partner as he was the client.

If you have still not received the horse's papers from the vendor, write to her by recorded delivery stating that if the papers are not sent to you within 14 days you will take action in the Small Claims Court for her breach of contract, the breach being that provision of the papers was part of the contract for the sale by her and the purchase, by you, of the horse.

If you feel that you can prove that you were misled by the vendor as to the true condition of the horse, and that the vendor must have known that the animal had been lame and had been fired, you might like to chance your arm and claim damages for misrepresentation, although I don't hold out much hope of you winning.

You will have to travel to the area where you bought the horse to bring any action.

question

Muck heap mess

Can I do anything about the huge manure heap, belonging to a livery yard and riding school, across the road from my property? The smell is indescribable at times.

answer

I suggest that you write to the owners of the stables, sending your letter by recorded delivery, stating what nuisance is being caused. Say that if the nuisance is not abated by them

within fourteen days you will seek an injunction.

If you can prove that you have suffered a financial loss as a result of the nuisance, e.g. business has suffered, you can also claim damages for that loss.

If you do bring an action in the County Court without the services of a solicitor, I'm sure that you will find the court staff helpful.

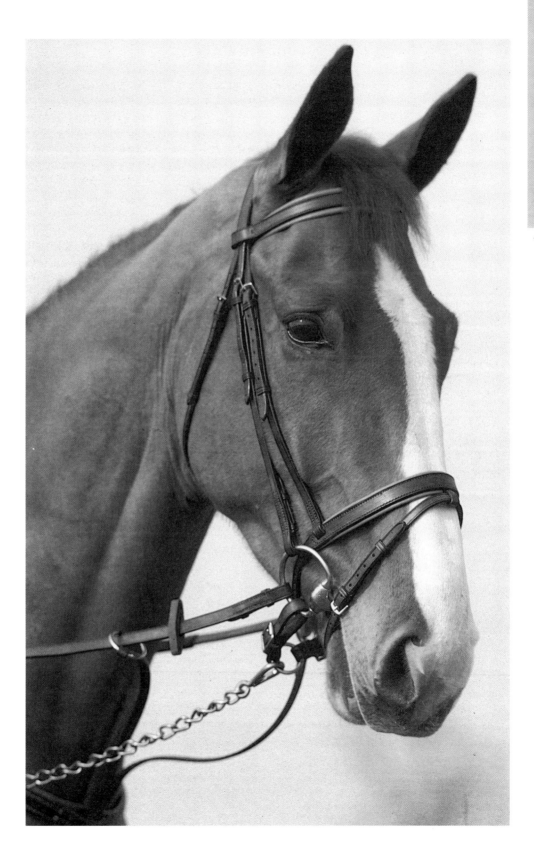

Loan commitment

question

What exactly is involved in having a horse on part-loan? What would be expected of me? Would it be useful to have a formal contract drawn up?

answer

It would be sensible to draw up some kind of agreement to safeguard the interests of both parties. The agreement should cover every eventuality you can think of – from who gets to ride when and for how long; whether you compete; who cares for the horse on a daily basis; costs (including who is responsible for veterinary and shoeing expenses, worming, replacing or repairing saddlery etc.).

The British Horse Society publish a useful free leaflet called *Buying, Leasing or Borrowing Horses* which gives a few pointers on loan agreements. It can be obtained from the British Horse Society, British Equestrian Centre, Stoneleigh, Kenilworth, Warwickshire, CV8 2LR. Enclose a large sae.

How much you pay each week or month depends on the arrangement you come to with the owner; he/she may decide just to charge you an unvarying flat rate, or alterna- tively ask you to split the costs or pay a per- centage of them – in which case the cost will vary depending on whether feed etc. is bought. If you have the latter arrangement, find out in advance roughly what the horse's running costs are so that you can budget for them – it is very easy to get caught out if you are not careful.

You should also agree to inform each other in advance if new purchases are to be made – after all you don't want to suddenly find you are liable for paying half the cost of a new saddle for a horse you do not own. If such purchases are likely to be made, it would be worth adding something into your written agreement about what happens if you do part company, i.e. sell the purchase and divide the money from it, or the horse's owner agrees to reimburse you for your share of it.

You should also consider a trial period of a month before committing yourself, to make sure that you are both going to be compati- ble – good friendships have been known to founder in such circumstances.

Fence injury

question

My horse caught itself on a large bolt which was sticking out of the fence surrounding the field where I keep him. He suffered a nasty injury just behind the girth.

The landowner called the vet to treat my horse, and admitted that they were liable for the injury. He said that he would waive my field rent for six weeks (£75) as compensa- tion. He also repaired the fence properly that same day.

Can I claim against the landowner for being negligent in respect of his duty of care? Or has he passed over his responsibility as he waived the rent?

My vet's bill was £350.

answer

It is fortunate that there is no dispute that the landowner has admitted liability; you can certainly claim against him for damages. The damages would include vet bills plus general damages for the loss of use of your horse whilst it recovered.

The landowner could argue that you accepted a rent-free period as full compensa- tion for your horse's injury. If you signed a document agreeing to this, or verbally accepted his offer, then you would have no further claim. If neither of these are the case, then you could claim in the Small Claims Court.

On the other hand, if stabling and grazing is difficult to get in your area and, apart from this incident, you have been happy with the facilities, you must consider whether you wish to upset such an arrangement by suing the landowner.

Livery death

The owner of the land where I kept my horse along with others, left a vehicle in the field which contained boxes of toxic insecticide pellets. Unfortunately my horse chewed open one of the boxes and ate some of the contents. Sadly she had to be destroyed later that day, despite my vet's attempts to save her.

Two other horses, belonging to someone else, were also affected, although they recovered.

Can I claim against the landowner for compensation and would I be successful? My mare was insured and I have put in a claim – although I feel it will not be enough to compensate for my loss.

Could the other owners sue the landowner for the veterinary fees they incurred?

There is an implied duty of care on the landowner's part, if he accepts rent from you, to see that your horse comes to no harm. However, as your horse chewed open a closed box to eat the poison, the landowner could claim that he did not know, and had no rea-

son to believe, that your horse could and would chew open the box. It would be necessary for you to prove that the landowner should have foreseen this possibility and failed to take action to prevent it.

Your insurance company, if they pay out your claim, may consider taking action against the landowner.

If you took action against him yourself it would be to reclaim vet fees, the value of the horse and general damages for the loss of your horse. I imagine that the claim would be heard in a County Court, rather than a Small Claims Court, and this could be an expensive business.

The owners of the other horses may feel like claiming against the landowner for recovery of vet fees, but I cannot say for sure that they would be successful. As far as your case goes, you have a fifty-fifty chance of success.

Yard owners who rent out grazing have a duty of care to ensure that horses come to no harm while in their fields

165

Who pays for damage?

I keep my horse on DIY livery at a farm. Recently my horse became upset when his field companion was briefly taken out of the field. My horse broke out of the field, damaging a galvanised gate beyond repair in the process. The farm owners say that I must pay for a replacement gate. Is this correct?

I presume that you do not have a written agreement with the farmer in respect of the grazing: if you did have such an agreement, it could well specify who is responsible for the damage.

I'm afraid that unless your horse's field companion was taken out of the field by the farmer, and the farmer was aware that your horse, as a consequence, was likely to get upset, you are likely to be held responsible for the damage caused by your horse.

Do check any insurance policy you have in respect of your horse to see if it is covered for damage to property.

Neighbour trouble

How can I protect my horses from my neighbour's weedkiller that has been sprayed on my side of a hedge and pasture? A few weeks ago my pony became ill, but my vet could not determine the cause.

Now my neighbour has started to spray another hedge, also bordering my field, and I suspect, and am worried, that it will affect the horses again.

I'm afraid to complain to the neighbour as I know he doesn't like horses. He has told me that he will continue to spray.

First of all, ask your vet if the the illness your pony suffered could, on all balance of probablities, have been caused by the weedkiller. If the vet is of this opinion and is prepared to say so in court if necessary, then you would have cause for nuisance against your neighbour.

Although a landowner is entitled, within certain bounds, to do what he/she wishes with his/her land, care has to be taken that anything done to the land does not create a nuisance for neighbours. This includes spraying if the landowner knew, or should have foreseen, that the spray might drift on to adjoining land. If you can get the necessary expert evidence from your vet, you can then sue in your local county court for damages and recovery of vet's fees, and obtain an injunction restraining the landowner from committing the nuisance in future.

I would hesitate to suggest taking legal action in any dispute with a neighbour, unless it is the last resort. However, in view of your neighbour's attitude this may be the only recourse for you.

VAT on livery

I keep my horse on DIY livery at a local yard. I signed a livery agreement, but after I'd been there a while, the owner told me I had to pay VAT on my livery rent.

Do I have to pay VAT, even though the original livery agreement makes no mention of it?

If the yard owner is registered for VAT he will have to charge you VAT for the service he is providing you with, i.e. DIY livery. You, in turn, are entitled to a VAT receipt when you pay your rent. This receipt must include the yard owner's VAT registration number.

Not suitable

Earlier this year I purchased a 16hh cob type described for sale as 'a family horse, hunter and showjumper'. I bought the horse after vetting for £2,500. The seller was a dealer.

You can imagine my horror when in early May the horse began to show all the signs of having a serious sweet itch problem. Despite taking all the usual precautions, including making his stable into a 'padded cell' as he threw himself around in a frenzy with the itching, the problem has advanced dramatically. Even with veterinary treatment and a strict stable management regime, the horse is almost unworkable in some conditions. I cannot see him being able to hunt due to the early starts, when the midges responsible are at their worst. The horse is clearly not suitable for the purpose for which I bought him.

Luckily I have made contact with a groom who used to work at the dealer's yard. The groom confirms that the horse suffered badly from sweet itch the summer before I bought him, and got worse through the winter.

Have I a legal right to demand a refund?

If the dealer knew, which I imagined he did, the purpose for which you wanted the horse, obviously you have a case under the Sale of Goods Act 1979 as the horse is not fit for the purpose for which you purchased it.

You are fortunate in having contact with the groom who worked at the dealer's yard; presumably he is willing to back up your evidence with evidence of his own that the horse suffered from sweet itch in the previous summer, so that the dealer cannot claim he was unaware of that fact.

In my opinion you have a good chance of suing the dealer for damages, plus interest, and winning in the County Court. First, however, I should get a statement, sworn if possible, from the groom and then write to the dealer setting out your case and saying you have the necessary evidence.

Hopefully the dealer will see sense and settle without you having to resort to a court case.

Misplaced trust

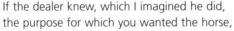

I recently sold a yearling. The buyers paid some cash and a cheque which I was told to cash at the end of the month when the buyer's wages were paid into her bank account.

To cut a long story short, the owner did not have the cash in the bank to complete payment for the pony and I am still waiting for it. I know I was silly to trust the buyer, but is there anything I can do to recover my money?

I suggest you write to the buyer, sending the letter by recorded delivery, saying that if the money is not paid within seven or 14 days you will take action for recovery in the Small Claims Court.

If the money is not forthcoming, or a satisfactory and reliable offer for payment made, go to your local County Court and take out a summons in the Small Claims Court for the sum involved, plus costs and interest.

Small Claims Courts are meant for settling claims like yours without recourse to lawyers, but if the sum owed is more than £1,000 the case will have to be dealt with in the County Court. If the case is for a straightforward debt you should not need the services of a lawyer.

You'll find court officials most helpful when making enquiries as to how to go about claiming in either the Small Claims or the County Court.

FINANCIAL AND LEGAL

question **Q**

Honesty pays!

I am planning to sell my 14-year-old TB gelding but he has a few problems and I am not sure which ones to admit to. He is a headshaker, is slightly cold backed, has slight COPD so his hay has to be soaked, he weaves and windsucks. On his plus side he is a good jumper, is 100% in traffic, to box, shoe and catch and he has lovely stable manners.

When I bought him I was not told of his problems. How much should I expect to get for him?

answer **A**

You may find the chapters on 'The Purchase of Horses and Veterinary Certification' and 'The Legal Implications of the Purchase of a Horse' in Hayes' 'Veterinary Notes for Horse Owners' of interest as regards your situation; you should be able to find this book in the reference section of your library.

Whatever the legal implications, do not imagine that you can con a vet inspecting him prior to purchase; if he does not pick up all the problems you have described, (s)he will certainly spot most of them, and you will have wasted your time and everybody else's if the prospective purchaser then decides not to go ahead with the sale.

Even if they would have been happy to put up with these problems, they may well be put off, wondering what else you haven't told them about. You would be far better to be honest about him from the start; by all means concentrate on his good qualities in any ads you place for him eg good to hack, traffic etc, but you should tell people either when they come to try him out or, if they are travelling a long distance to view, over the phone to save

Be truthful about your horse's little foibles

them a wasted trip.

Being honest will not only ensure you are legally in the clear, but if you care at all about him, you will want to know that whoever buys him knows his problems and will be prepared to care for him properly from the start, rather than finding out by trial and error.

Although you may find that you will not get much money for him with these problems, if he is as well mannered and sensible as you say, he should be able to find a suitable home, which surely is more important than making a profit.

Like cars, older horses rarely appreciate in value, and this is something you should have considered when initially purchasing him. Look through ads in horsy magazines for an idea of a realistic price to ask for him.

Pregnancy problem

question

I recently sold my mare and was extremely shocked when they rang up some weeks later and told me that she was pregnant. I had no idea my mare was in foal, and can only think this happened when a stallion, owned by the livery yard where I used to keep her, got in the field with the livery horses, including mine.

Can I or the new owners of my horse claim against the livery yard?

answer

The new owner of your mare has no claim against your old livery yard as there was no contractual relationship between them.

For you to claim, you would have to prove that the stallion was indeed the sire of your mare's foal. Proving this would be strengthened by blood testing. If the case went to court a judge may well order such a test if the stallion's owner denied his horse was the sire.

If you suffered any damage when you owned the mare, through her being in foal, such as incurring vet fees, being laid off work due to illness or through being in foal, you may be able to recover damages for the loss of her services.

On the other hand, the owner of the stallion could argue that you have a valuable asset in the foal, the value of which could be offset against any damages you might be awarded.

Access worry

question

There is a public footpath, via a stile and a gate, through the field where I keep my horse. Am I within my legal rights to padlock the gate to stop people leaving it open?

answer

I do not think that you have the right to padlock the gate to the public footpath. This is because it is possible that the footpath will be used by elderly and physically handicapped people who would be unable to negotiate the stile.

You don't say who owns the field. If rented, ask the owner if you or he can put up a sign requesting the gate to be shut.

Am I to blame?

question

Recently when out riding my horse, some other riders galloped up behind me and one of them banged into the back of me. My horse kicked out in defence, and broke the other horse's leg. The horse had to be put down.

That evening, the parents of the horse's owner rang and told me that I had to pay them £1000 for a new horse or they would take me to court.

Where do I stand – it was not my fault that the girl could not control her horse. Can they take me to court?

answer

Yes they can, but whether or not they would win the case is a different matter. From what you say, it was entirely the fault of the rider of the horse which had to be destroyed due to her being either unable to control the animal, or by riding in a reckless and irresponsible manner.

I have a feeling that the threat to take legal action is a 'try on' and if you call their bluff by refusing to be stampeded into paying them £1000, I doubt that they would follow through with their threat.

If you have further problems, I suggest that you consult a solicitor.

170

question

Fence fracas

The field boundary fence between the livery yard where I keep my horse and the adjoining land, which belongs to a neighbouring riding school, is in a state of disrepair. The riding school own the fence and are responsible for its upkeep. However, despite being asked repeatedly, they have failed to repair it. Recently some of their horses pushed their way through the fence and got in to the field with my horses, resulting into two of our horses being injured.

Your advice would be appreciated.

answer

I suggest that you and the other owners of

horses in the livery, together with the livery yard owner, share the cost of consulting a solicitor.

Ask the solicitor to write a letter to the riding school, warning them that if they fail to repair the fence they will be held responsible for any injury, due to the fence disrepair, to horses in the livery stable.

This may seem an excessive step to take, but it seems that the riding school need to be threatened with drastic action if they are to carry out their obligations.

question

Noisy neighbour

I keep my horses at a small DIY livery yard. One of the other livery owners has recently bought a horse that was known to be a 'door banger' before she purchased it.

It kicks the door so much that we have politely objected twice and have even offered to fix thick padding to the horse's door. The owner then put some thin padding on the door, but this has not deadened the noise at all.

My mare has now started to copy the other horse and is kicking her door.

What are my legal rights regarding situations such as this? If I pursue the matter with the yard owner, can she ask me to leave?

answer

You have a legal right to expect that your horse will be well cared for and kept free from the possibility of injury, as well as from being upset and made nervous, which may result from the other horse's habit of door banging.

If you do pursue the matter further with the yard owner, she has every right to ask you to leave by giving you the appropriate notice. If you pay weekly, the notice is likely to be a week; if you pay monthly, you'll get a month's notice to leave.

On the other hand, if you have a friendly relationship with the yard owner and that the

facilities are good. Why not, in the interest of harmonious relations, have another word and repeat your offer of putting thick carpet on the door banger's door?

Point out, if necessary, that it would be in the interest of the yard owner to protect the animal and the door, because if the horse suffers injury as a result of the banging, and the yard owner knew of the possibility of injury being sustained, she may be held wholly or partially to blame.

TOP TIP

Buyer Beware
When buying a horse privately remember the rule 'buyer beware'.

A veterinary examination, carried out by your vet, not the vendor's, is recommended – but do remember that this certifies the animal as found at the time of examination only and cannot be a guarantee as to the horse's future soundness or performance.

Loan legalities

I am hoping to buy my first horse later this year and am at present having stable management lessons. I feel that it may be prudent to have a horse on loan first, with the option to buy rather than buying one first and then finding I cannot cope.

Where do I stand legally with a horse on loan? What happens if there is an accident or the horse becomes ill? Do I still need insurance? Will I need to have a legal agreement drawn up?

If you decide to buy a horse, have the animal examined by a vet and tell the seller what you intend to use the animal for, i.e. general riding or something more specific such as jumping, hunting, etc. Be sure that the vet examines the horse to see that it is fit for the purpose for which you require the animal.

Ask the seller for a receipt and for a warranty that the age of the horse is accurate, that it is free from vice and fit for the purpose that you want it for. If the seller is honest he/she should not object to giving such an assurance. If he/she is unwilling to give an assurance then think again!

If you get a horse on loan with the option to buy, similar safeguards as outlined above should be incorporated into a loan agreement. It is also important to establish, and put in writing, the terms of the loan which should include: length of loan; how much you will pay; who is responsible for insurance and vet fees; where the horse will be stabled and grazed; what you can and cannot use the animal for during the length of the loan; and whether any other persons, other then yourself, will be allowed to ride the animal.

Temporary accommodation

Would I be allowed to put either a caravan or a portable building on the land where I graze my horses, sheep and goats? I do not want to live in the caravan – just use it as a base to have a telephone, kettle and toilet as I live a couple of miles away from the field.

Assuming that you own the land, or have the landowner's permission, I see no reason why you should not have a caravan on the site. A

portable building may be subject to planning consent, and so too could the caravan in certain circumstances. Much would depend on planning guidelines laid down by your particular local authority.

I suggest that you contact your local planning department and ask their advice. I would be surprised if they said no; if they do, you have a right of appeal.

TOP TIP

Clear Agreements
Whether you are loaning out a horse, sharing with a friend, taking a horse on loan, buying a livery service...do get your agreement in writing. This saves so much hassle later on as all parties know exactly where they stand.

Always have a horse vetted by your own vet before purchase. Ensure your vet knows what purpose you intend to use the horse for – this should be included on the vetting certificate.

Riding school loan

I need to loan my mare out this year and have been approached by a local riding school who are interested in having her. However, I know very little about loaning! What should I expect the riding school to pay for? Where do I stand regarding insurance and vet bills, i.e. what insurance cover should my mare have and who pays for it, and who pays for her vaccinations and wormers?

Do I have to supply tack with my horse? Would it be advisable to have a contract with the riding school, stating who pays for what, responsibilities and length of loan? Should I have a solicitor draw up the contract?

answer

In my view, if the school is making money by the use of your horse they should pay for all her expenses, including insurance and vet bills. It is up to you whether or not you supply tack with the horse.

It is extremely advisable to draw up a contract setting out the terms of the loan and exactly what the riding school is held responsible for. Include the length of notice given by each party for the loan termination.

You may also like to put into the agreement any restrictions you feel are necessary for the well-being of your horse, such as how many hours a day she should be ridden and whether or not she can be jumped or galloped.

Do have a solicitor to draw up an agreement – you can split the cost between you and the riding school. Ring solicitors to ask for a quote.

When loaned to a good riding school, your horse will usually benefit from being well cared for and schooled

172

Stay ahead of the field...

...by reading *Your Horse* magazine, Britain's biggest selling horse monthly. Each issue is packed with invaluable information on horse care, riding advice and veterinary guidance to ensure *your* horse remains happy and healthy.

AVAILABLE NOW AT ALL GOOD NEWSAGENTS

If you have enjoyed *Horse Answers* you may be interested in the following Boxtree titles:

1 85283 916 3	*Countrywomen*	£14.99
0 7522 1609 0	*True Nature of the Cat*	£9.99
0 7522 1613 9	*The Daily Telegraph Room Service*	£8.99
1 85283 438 2	*The World's Best Trout Flies*	£19.99

All these books are available at your local bookshop or newsagent, or can be ordered direct from the publisher. Just tick the titles you want and fill in the form below. Price and availability change without notice.

Littlehampton Book Services, 14 Eldon Way, Lineside Industrial Estate, Littlehampton, BN17 7HE
Please a send cheque or postal order for the value of the book, and add the following for postage and packing:
UK including B.F.P.O. – £1.00 for one book, plus 50p for the second book, and 30p for each additional book ordered up to a £3.00 maximum.
OVERSEAS INCLUDING EIRE – £2.00 for the first book, plus £1.00 for the second book, and 50p for each additional book ordered.

OR please debit this amount from my Access/Visa Card (delete as appropriate)

Card Number   Amount £.

Valid From Date   Expiry Date

Signed   Card holder's Name

Card holder's Address

Delivery Address (if different from above)